SAFe® 5.0 Distilled

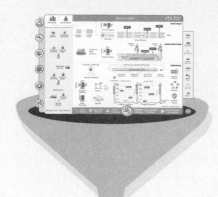

SAFe® 5.0

SAFe®
DISTILLED

**ACHIEVING BUSINESS
AGILITY WITH THE
SCALED AGILE FRAMEWORK®**

**Richard Knaster
Dean Leffingwell**

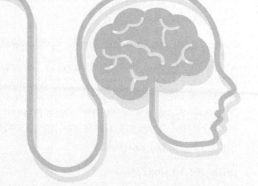

◆▾ Addison-Wesley

For information about buying this title in bulk quantities, or for special sales opportunities (which may include electronic versions; custom cover designs; and content particular to your business, training goals, marketing focus, or branding interests), please contact our corporate sales department at corpsales@pearsoned.com or (800) 382-3419.

For government sales inquiries, please contact governmentsales@pearsoned.com.

For questions about sales outside the U.S., please contact intlcs@pearson.com.

Visit us on the Web: informit.com/aw

Library of Congress Control Number: 2020936580

Copyright © 2020 Scaled Agile, Inc.

Cover design and illustration by Regina Cleveland

ISBN-13: 978-0-13-682340-7

ISBN-10: 0-13-682340-8

15 2022

From Richard

We dedicate this book to the Scaled Agile community,
who have contributed to the success of SAFe and applied it to
improve value, quality, and flow, and to make work more engaging and fun.
And to the amazing people at our company, Scaled Agile Inc., who help
make the world a better place, every day.

From Dean

This book is dedicated to my teammates:
Richard Knaster, Inbar Oren, Steve Mayner,
Harry Koehnemann, Luke Hohmann, Andrew Sales,
Yolanda Berea, and Risa Wilmeth.
"Nothing beats an Agile team."

Contents

Preface

When the Scaled Agile Framework (SAFe) was introduced to the public in 2011, we passionately believed that it had the potential to change the way the largest enterprises in the world would develop software and systems that deliver value.

Today, we can say unequivocally that SAFe has lived up to its promise. Hundreds of the world's largest brands now depend on SAFe to stay competitive in an ever-disruptive marketplace. More than 300 business partners, large and small, deliver SAFe training and services worldwide. As of early 2020, more than 600,000 individuals have gained personal knowledge and enhanced their careers by training and certifying in SAFe practices. That's a big responsibility, and we take it very seriously.

As the demand for SAFe continues to grow, so do our efforts to support it. Through Scaled Agile, Inc.—the company behind SAFe—we are continually creating, refining, and delivering tools, resources, and learning events to help enterprises achieve the best possible results with SAFe.

- *The SAFe website*. A freely available knowledge base of proven, integrated principles and practices for Lean, Agile, and DevOps. For more information, go to: scaledagileframework.com.

- *Learning and certification*. A comprehensive role-based curriculum for successfully implementing SAFe, which now includes 13 courses and certifications (scaledagile.com/learning).

- *SAFe community platform*. Continuous learning, tools, and connections for SAFe professionals with Communities of Practice for each role, as well as e-learning, videos, toolkits, collaboration forums, assessments, and resources for professional development (scaledagile.com/community).

- *Scaled Agile partner network*. Worldwide SAFe expertise and support through more than 300 partners (scaledagile.com/find-a-partner).

- *Global and regional SAFe summits*. In 2020, summit events will be held in the United States and Europe (safesummit.com). The latter event will be held virtually due to COVID-19.

The success of SAFe is a direct result of practicing what we preach. We run our entire business—not just product development—with SAFe. That includes sales, marketing, IT, framework development, learning and certification, community platform, accounting, finance, and more.

Our walls are plastered with Kanban boards, sticky notes, objectives, and backlogs, and we plan, iterate, and deliver as we prescribe in SAFe. But most importantly, we have made business agility a part of our company's DNA with an intense focus on a *continuous learning culture*. We never assume that we have all the answers, and we do our best to listen to our detractors as much as our enthusiasts; indeed, we find motivations in both!

Development of SAFe was and is driven by fast feedback and a relentless pursuit of the best possible framework along with the highest-quality training, certification, and customer experience available on the market. And of course, future versions of the framework are always in development.

We're grateful to the thousands of forward-thinking individuals who have been instrumental in proving and realizing SAFe's potential: the enterprise adopters and practitioners who are doing the heavy lifting in applying SAFe in enterprises, as well as the partners, consultants, and trainers who support them.

It's a wonderful thing we've all built together, and we are inspired to continuously evolve SAFe to provide value to the industry—better systems, better business outcomes, and better daily lives for the people who build and use the world's most important systems.

Why SAFe?

Welcome to the age of software and digital—an interconnected, real-time world in which every industry depends on technology and every organization is (at least in part) a software company. To remain competitive, enterprises need to digitally transform their operations, business solutions, and customer experience.

But the challenge many enterprises face is that their current business models, organizational hierarchy, and technology infrastructure can't keep pace with the rapid change required. While Agile development has provided significant improvements to many organizations, by itself it is not enough. What began in software development must now be scaled and expanded to encompass the entire enterprise, changing how people work and how every aspect of the business operates. Put simply, enterprises need *business agility*, the determining factor that will decide the winners and losers in the digital economy.

By empowering people to make quick decisions, including allocating resources and aligning the right people around the right work, business agility permits companies to capitalize on emerging opportunities. Achieving this level of agility requires mastering not one but two business operating systems.

- The first system is traditionally hierarchical and is common to most enterprises. It provides the necessary efficiency, stability, governance, people operations, and other scalable aspects needed to survive in the marketplace and deliver the current mission.

- The second system is a *customer-centric, value stream network*, which is able to quickly deliver innovative business solutions to a faster-moving marketplace.

SAFe helps you implement this second operating system, enabling your enterprise to do the following:

- Quickly adapt and respond to emerging competitive threats

- Efficiently identify and deliver incremental customer value

- Maintain quality in an evolving and innovative product and solution portfolio

Moreover, you will be able to optimally organize teams around value and reorganize quickly in response to changing business needs. The result is that your company will achieve the business agility needed to survive and thrive in the digital age.

A growing number of Global 2000 enterprises have found the answer in SAFe. The framework integrates the iterative development practices of Agile and the culture, tools, and practices of DevSecOps with the mindset of Lean and flow, which focuses on minimizing waste and delays while maximizing customer value. With SAFe, organizations can better link strategy with execution, innovate faster and deliver high-quality solutions to the market more quickly. This has proven to be a powerful advantage that enables businesses to leverage digital disruption to their advantage.

As case studies on the SAFe website (scaledagileframework.com) show, many enterprises—large and small—are getting extraordinary business results from adopting SAFe.

These results typically include the following:

- 10–50 percent happier, more-motivated employees

- 30–75 percent faster time-to-market

- 25–75 percent defect reduction

- 20–50 percent increase in productivity

As you can imagine, with results like those, SAFe is spreading rapidly around the world. Leading surveys and research organizations cite SAFe as the preferred method for scaling Agile. SAFe is by far the most commonly considered and adopted scaling framework.

About This Book

"SAFe® Distilled *is the book we've all been waiting for. It breaks down the complexity of the framework into easily digestible explanations and actionable guidance. A must-have resource for beginners as well as seasoned practitioners."*

— Lee Cunningham, senior director, Enterprise Agile Strategy at
  CollabNet VersionOne

The SAFe knowledge base at scaledagileframework.com is an invaluable resource for people who build software and systems and business solutions; however, navigating the guidance can be daunting for the uninitiated. SAFe is a robust framework supported by hundreds of web pages. Where do you start? In what order should you read the articles? What information is really important to you and when?

We get it. There's a Wikipedia aspect to the SAFe body of knowledge that can be difficult to navigate. It doesn't really tell its own story, and that's why we wrote *SAFe® 5.0 Distilled: Achieving Business Agility with the Scaled Agile Framework*.

The book is divided into three parts.

- ***Part I: Competing in the Age of Software*** introduces business agility and why businesses need SAFe. It describes how SAFe leverages four main bodies of knowledge—Agile, DevOps, Lean product development, and systems thinking—to achieve better business outcomes. This part also introduces SAFe to help you understand the basics of the framework and to serve as a foundation for your learning journey.

- ***Part II: The Seven Core Competencies of the Lean Enterprise*** describes the competencies needed to achieve business agility. Each competency is a set of related knowledge, skills, and behaviors that enable enterprises of all sizes to thrive and survive in the age of software and digital. There is a chapter for each competency, and each integrates knowledge from many different SAFe articles to provide a complete but concise story.

- *Part III: Implementing SAFe, Measure and Grow* describes how to implement the framework's principles, practices, and activities. Here you will learn a step-by-step approach for adopting SAFe and how to measure, grow, and accelerate the benefits of your Lean-Agile implementation to achieve business agility.

We also believe that building the world's most important systems should be fun, too! Perhaps that's the real reason we wrote this book.

—*Richard Knaster and Dean Leffingwell*

Register your copy of *SAFe® 5.0 Distilled* on the InformIT site for convenient access to updates and/or corrections as they become available. To start the registration process, go to informit.com/register and log in or create an account. Enter the product ISBN (9780136823407) and click Submit. Look on the Registered Products tab for an Access Bonus Content link next to this product, and follow that link to access any available bonus materials. If you would like to be notified of exclusive offers on new editions and updates, please check the box to receive email from us.

Acknowledgments

First and foremost, this is a book about SAFe, and therefore the authors are deeply indebted to all those who have contributed to the development of the framework. There are more than 150 books and authors who (knowingly or unknowingly) contributed to the bodies of knowledge that under SAFe. In addition, there are another 100 or so contributors, reviewers, commenters, editors, graphic designers, etc., who make SAFe what it is. But if we were to take time to thank all those who contributed, we wouldn't be able to call this book "distilled." Fortunately, the SAFe Contributors page (scaledagileframework.com/contributors) acknowledges those contributions, so we needn't repeat them here.

However, it is appropriate to thank all those who contributed directly to this particular work: framework team members Steven Mayner, Harry Koehnemann, Luke Hohmann, Inbar Oren, Andrew Sales; senior graphic designer Risa Wilmeth; and technical editor Alan Sharavsky. Finally, a special thanks to our Addison-Wesley team: executive editor Greg Doench, content producer Julie Nahil, and copy editor Kim Wimpsett.

About the Authors

Richard Knaster, SAFe Fellow, Principal Consultant, Scaled Agile, Inc.

Richard has more than 30 years' experience in software and systems development, in roles ranging from developer to executive, and has been leading large-scale Agile transformations for well over 15 years. Richard actively works on advancing SAFe's Lean-Agile methods as a SAFe Fellow. As a principal consultant for Scaled Agile, Inc., he is passionate about helping organizations create a better environment to deliver value, improve quality, and enhance flow, all while making work more engaging and fun.

Dean Leffingwell, creator of SAFe, Chief Methodologist, Scaled Agile, Inc.

Widely recognized as one of the world's foremost authorities on Lean-Agile best practices, Dean Leffingwell is an author, serial entrepreneur, and software and systems development methodologist. His best-selling books, *Agile Software Requirements: Lean Requirements Practices for Teams, Programs, and the Enterprise* and *Scaling Software Agility: Best Practices for Large Enterprises*, form much of the basis of modern thinking on Lean-Agile practices and principles. He serves as Chief Methodologist to Scaled Agile, Inc., which he cofounded in 2011.

Part I
Competing in the Age of Software

"In the age of software, every business is a software business. Agility isn't an option, or a thing just for teams; it is a business imperative."

—Dean Leffingwell, creator of SAFe

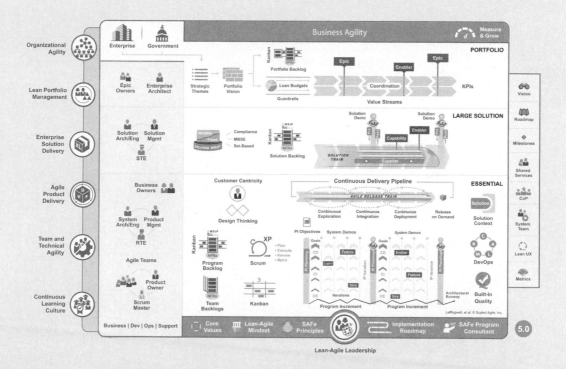

Introduction

Part I of this book introduces why businesses need SAFe, the challenges of software and systems development, and how it leverages four main bodies of knowledge—Agile, DevOps, Lean product development, and systems thinking—to achieve better business outcomes. Also, this part introduces the Scaled Agile Framework (SAFe) that serves as a foundation for your learning journey.

Business Agility

"Those who master large-scale software delivery will define the economic landscape of the 21st century."
   —Mik Kersten, *Project to Product*

Business agility is the ability to compete and thrive in the digital age by quickly responding to market changes and emerging opportunities with innovative business solutions. Achieving business agility requires that everyone involved in delivering solutions use Lean and Agile practices to continually create innovative, high-quality products and services faster than the competition. Such solution delivery typically requires active participation from business and technology leaders, Agile teams, and representatives from IT operations, legal, marketing, finance, compliance, security, and others.

Competing in the Age of Software

In her book, *Technological Revolutions and Financial Capital*, Carlota Perez describes the recurring patterns and changes that have emerged from five revolutions (e.g., age of oil and mass production) illustrated in Figure 1-1. Her research concludes that they occur every generation or so and have a profound impact on society.

First, they cause a massive influx of financial capital (investment), which then results in new production capital (goods and services). Second, they cause market disruption, social change, and a new economic order.

These truly 'world-shaking' technology disruptions typically occur in three distinct phases.

1. *Installation period*. New technology and financial capital combine to create a 'Cambrian explosion' of new entrants.

2. *Turning point*. Existing businesses either master the new technology or decline and become relics of the last age.

3. *Deployment period.* Production capital of the new technology giants starts to overtake existing businesses. This changes society in fundamental ways.

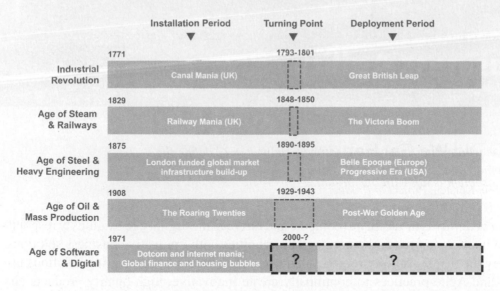

Figure 1-1. Technological revolutions over the past few centuries[1]

As Figure 1-1 illustrates, the installation period has already occurred for the age of software and digital. What, perhaps, is less clear is whether we are at the turning point or deployment period.

However, we are already seeing examples of tech giants overtaking existing businesses and changing society in fundamental ways. The rapid pace of technological change indicates that we are passing through the turning point or more likely we are already in the deployment period.

One might simply look at the massive market capitalizations of Google, Apple, Amazon, Baidu, Salesforce, or Tesla (all companies that didn't exist just 20 to 30 years ago) as strong evidence that we are in the deployment period. It's abundantly clear that every enterprise must prepare for the inevitable business and societal change brought on by the digital age.

In his book *Project to Product*, Mik Kersten analyzes Perez's work and notes that the technological challenge facing our world economy is that "the productivity of

1. Carlota Perez, *Technological Revolutions and Financial Capital: The Dynamics of Bubbles and Golden Ages* (Edward Elgar Publishing, 2002).

software delivery at enterprise organizations falls woefully behind that of the tech giants, and the digital transformations that should be turning the tide are failing to deliver business results."[2]

Kersten's insightful analysis points to an undeniable truth—that many large and successful enterprises today face a daunting existential crisis. The capabilities and physical assets that made these organizations successful, such as brick-and-mortar retail stores, manufacturing, distribution, real estate, local banking, and insurance centers, will no longer be adequate, by themselves, to ensure survival in this new era.

How Did We Get Here?

"The problem is not with our organizations realizing that they need to transform; the problem is that organizations are using managerial frameworks and infrastructure models from past revolutions to manage their businesses in this one."[3]
   —Mik Kersten

Most leaders in traditional organizations are well aware of the threat of digital disruption, and yet many of them fail to make the transition to survive and thrive in the next revolution. The question we have to ask is, why?

In his recent book, *Accelerate: Building Strategic Agility for a Faster-Moving World*, organizational researcher and author John P. Kotter describes how successful enterprises didn't originate as large, cumbersome, and unable to survive a rapidly changing market. Rather, these organizations typically began life as a fast-moving, adaptive network of motivated individuals aligned to a common vision and focused on the needs of their customers. At this stage, roles and reporting relationships are fluid, and people naturally collaborate to identify customer needs, explore potential solutions, and deliver value in any way they can. In other words, it's an adaptive 'entrepreneurial network' of people working toward a shared, customer-centric purpose (Figure 1-2).

---

2. Mik Kersten, *Project to Product* (IT Revolution Press, 2018).
3. Ibid.

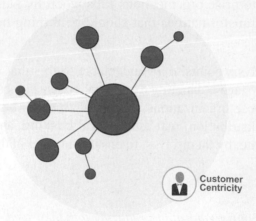

Figure 1-2. New enterprises start as a customer-focused network

As the enterprise achieves its goals, it naturally wants to expand on its success and grow. This means individual responsibilities need to become clearer to ensure that critical details are carried out. Taking on these responsibilities requires gaining expertise, hiring specialists, forming departments for efficiency, and developing policies and procedures to ensure legal compliance and driving repeatable, cost-efficient operations. As a result, businesses start to organize by function. Silos begin to form. Meanwhile, operating in parallel, the network continues to seek new opportunities to deliver value (Figure 1-3).

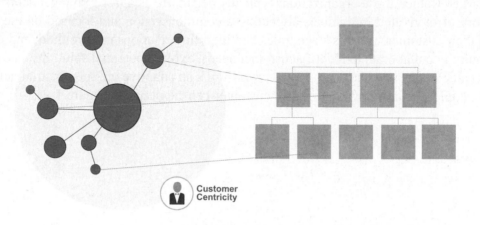

Figure 1-3. Growing hierarchical structure running in parallel with an entrepreneurial network

The organization's hierarchy grows faster and larger to achieve ever-increasing economies of scale. But naturally, the practices and responsibilities needed to run a large business begin to conflict with the entrepreneurial network. With the power, influence, and responsibility of current revenue and profitability, the hierarchy collides with the faster-moving, more adaptive, entrepreneurial network. The result? The network gets crushed by the hierarchy. Customer centricity is one of the casualties (Figure 1-4).

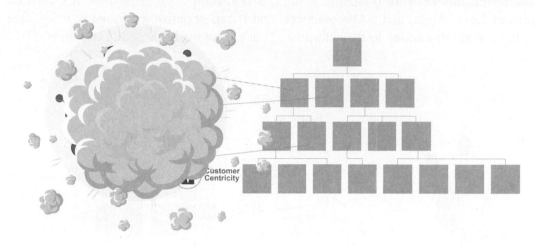

Figure 1-4. Entrepreneurial network collides with a growing hierarchy

Still, as long as the market remains relatively stable, the economies of scale and revenue provide a protective barrier against competitors, and the enterprise can enjoy continued success and growth. However, when customer needs shift dramatically or when a disruptive technology or competitor emerges, the organization lacks the agility to respond. Years of market domination and profitability can vanish, seemingly overnight. The company's very survival is now at stake.

Kotter notes that the organizational hierarchies that we've built over the past 50 years have done a great job of providing time-tested structures, practices, and policies. They support the recruiting, retention, and growth of thousands of employees across the globe. Simply put, they largely work and are still needed. But the question becomes, how do we organize and reintroduce the entrepreneurial network? In addressing the dilemma, Kotter points out, "The solution is not to trash what we know and start over but instead to reintroduce a second system." This model, which Kotter calls a *dual operating system*, restores the speed and innovation of the entrepreneurial network while leveraging the benefits and stability of the hierarchical system.

So, how do we create such a dual operating system? We will describe that in the next section.

SAFe: The Value Stream Network for Business Agility

Implementing the Scaled Agile Framework (SAFe) offers a way for enterprises to realize the second operating system and regain the focus on customers, products, innovation, and growth (Figure 1-5).

Moreover, this network operating system, SAFe, on the left is *flexible*. It's built on proven Lean, Agile, and SAFe practices, and it can organize and quickly reorganize with minimal disruption to the enterprise. That's what business agility demands.

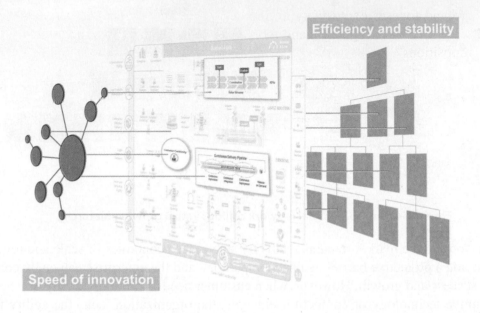

Figure 1-5. SAFe as the second value stream network operating system

However, implementing SAFe effectively requires organizations to gain a significant degree of expertise across seven core competencies. These will be briefly described in Chapter 2, Introduction to SAFe.

While each competency can deliver value on its own, the competencies are also interdependent. Consequently, real business agility can be achieved only when the enterprise achieves some amount of mastery of all. It's a tall order, but the path is clear.

Summary

The age of software and digital transformation threatens the very existence of many enterprises across the globe. Put simply, the organizational structures, management methods, and way of working that created success in the past cannot keep up with an increasingly digital future. In order to survive, enterprises must create, evolve, and master a dual operating system. One looks like a fairly traditional hierarchy, with familiar roles and responsibilities, but is leaner and follows more Agile practices. The second is a more adaptive and flexible entrepreneurial network that is Lean and Agile to its core and focuses exclusively on the customers and opportunities the market presents. This network organizes and reorganizes continuously to address changing value propositions.

Together, these two operating systems provide stability and operational strength coupled with a dynamic network that continually addresses new opportunities with innovative technology-based business solutions. The result is a Lean enterprise that is ready to thrive in the digital age.

2

Introduction to SAFe

"If you can't describe what you are doing as a process, you don't know what you're doing."

— W. Edwards Deming

In Chapter 1, we introduced the concept of *business agility* and its importance to competing in today's fast-paced digital world. It explored the need for a dual operating system, one for stability and execution and another for innovation and growth. It introduced SAFe as the entrepreneurial and flexible second operating system that helps enterprises achieve the goals of stability, execution, and innovation. This chapter provides a brief overview of SAFe and discusses how it helps organizations achieve business agility.

What Is SAFe?

SAFe for Lean Enterprises is an online knowledge base of proven, integrated principles, practices, and guidance that brings the power of Lean, Agile, and DevOps to the people building the world's most important systems. The goal of SAFe is to help enterprises become thriving digital age businesses that deliver competitive systems and solutions to its customers in the shortest sustainable lead time.

Why Implement SAFe?

"We had multiple waterfall efforts, third-party integration, and a hard, regulatory mandate that made coordination and execution exceptionally difficult. SAFe provided the agility, visibility, and transparency needed to ensure we could integrate with the numerous other efforts, get predictable in our delivery, and ensure timelines are met."

— David McMunn, the director of Fannie Mae's Agile Center of Excellence (COE)

As described in Chapter 1, enterprises have to learn how to adapt quickly to the digital age or become extinct, no matter their size, their strength, or how smart they are. Business agility isn't an option; it's a business imperative. Even businesses that don't consider themselves Information Technology (IT) or software companies are now all highly dependent on their ability to rapidly produce new, high-quality, innovative technology-based products and services.

The mission of Scaled Agile Inc. (SAI) is to help enterprises thrive in the digital age. We do that through the development and publication of the SAFe knowledge base, as well as accompanying certification, training, courseware, community resources, and a global network of more than 300 tooling and service partners.

Improving System Development Outcomes

SAFe draws from four primary bodies of knowledge—Agile, DevOps, Lean product development, and systems thinking—and leverages more than a decade of real-world customer experience. It helps enterprises answer the following types of questions:

- How do we align technology development to business strategy?

- How do we deliver new value on a predictable schedule so that the rest of the business can plan?

- How do we improve the quality of our solutions and delight our customers?

- How do we scale Agile practices across the enterprise to deliver better results?

- How do we reorganize around value to avoid the delays inherent in a traditional, functional structure?

- How do we create an environment that fosters collaboration, innovation, and relentless improvement?

- How do we encourage people to take risks, think creatively, and embrace continuous learning?

By adopting SAFe—and applying its well-described set of values, principles, and practices—the enterprise can address these questions and realize greater business and individual benefits.

SAFe enables business agility and improves business outcomes for organizations of all sizes across the world. It has produced dramatic improvements in time to market, employee engagement, higher quality, higher customer satisfaction, and overall improved economic outcomes. It also helps create cultures that are more productive, rewarding, and fun.

Figure 2-1 highlights these benefits as derived directly from customer case studies.

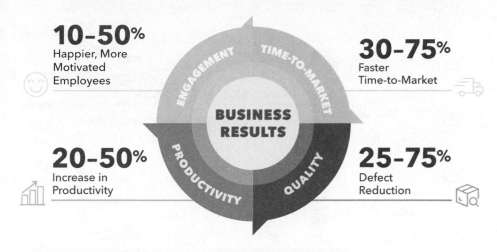

Figure 2-1. SAFe business benefits (source: scaledagile.com/customer-stories)

The Big Picture

Before an enterprise can gain the substantial business benefits shown in Figure 2-1, it has to transform itself into a Lean-Agile enterprise. This transformation requires developing enterprise core competencies that enable a new style of leadership, new ways of thinking and working, and a culture focused on value delivery and continuous improvement.

SAFe's extensive body of knowledge describes the roles, responsibilities, artifacts, and activities necessary to implement enterprise-scale Lean-Agile development. SAFe synchronizes alignment, collaboration, and delivery for large numbers of Agile business and technical teams. Scalable and configurable, SAFe supports smaller-scale solutions employing 50–125 practitioners, as well as complex systems that require thousands of people to build and maintain.

The SAFe website features an interactive *Big Picture* graphic with tabs to select each configuration, as shown in Figure 2-2.

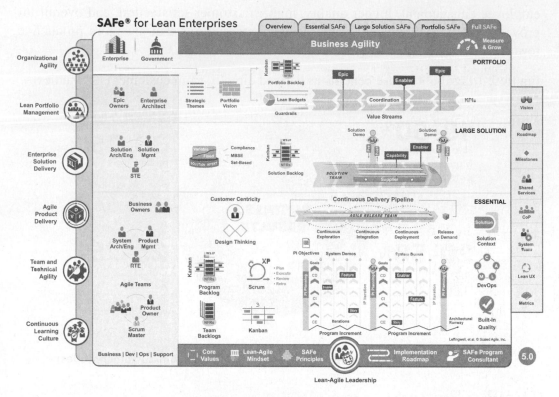

Figure 2-2. The SAFe Big Picture

This graphic provides a visual overview and is the primary user interface to the SAFe knowledge base. Each icon of the image is clickable and provides an entry to the extensive SAFe guidance, which includes the following: the seven core competencies of the Lean enterprise, the four configurations that support a full range of development and business environments, and the foundational principles, values, mindset, roles, artifacts, and implementation elements that make up SAFe. Each of these elements is described next.

Overview Tab

SAFe includes an Overview tab, as illustrated in Figure 2-2. When you click on it, the image in Figure 2-3 is displayed. It provides a simplified view of SAFe's seven core competencies and the twenty-one dimensions that enable business agility. The customer is the focal point for all competencies, while Lean-Agile leadership is foundational. This overview is a useful tool for providing an initial orientation to SAFe and for framing executive briefings.

The road to business agility is a journey, not a destination. To this end, the Measure & Grow link (top right) offers access to a guidance article, which describes how SAFe portfolios evaluate their progress toward business agility and determine the next improvement steps. This topic is further explored in Chapter 16, Measure, Grow, and Accelerate.

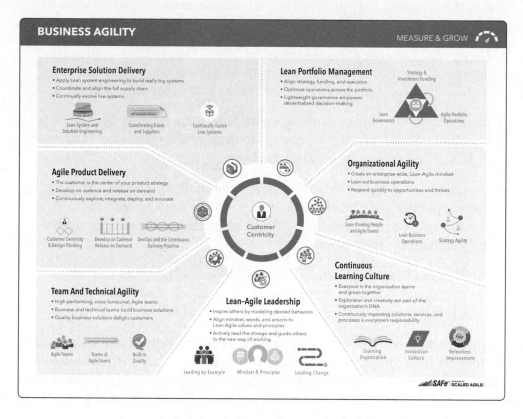

Figure 2-3. The SAFe Overview tab

The seven core competencies are the 'primary lens' for understanding and implementing SAFe. Each is a set of related knowledge, skills, and behaviors, which together enable enterprises to achieve business agility by delivering the best quality and value in the shortest sustainable lead time. The following is a summary of each:

- **Lean-Agile Leadership** describes how Lean-Agile leaders drive and sustain organizational change by empowering individuals and teams to reach their highest potential.

- **Team and Technical Agility** describes the critical skills and Lean-Agile principles and practices that high-performing Agile teams use to create innovative business solutions for their customers.

- **Agile Product Delivery** is a customer-centric approach to defining, building, and releasing a continuous flow of valuable products and services to customers and users.

- **Enterprise Solution Delivery** describes how to apply Lean-Agile principles and practices to the development of the world's largest and most sophisticated software applications, networks, and cyber-physical systems.

- **Lean Portfolio Management** aligns strategy and execution by applying Lean and systems thinking approaches to strategy and investment funding, Agile portfolio operations, and governance.

- **Organizational Agility** describes how Lean-thinking people and Agile teams optimize their business processes, evolve strategy with clear and decisive new commitments, and quickly adapt the organization as needed to capitalize on new opportunities.

- **Continuous Learning Culture** is a set of values and practices that encourage individuals—and the enterprise as a whole—to continually increase knowledge, competence, performance, and innovation.

Each core competency has an assessment that explores areas of opportunity and concern along its three dimensions. These assessments are located at the bottom of each competency article on the SAFe website. To obtain guidance on how to improve, each assessment has a set of recommendations or 'grows,' which are also linked from the individual competency articles.

SAFe Configurations

Configurable and scalable, SAFe allows each organization to adapt the framework to its own business needs (Figure 2-4). With four out-of-the-box configurations, SAFe supports the full spectrum of solutions, from those requiring a small number of teams to those complex systems that require hundreds—and even thousands—of people to build and deliver.

The configurations can be accessed with the tabs shown in Figure 2-2, and each configuration is briefly described next.

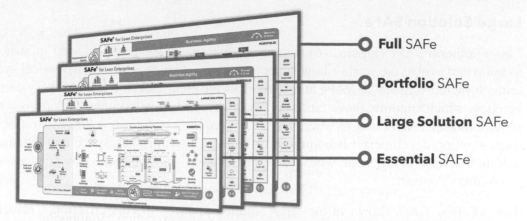

Full SAFe

Portfolio SAFe

Large Solution SAFe

Essential SAFe

Figure 2-4. SAFe configurations

Essential SAFe

Essential SAFe (Figure 2-5) contains the minimal set of roles, events, and artifacts required to continuously deliver business solutions. It is built on the principles and practices found in the competencies of Lean-Agile leadership, team and technical agility, and Agile product delivery. It is the basic building block for all other SAFe configurations and is the simplest starting point for implementation.

The Agile Release Train (ART) is a fundamental organizing structure in Essential SAFe, where Agile business and technical teams, key stakeholders, and other resources are dedicated to an important, ongoing solution mission. The ART's long-lived, flow-based, self-organizing nature is what powers SAFe and ultimately enables business agility. Most trains are virtual organizations that cut across organizational and geographic boundaries.

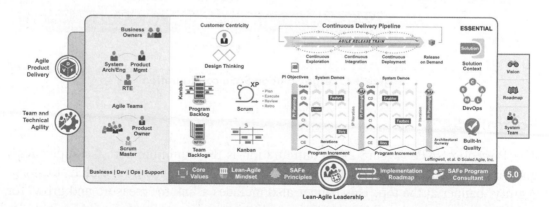

Figure 2-5. Essential SAFe

Large Solution SAFe

Large Solution SAFe (Figure 2-6) describes additional roles, practices, and guidance to build and evolve the world's largest applications, networks, and cyber-physical systems. It includes Essential SAFe and introduces the enterprise solution delivery competency, which supports those building the largest and most complex solutions that require multiple ARTs and suppliers but do not require portfolio-level considerations. Such solution development is common for industries such as aerospace and defense, automotive, and government, where the large solution—not portfolio governance—is the primary concern.

The Solution Train, shown in the large solution level, is the organizational vehicle that coordinates the efforts of multiple ARTs and suppliers to deliver these large and complex systems. The value delivered by Solution Trains can range from core banking applications in global financial institutions to jet fighters and satellite systems.

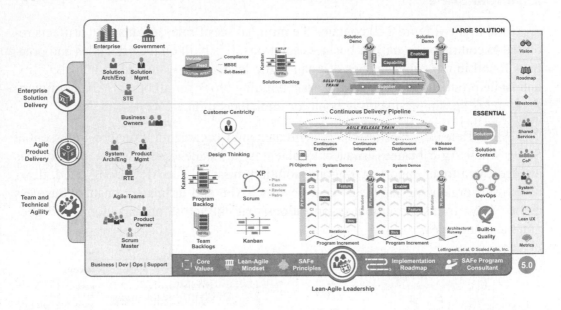

Figure 2-6. Large Solution SAFe configuration

Portfolio SAFe

The Portfolio SAFe (Figure 2-7) configuration is the minimum set of competencies and practices that can fully enable business agility, as indicated by the blue 'Business Agility' banner at the top. This banner also includes a link to 'measure and grow' for guidance on conducting SAFe business agility assessments. Portfolio SAFe includes the Essential SAFe competencies and adds the competencies of Lean portfolio management, organizational agility, and continuous learning culture.

The configuration aligns portfolio execution to enterprise strategy and organizes development around the flow of value through one or more value streams. It provides principles and practices for portfolio strategy and investment funding, Agile portfolio operations, and Lean governance. It helps assure that the value stream and its trains are focused on building the right things with the appropriate level of investments needed to meet strategic objectives.

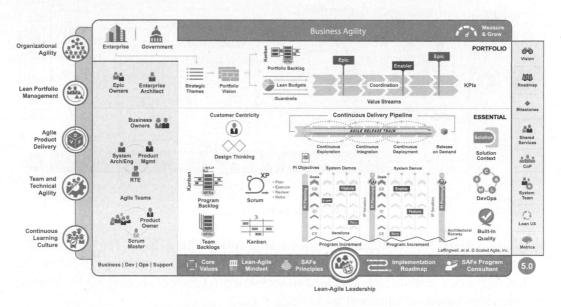

Figure 2-7. Portfolio SAFe configuration

Full SAFe

Full SAFe (Figure 2-8) is the most comprehensive configuration, including all seven core competencies needed for business agility. It is used by the world's largest enterprises to maintain portfolios of large and complex solutions. In some cases, multiple instances of various SAFe configurations may be required.

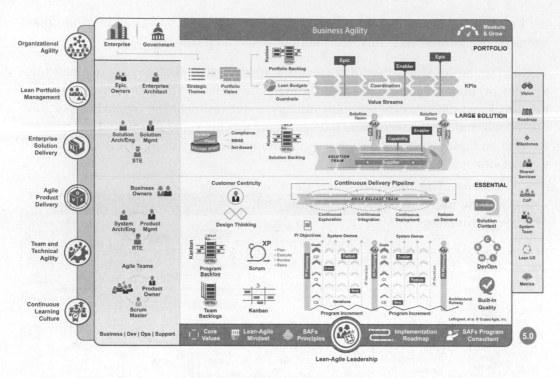

Figure 2-8. Full SAFe configuration

In addition to the four configurations, the framework includes SAFe for Government, which is a set of success patterns for implementing Lean-Agile practices in the public sector. It offers a landing page that hosts a series of government specific SAFe articles, and provides videos, events, and other resources.

You can find more information about the government specific practices at www.scaledagileframework.com/government/.

The Spanning Palette

The *spanning palette* contains various roles and artifacts that may apply to a specific team, ART, large solution, or portfolio context. An essential element of SAFe's flexibility and configurability, the spanning palette permits organizations to apply only the items needed for their configuration.

Figure 2-9 illustrates two versions of the spanning palette.

The small palette is used by the Essential SAFe configuration, while the larger one serves all other configurations. However, since SAFe is a framework, which is meant to be adapted to your context, enterprises can apply any of the elements from the larger spanning palette to Essential SAFe.

The following are brief descriptions of each spanning palette element:

- **Vision**. The vision describes a future view of the solution to be developed, reflecting customer and stakeholder needs, as well as the features and capabilities that are proposed to address those needs.

- **Roadmap**. The roadmap communicates planned ART and value stream deliverables and milestones over a timeline.

- **Milestones**. A milestone is used to track progress toward a specific goal or event. SAFe describes fixed-date, Program Increment (PI), and learning milestones.

- **Shared Services**. Shared services represent the specialty roles that are necessary for the success of an ART or Solution Train but that cannot be dedicated full-time to any specific train.

- **CoP**. A Community of Practice (CoP) is an informal group of team members and other experts that has a mission of sharing practical knowledge in one or more relevant domains.

- **System Team**. The system team is a special Agile team that provides assistance in building and using the continuous delivery pipeline and, where necessary, validating full end-to-end system performance.

Figure 2-9. Spanning palette

- **Lean UX**. Lean User Experience (UX) is the application of Lean principles to user experience design. It uses an iterative, hypothesis-driven approach to product development, through constant measurement and learning loops (build-measure-learn).

- **Metrics**. The primary measure in SAFe is the objective evaluation of working solutions. Moreover, SAFe defines some additional intermediate and long-term measures that teams, ARTs, and portfolios can use to measure progress.

The Foundation

The *foundation* contains the supporting principles, values, mindset, implementation guidance, and leadership roles needed to deliver value successfully at scale. Each foundation element, as shown in Figure 2-10, is briefly described next.

Figure 2-10. SAFe foundation

- **Lean-Agile leaders**. Management has the ultimate responsibility for business outcomes. Leaders are trained in SAFe and in turn become trainers of these leaner and more agile ways of thinking and operating. To this end, SAFe describes a new style of leadership exhibited by the enterprise's new 'Lean-thinking manager-teachers.'

- **Core values**. Four core values of alignment, built-in quality, transparency, and program execution define the belief and value system for SAFe.

- **Lean-Agile mindset**. Lean-Agile leaders are lifelong learners and teachers who understand, embrace, and foster Lean and Agile principles and practices across the enterprise.

- **SAFe principles**. SAFe practices are grounded in 10 principles that synthesize Agile methods, Lean product development, DevOps, systems thinking, and decades of field experience.

- **Implementation roadmap**. Implementing the changes necessary to become a Lean-Agile technology enterprise is a substantial change for most companies. SAFe provides an implementation roadmap to help guide organizations on this journey

- **SAFe Program Consultants (SPCs)**. SPCs are certified change agents who combine their technical knowledge of SAFe with an intrinsic motivation to improve their company's software and systems development processes.

The SAFe Implementation Roadmap

The SAFe implementation roadmap (Figure 2-11) provides a proven method for achieving the desired organizational change. It is generally based on the principles in

John P. Kotter's eight-step model for leading change. As leaders strive for successful change, this roadmap helps them 'know the way.'

While no two SAFe adoptions are identical and they rarely follow a perfectly sequential step-by-step process, businesses typically get the best results when they follow a path similar to that shown in the SAFe implementation roadmap.

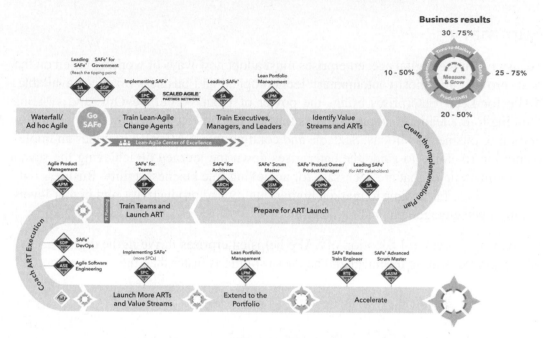

Figure 2-11. SAFe implementation roadmap

Measure and Grow

Measure and grow is the term we use to describe how SAFe portfolios evaluate their progress on the journey toward business agility and determine the next improvement steps.

It describes how to *measure* the current state of a portfolio and *grow* to improve overall business outcomes.

Measure and grow are accomplished via two separate assessment mechanisms, designed for significantly different audiences and different purposes.

> *1. **The SAFe Business Agility Assessment*** is designed for LPM and portfolio stakeholders to assess their overall progress on the ultimate goal of true business agility.

2. **The SAFe Core Competency Assessments** are used to help teams and trains improve on the technical and business practices they need to help the portfolio achieve that larger goal.

Each assessment follows a standard process pattern of *running the assessment, analyzing the results, taking action, and celebrating the victories*.

Summary

To survive in the digital age, enterprises must adopt new ways of working based on the best, proven, and most contemporary technological and business practices available. SAFe for Lean Enterprises brings the power of Lean, Agile, DevOps, and systems thinking to the leaders and practitioners that are responsible for building the next generation of business solutions. Scalable and configurable, SAFe also provides an implementation roadmap to guide the enterprises down the journey of achieving the seven core competencies that are necessary for achieving true business agility. Business outcomes include faster time to market, higher quality and productivity, and higher levels of employee engagement and motivation.

In this way, successful adoption of SAFe helps enterprises thrive in the digital age by delivering innovative technical and business solutions faster than the competition.

3

Lean-Agile Mindset

"In a growth mindset, people believe that their most basic abilities can be developed through dedication and hard work—brains and talent are just the starting point. This view creates a love of learning and a resilience that is essential for great accomplishment."
 —Dr. Carol S. Dweck, Author and Stanford psychology professor

The Lean-Agile mindset is the combination of beliefs, assumptions, attitudes, and actions of leaders and practitioners who embrace the concepts of the Agile Manifesto and Lean thinking and apply it in their daily lives.

This mindset provides the foundation for adopting and applying Scaled Agile Framework (SAFe) principles and practices, as well as an enhanced company culture that enables business agility. It offers leadership the tools needed to support a successful transformation, helping individuals and the entire enterprise achieve their goals.

Mindset Awareness and Openness to Change

A mindset is the mental lens through which we see and interpret the world. It's how the human mind simplifies, categorizes, and makes sense of the vast amount of information it receives each day.

Dr. Dweck's quote reminds us that our mindsets are the foundation for achieving success and happiness in life. With the right mindset, anything is possible.

Our mindsets are formed through a lifetime of structured (classes, reading) and unstructured (life events, work experience) learning. Together, this learning resides deep in our subconscious mind; represents our long-held beliefs, attitudes, and assumptions; and influences the decisions and actions we make every day.

As a result, we are often unaware of how our mindset affects how we do our work and how we interact with people. But if a mindset is made from all this learning and experience, can a mindset be changed? The good news, according to Dr. Dweck, is that mindsets can, indeed, be changed.

The next question becomes, how? It begins with an awareness of fixed and growth mindsets. Some individuals may appear to have a relatively 'fixed' mindset, while others are more open to change and 'growth,' as Figure 3-1 illustrates.

For example, many beliefs are developed from business school and on-the-job experience that are grounded in waterfall, phase-gated, and siloed ways of working. Approaching this situation with a fixed mindset says the organization is the way it is, and no matter what you do it will never change. A growth mindset says you can create change if you work hard, adapt to feedback, and implement strategies for personal development.

Put simply, Henry Ford said, "Whether you think you can, or you think you can't—you're right." Adopting a new mindset requires a belief that new abilities can be developed with time and effort. In this case, leaders must remain open to the possibility that existing mindsets based on traditional management practices need to evolve to guide the organizational change required to become a Lean enterprise.[1] The next two sections describe the key elements of the Lean-Agile mindset we need to achieve.

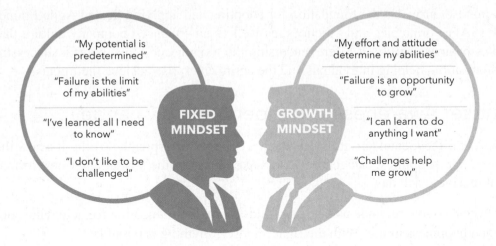

Figure 3-1. Adopting a new mindset requires a belief that new abilities can be developed with effort

---

1. Allen Ward and Durward Sobeck, *Lean Product and Process Development*. Lean Enterprise Institute, 2014.

Thinking Lean and Embracing Agility

To begin this journey of change and instill new habits into the culture, leaders and managers need to learn and adopt the Lean-Agile mindset (Figure 3-2).

House of Lean	Agile Manifesto

House of Lean

VALUE

Respect for people and culture | Flow | Innovation | Relentless improvement

LEADERSHIP

Value in the shortest
sustainable lead time

Agile Manifesto

Individuals and interactions over processes and tools

Working software over comprehensive documentation

Customer collaboration over contract negotiation

Responding to change over following a plan

*That is, while there is value in the items on the
right, we value the items on the left more.*

Figure 3-2. The aspects of a Lean-Agile mindset

Thinking Lean and embracing agility combine to make up a new management approach, one that improves workplace culture by providing the concepts and beliefs that leaders need to guide a successful business transformation. In turn, this helps individuals and enterprises achieve their goals.

Thinking Lean

Lean was originally developed to streamline manufacturing.[2] However, the principles and practices of Lean thinking are now deeply embedded and applied to the development of products, software, and systems. The SAFe House of Lean (shown in Figure 3-2) was inspired by the Toyota House of Lean, to illustrate these concepts simply.

Goal: Value

The 'roof' of the house represents value, and the goal is to *deliver the maximum value in the shortest sustainable lead time, while providing the highest possible quality to customers and society*. High morale, psychological and physical safety, and customer delight are additional goals and benefits.

---

2. James P. Womack, Daniel T. Jones, and Daniel Roos, *The Machine That Changed the World: The Story of Lean Production—Toyota's Secret Weapon in The Global Car Wars that is Revolutionizing World Industry* (Free Press, 2007).

Pillar 1: Respect for People and Culture

Respect for people and culture is a basic tenet of Lean. SAFe enables people to evolve their own practices and improvements. Management challenges them to change and may guide them on the journey. However, individuals and teams learn problem-solving and reflection skills and are accountable for making the appropriate improvements.

The driving force behind this new behavior is a generative culture, which is characterized by a positive, safe, and performance-centric environment.[3] Leaders need to embrace this change and adopt it first, modeling the new ways of thinking and behaving for others to learn and follow.

Respect for people and culture is also extended to relationships with suppliers, partners, customers, and the broader community; all of these parties are vital to the long-term success of the enterprise. When there's real urgency for change, culture improves naturally. First, understand and implement SAFe values and principles. Second, deliver winning results. Cultural change will surely follow!

Pillar 2: Flow

The key to successfully executing SAFe is to establish a continuous flow of work that supports incremental value delivery based on constant feedback and adjustment. Continuous flow enables faster sustainable value delivery, effective built-in quality practices, relentless improvement, and evidence-based governance based on working solutions.

These principles of flow are an important part of the Lean-Agile mindset:

- Understanding the full value stream

- Visualizing and limiting Work In Process (WIP)

- Reducing batch sizes

- Managing queue lengths

- Eliminating waste and removing delays

Additionally, achieving a faster flow of value requires shifting from a 'start-stop-start' project management process to an Agile product delivery approach, which is aligned to long-lived value streams.

---

3. Accelerate: The 2018 State of DevOps Report. http://services.google.com/fh/files/misc/state-of-devops-2018.pdf

Lean-Agile principles provide a better understanding of the development process by incorporating new thinking, tools, and techniques. Leaders and teams can use them to move from a phase-gated approach to a DevOps approach with a continuous delivery pipeline that extends flow to the entire value delivery process.

Pillar 3: Innovation

Flow builds a solid foundation for value delivery. But without innovation, both the product and the process will stagnate. To support this critical part of the SAFe House of Lean, Lean-Agile leaders do the following:

- Hire, coach, and mentor innovation and entrepreneurship in the organization's workforce.

- 'Go see' and visit the actual workplace (known as 'gemba'), where the products and solutions are created and used. As Taiichi Ohno put it, "No useful improvement was ever invented at a desk."

- Provide time and space for people to be creative to enable purposeful innovation. This can rarely occur in the presence of 100 percent utilization and daily firefighting. SAFe's Innovation and Planning (IP) iteration is one such opportunity.

- Apply continuous exploration, the process of constantly exploring the market and user needs, getting fast feedback on experiments, and defining a vision, roadmap, and set of features that bring the most promising innovations to market.

- The facts are friendly. Validate innovations with customers and then 'pivot without mercy or guilt' when fact patterns change.

- Couple strategic thinking with local team-based innovations to create an 'innovation riptide' that can power a tidal wave of new products, services, and capabilities.

Pillar 4: Relentless Improvement

Relentless improvement is the fourth pillar of the SAFe House of Lean. It guides the business to become a learning organization through continuous reflection and adaptation. A 'constant sense of competitive danger' drives the aggressive pursuit of improvement opportunities. Leaders and teams systematically do the following:

- Optimize the whole, not just the parts, of the organization and the development process.

- Reinforce the problem-solving mindset throughout the organization, where all are empowered to engage in daily improvements to the work.

- Reflect at key milestones to openly identify and address process shortcomings at all levels.

- Apply Lean tools and techniques to determine the fact-based root cause of problems and apply effective countermeasures rapidly.

- Base improvements on facts. Consider facts carefully and then act quickly.

Chapter 11, Continuous Learning Culture, will provide additional perspective on the importance of innovation and relentless improvement in achieving business agility.

Foundation: Leadership

As with any significant organizational change, the enterprise's managers, leaders, and executives are responsible for the adoption and success of the Lean-Agile transformation. Their leadership is the foundation of Lean and is the starting point for individual, team, and enterprise success. Successful leaders are trained in these new and innovative ways of thinking and exhibit the principles and behaviors of Lean-Agile leadership.

From a leadership perspective, Lean is different than Agile. Agile was developed as a team-based process for a small group of cross-functional, dedicated individuals who were empowered, skilled, and needed to build working functionality in a short timebox. Management, however, was not part of this definition. But, excluding management from the new way of working doesn't scale in an enterprise.

By contrast, in Lean, managers are leaders who embrace the values of Lean, are competent in the basic practices, and teach these practices to others. They proactively eliminate impediments and take an active role in supporting organizational change and facilitating relentless improvement. Chapter 5, Lean-Agile Leadership, is dedicated to this topic.

Embracing Agility

The right half of the Lean-Agile mindset (Figure 3-2) is, of course, Agile. Since it's a critical element of SAFe, the rest of this chapter is devoted to the values and principles of Agile.

A brief history of Agile is helpful to understand its intent. In the 1990s, responding to the many challenges of waterfall processes, some lighter-weight and more iterative development methods emerged. In 2001, many thought leaders of these frameworks came together in Snowbird, Utah. While there were differences of opinion on the specific merits of one method over another, the attendees agreed that their shared values and beliefs dwarfed the differences. The result was a *Manifesto for Agile Software Development*[4]—a turning point that clarified the new approach and started to bring the benefits of these innovative methods to the whole development industry. In the years since the manifesto was first published, Agile has been adopted by domains outside of software development, including hardware systems, infrastructure, operations, and support. More recently, business teams outside of technology have also embraced Agile principles for planning and executing their work.

The Values of the Agile Manifesto

Figure 3-3 illustrates the Agile Manifesto and is followed by a description of its four values.

Figure 3-3. *Manifesto for Agile Software Development*

---

4. Manifesto for Agile Software Development, http://agilemanifesto.org/.

We Are Uncovering Better Ways

The first phrase of the manifesto deserves emphasis: "We are uncovering better ways of developing software by doing it and helping others do it."

We interpret this as describing an ongoing journey of discovery to increasingly embrace Agile behaviors, a journey with no end. SAFe is not a fixed, frozen-in-time framework. As we uncover better ways of working, we adapt the framework, as evidenced by more than six major releases as of this writing.

Where We Find Value

We'll discuss the values shortly, but the final phrase of the manifesto is also important and sometimes overlooked: "That is, while there is value in the items on the right, we value the items on the left more."

Some people may misinterpret the value statements as a binary decision between two choices (e.g., working software versus comprehensive documentation), but that's not the intended meaning. Both items have value; however, the item on the left has more value (i.e., working software). The Agile Manifesto is not rigid or dogmatic. Instead, it embraces the need to balance the values based on the context.

Individuals and Interactions over Processes and Tools

Deming notes, "If you can't describe what you are doing as a process, then you don't know what you are doing." So, Agile processes in frameworks like Scrum, Kanban, and SAFe do matter. However, a process is only a means to an end. When we're captive to a process that isn't working, it creates waste and delays. So, *favor individuals and interactions* and then modify processes accordingly.

In a distributed environment, tools are critically important to assist with communication and collaboration (e.g., video conferencing, text messaging, ALM[5] tools, and wikis). This is especially true at scale. However, tools should supplement, rather than replace, face-to-face communication.

Working Software over Comprehensive Documentation

Documentation is important and has value. But creating documents for the sake of complying with potentially outdated corporate governance models has no value. As

---

5. ALM: application life-cycle management.

part of a change program, governance, often captured by documentation standards, needs to be updated to reflect the Lean-Agile way of working. Rather than create detailed documentation too early—especially the wrong kind—it's more valuable to show customers working software to get their feedback. Therefore, favor *working software*. And document only what's truly needed.

Customer Collaboration over Contract Negotiation

Customers are the ultimate deciders of value, so their close collaboration is essential in the development process. To convey the rights, responsibilities, and economic concerns of each party, contracts are often necessary—but recognize that contracts can over-regulate what to do and how to do it. No matter how well they're written, they don't replace regular communication, collaboration, and trust. Win–lose contracts usually result in poorer economic outcomes and distrust, creating short-term relationships instead of long-term business partnerships. Instead, contracts should be win-win propositions that favor *customer collaboration*.

Responding to Change over Following a Plan

Change is a reality that the development process has to reflect. The strength of Lean-Agile development is in how it embraces change. As the system evolves, so does the understanding of the problem and the solution domain. Business stakeholder knowledge also improves over time, and customer needs evolve as well. Indeed, those changes in understanding add value to our system.

Of course, the manifesto phrase "over following a plan" indicates that *there is in fact a plan*! Planning is an important part of Agile development. Indeed, Agile teams and ARTs plan more often and more continuously than their counterparts using a waterfall process. However, plans need to adapt as new learning occurs, new information becomes available, and the situation changes.

Agile Manifesto Principles

The Agile Manifesto (Figure 3-4) has 12 principles that support its values.[6] These principles take those values a step further and specifically describe what it means to be Agile.

Most of these principles are self-explanatory. They need no elaboration, except for a discussion of applying the Agile Manifesto at scale, which is covered next.

---

6. http://agilemanifesto.org/principles.html

The combination of values and principles in the manifesto creates a framework for what the Snowbird attendees believed was the essence of Agile. The industry is better for the extraordinary business and personal benefits made possible by this new way of thinking and working. We are grateful for it.

The Principles of the Agile Manifesto

1. Our highest priority is to satisfy the customer through early and continuous delivery of valuable software.

2. Welcome changing requirements, even late in development. Agile processes harness change for the customer's competitive advantage.

3. Deliver working software frequently, from a couple of weeks to a couple of months, with a preference for the shorter timescale.

4. Business people and developers must work together daily throughout the project.

5. Build projects around motivated individuals. Give them the environment and support they need, and trust them to get the job done.

6. The most efficient and effective method of conveying information to and within a development team is face-to-face conversation.

7. Working software is the primary measure of progress.

8. Agile processes promote sustainable development. The sponsors, developers, and users should be able to maintain a constant pace indefinitely.

9. Continuous attention to technical excellence and good design enhances agility.

10. Simplicity—the art of maximizing the amount of work not done—is essential.

11. The best architectures, requirements, and designs emerge from self-organizing teams.

12. At regular intervals, the team reflects on how to become more effective, then tunes and adjusts its behavior accordingly.

agilemanifesto.org

Figure 3-4. The principles of the Agile Manifesto

Applying the Agile Manifesto at Scale

The brief document that launched this massive movement is more than 19 years old. Since then, not one word has changed. So, it's fair to ask, given all the advancements in the last 19 years, is the Agile Manifesto still relevant? Or should it be treated like a historical document that has long since served its purpose?

What's more, Agile was defined for small, fast-moving, software-only teams. That raises other valid questions: Does the Agile Manifesto scale? Does it meet the needs of enterprises developing the biggest and most complex software and systems? Does it serve the needs of systems that require hundreds of people to build them and have unacceptably high costs of failure?

Rather than judge the ability of Agile to remain relevant on its own, what better way to assess the manifesto's practicality than by asking the people actively engaged in building these new systems? Specifically, we routinely ask SAFe students to do an exercise in class, as described in Figure 3-5.

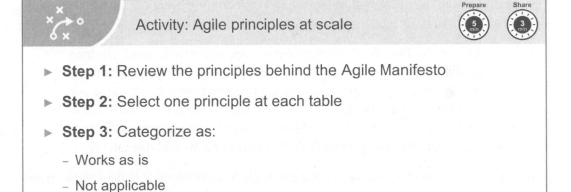

Figure 3-5. Agile Manifesto class exercise

The typical response is that principles 1, 3, 5, 7, 8, 9, 10, and 12 'work as is.' The conclusion is that most Agile principles scale without requiring any rethinking, and indeed, *most need even more emphasis* when applied at scale. The other principles typically foster a little more discussion, as highlighted here:

- *Principle #2—Welcome changing requirements, even late in development. Agile processes harness change for the customer's competitive advantage.* The comments here are, 'It just depends.' In some cases, the cost of change for some types of late modifications may create situations that are not feasible. For example, can we change the optical resolution of a geophysical satellite a few months before launch? Probably not, unless it's driven purely by software.

- *Principle #4—Business people and developers must work together daily throughout the project.* Most are certainly willing to comply with the spirit of this concept. However, there are limitations on the economic practicality and convenience of daily on-site feedback from customers though we fully agree with the sentiment.

- *Principle #6—The most efficient and effective method of conveying information to and within a development team is face-to-face conversation.* Everyone agrees with the intent of this principle. SAFe addresses this point, in part, with Agile team iteration planning and periodic face-to-face Program Increment (PI) planning events. Such events meet many of the needs for efficient communication at scale.

- *Principle #11—The best architectures, requirements, and designs emerge from self-organizing teams.* Nearly everyone agrees with this principle—depending on how you define a team and the subject and scope of the decisions! Everyone agrees that when you consider an Agile Release Train (ART) as the team, the addition of some architectural and other governance can absolutely create the best requirements and design.

The conclusion from this exercise is that the Agile Manifesto *does indeed scale*. However, many principles require increased emphasis at scale, while others require a more expanded perspective. The Agile Manifesto remains as relevant today as ever, perhaps even more so. We're fortunate to have it, and it plays a vital role in SAFe.

SAFe integrates the values and principles of the Agile Manifesto and Lean throughout the framework. Lean-Agile leaders advance their adoption by first gaining in-depth knowledge through self-study, training, applying what they learn, and discussing breakthroughs and challenges with their peers. Leaders also support their teams as they embrace the Lean-Agile mindset by providing training and coaching and by being a role model for others to follow.

Summary

Mindset drives people's behavior and actions. Moving to a Lean-Agile development paradigm will typically require a change in mindset. Not only are the practices different, but the entire belief system—including core values, culture, and leadership philosophies—is different as well. To begin the Lean-Agile journey and instill new habits into the culture, everyone must adopt the values, mindset, and principles provided by SAFe, Lean thinking, and the Agile Manifesto. This new mindset creates the foundation needed for a successful Lean-Agile transformation.

SAFe Principles

"The impression that 'our problems are different' is a common dis-ease that afflicts management the world over. They are different, to be sure, but the principles that will help to improve the quality of product and service are universal in nature."
— W. Edwards Deming

Why Focus on Principles?

The Scaled Agile Framework (SAFe) is based on a set of Lean-Agile principles—the core beliefs, fundamental truths, and economic values that drive effective roles and practices. It is based on principles because they are enduring. No matter the situation, they stand the test of time and can be applied universally. Principles inform SAFe prac-tices—a specific activity, action, or way of accomplishing something.

But a practice that works in one situation may not necessarily apply or work in an-other. Therefore, before an enterprise can apply SAFe practices, it requires an un-derstanding of its underlying principles. This chapter describes the following SAFe Lean-Agile principles:

1. Take an economic view.
2. Apply systems thinking.
3. Assume variability; preserve options.
4. Build incrementally with fast, integrated learning cycles.
5. Base milestones on objective evaluation of working systems.
6. Visualize and limit Work In Process (WIP), reduce batch sizes, and manage queue lengths.
7. Apply cadence; synchronize with cross-domain planning.
8. Unlock the motivation of knowledge workers.

9. Decentralize decision-making.

10. Organize around value.

Principle #1: Take an Economic View

"While you may ignore economics, it won't ignore you."
    —Don Reinertsen, *Principles of Product Development Flow*

Delivering the best value and quality for people and society in the shortest sustainable lead time requires a fundamental understanding of the economics of building systems. Everyday decisions must be made in a proper economic context. Two Lean-Agile practices are essential to this principle: to deliver incrementally, early, and often, and to apply a comprehensive economic framework.

Deliver Early and Often

Most organizations embrace Lean-Agile development because their existing processes aren't producing the results they need, or because they anticipate that they won't work in the future. By choosing a Lean-Agile path, they're embracing a model based on incremental development and early and continuous value delivery, as Figure 4-1 illustrates.

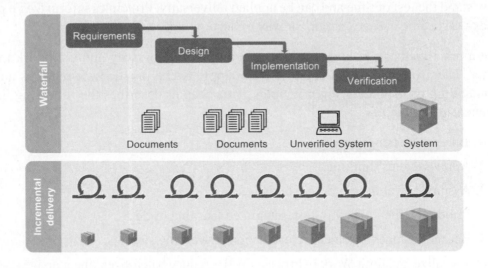

Figure 4-1. Moving to early and continuous delivery of value

The ability to deliver early and often has a direct economic benefit, as illustrated in Figure 4-2.

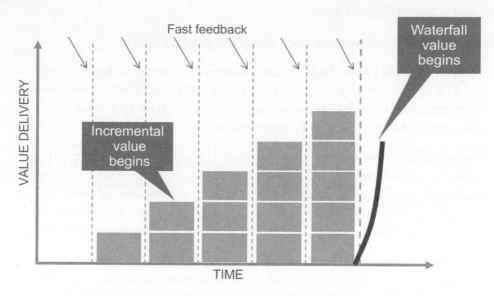

Figure 4-2. The accumulating value of incremental delivery

This figure shows how Lean-Agile methods deliver value to the customer much earlier in the process and accumulate additional value over time. Conversely, with the waterfall model, value can't even begin to accrue until the end of the development cycle. Also, the figure above doesn't even take into account the advantage of far faster feedback or the probability that the waterfall delivery would not occur on time. Simply put, even a perfectly executed waterfall project (and there aren't so many of those) can't compete economically with an Agile approach.

Moreover, as long as the quality is high enough, products and services offered to the market early are typically more valuable than if they were delivered later. After all, if they arrive ahead of the competition, products are worth a premium as they aren't available from anyone else. Even a Minimum Viable Product (MVP) can be worth more to an early buyer than a more full-featured product delivered later.

Apply a Comprehensive Economic Framework

Every SAFe portfolio requires an economic framework—a set of decision guidelines that align everyone with the financial objectives of a portfolio and inform the decision-making process. After all, teams and Agile Release Trains (ARTs) make many decisions every day, influencing economic outcomes. Without proper guidance, self-organizing teams will just make their 'best guess.' As a result, teams may make choices that are not aligned with the core economics of the system, creating the potential for technical debt, rework, waste, and a lack of fitness for use.

SAFe's economic framework contains these four primary elements:

- ***Operating within Lean budgets and guardrails***. These guardrails include guiding investments by horizon, optimizing value and solution integrity with capacity allocation, approving significant initiatives (portfolio epics), and continuous business owner engagement.

- ***Understanding economic trade-offs***. Everyone involved in building solutions needs to understand the trade-offs between development expense, lead time, product cost, value, and risk. Changing any one of these five variables can have an impact on one or more of the others. Understanding how each variable influences the others is vital to making good decisions.

- ***Leveraging suppliers***. Outsourcing labor can provide a cost-efficient way to add personnel, especially if the need is temporary or the demand is highly variable. A supplier may provide specific hardware, software, or skills needed for the solution.

- ***Sequencing jobs for the maximum benefit***. In a flow-based system, job sequencing, rather than prioritization based on speculative return on investment, produces the best economic outcome. To that end, Weighted Shortest Job First (WSJF) is used to prioritize backlogs by calculating the relative Cost of Delay (CoD) and job duration.

Principle #2: Apply Systems Thinking

"A system must be managed. It will not manage itself. Left to themselves, components become selfish, independent profit centers and thus destroy the system ... The secret is cooperation between components toward the aim of the organization."
— W. Edwards Deming

Deming observed that addressing the challenges in the workplace and the marketplace requires an understanding of the systems within which workers and users operate. Such systems are complex, and they consist of many interrelated components. But optimizing a component does not optimize the system. To improve, everyone must understand the larger aim of the system. In SAFe, systems thinking is applied to the solution being developed, and the organization that builds the system.

Figure 4-3 illustrates the three primary aspects of systems thinking.

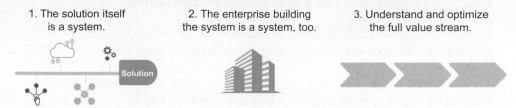

Figure 4-3. Aspects of systems thinking

Understanding these concepts helps leaders and teams navigate the complexity of solution development, the organization, and the larger picture of total time to market. Each aspect is described in the following sections.

The Solution Is a System

Solution Each value stream produces one or more solutions, which are the products, services, or systems delivered to internal or external customers. When it comes to these systems, Deming's quote that "a system must be managed" leads to these critical insights:

- Team members should clearly understand the boundaries of the system and how it interacts with the environment and the systems around it.

- Optimizing a solution component does not optimize the system as a whole.

- The value of a system passes through its interconnections.

- A system can evolve no faster than its slowest integration point.

The Enterprise Building the System Is a System, Too

There's a second aspect to systems thinking: the people, management, and processes of the organization that develop the system are also a system. The understanding that systems must be managed applies in this case as well. Otherwise, the components of the organization building the system will optimize locally and become selfish, limiting the speed and quality of value delivery. While these insights apply directly here, there is more to consider:

- Since building systems is a social endeavor, leaders should create an environment where people can collaborate on building better systems.

- Suppliers and customers are integral to the value stream. They need to be treated as partners, based on a long-term foundation of trust.

- Optimizing individual teams or functional departments does not necessarily enhance the flow of value through the enterprise.

- Accelerating value flow requires eliminating silos and creating cross-functional organizations, such as ARTs and Solution Trains.

Understand and Optimize the Full Value Stream

Value streams are fundamental to SAFe. A SAFe portfolio is a collection of development value streams, each of which delivers one or more solutions to the market. Each value stream (Figure 4-4) consists of the steps necessary to integrate and deploy a new concept through a new or existing system.

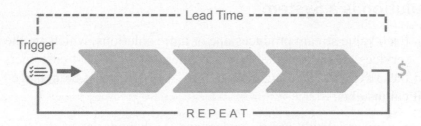

Figure 4-4. A value stream from 'concept to cash'

Understanding and optimizing the full value stream—the third aspect of systems thinking—is the only way to reduce the total time it takes to go from concept to cash.[1]

---

1. Mary Poppendieck and Tom Poppendieck, *Implementing Lean Software Development* (Addison-Wesley, 2006).

Only Management Can Change the System

"Everyone is already doing their best; the problems are with the system … only management can change the system."
  —W. Edwards Deming

This Deming quote prepares us for a final set of insights. Systems thinking requires a new approach to management as well. Lean-thinking managers are systematic problem-solvers, who take the long view, proactively eliminate impediments, and lead the changes necessary to improve the systems that limit performance. They exhibit and teach systems thinking and Lean-Agile values, principles, and practices. Moreover, such leaders foster a continuous learning culture that includes relentless improvement in the application of systems thinking.

Principle #3: Assume Variability; Preserve Options

"Generate alternative system-level designs and subsystem concepts. Rather than try to pick an early winner, aggressively eliminate alternatives. The designs that survive are your most robust alternatives."
  —Allen C. Ward, *Lean Product and Process Development*

Traditional design and life-cycle practices encourage choosing a single design-and-requirements option too early in the development process. Unfortunately, if that starting point proves to be the wrong choice, then future adjustments take too long and can lead to a suboptimal outcome.

Figure 4-5 contrasts a traditional point-based design against a Set-Based Design (SBD) approach. In SBD, developers consider multiple design choices at the start. After that, they continuously evaluate economic and technical trade-offs—based on the objective evidence demoed at integration-based learning points. Then they eliminate the weaker options over time and ultimately converge on a final design, based on the knowledge gained to that point. The results of this approach are better designs and economic outcomes.

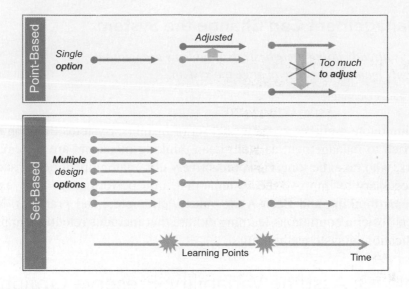

Figure 4-5. Moving to early and continuous delivery of value

Principle #4: Build Incrementally with Fast, Integrated Learning Cycles

"The epiphany of integration points is that they control product development and are the leverage points to improve the system. When the timing of integration points slips, the project is in trouble."
—Dantar P. Oosterwal, *The Lean Machine*

In traditional, phase-gated development, investment costs begin immediately and accumulate until a solution is delivered. Often, little to no actual value is provided before all of the committed features are available or the program runs out of time or money. What's more, the development process itself isn't set up or implemented to allow incremental capabilities to be evaluated by the customer. As a result, the risk remains until the end of the project when feedback can finally be obtained on the feature's fitness for purpose.

Integration Points Create Knowledge from Uncertainty

Lean principles and practices approach the problem differently by starting with a range of requirements and design options (Principle #3), which are considered while building the solution incrementally in a series of short timeboxes (iterations). Each iteration results in an increment of a working system that can be evaluated. Subsequent ones build on the previous increments, and the solution evolves until it's released. The knowledge gained from integration points helps establish technical viability, and can also serve as minimum viable solutions or prototypes for testing the market, validating usability, and obtaining objective customer feedback.

Integration Points Occur by Intent

The development process and the solution architecture must both be designed for frequent integration points. Each point creates a 'pull event' that pulls the various solution elements into an integrated whole, even though it addresses only a portion of the system intent. Integration points pull the stakeholders together as well, creating a routine synchronization that helps assure that the evolving solution addresses the real and current business needs, as opposed to the assumptions established at the beginning. Each integration point delivers its value by converting uncertainty into knowledge.

Faster Learning Through Faster Cycles

Figure 4-6 illustrates how integration points reinforce the basic Plan–Do–Check–Adjust (PDCA) scientific learning process, which helps control the variability of solution development. Like science, the system advances one cycle at a time.

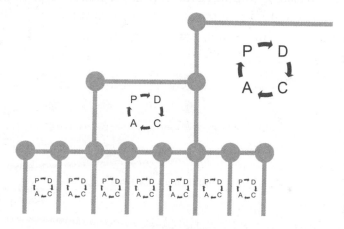

Figure 4-6. Nested integration points occur by intent using a fixed cadence

Moreover, the more frequent the integration points, the faster the learning. In complex systems development, local integration points are used to assure that each system element or capability is meeting its responsibilities to contribute to the overall solution intent. These local points are then integrated at the next higher system level. The larger the system, the more such integration levels exist. The more frequent it happens the faster you learn.

Principle #5: Base Milestones on Objective Evaluation of Working Systems

"There was, in fact, no correlation between exiting phase gates on time and project success ... the data suggested the inverse might be true."

—Dantar P. Oosterwal, *The Lean Machine*

Building today's large-scale systems requires substantial financial investment. Business Owners, customers, and developers need to collaborate to ensure that the proposed return on investment is consciously addressed throughout the development process, rather than hoping that everything will work out in the end.

However, as shown in Figure 4-7, the sequential, phase-gated development process that so many companies rely on to assess progress, reduce risk, and manage investment exposure doesn't always work that way. That's because this model has inherent flaws. The phase-gate model assumes that a point (known) solution exists, and requirements will not change as development occurs. Worse, in most cases, there isn't even a partial working solution available at the phase gates to demonstrate actual progress. As a result, real progress isn't known until the end, when the solution is integrated and tested, which often results in significant rework and delays.

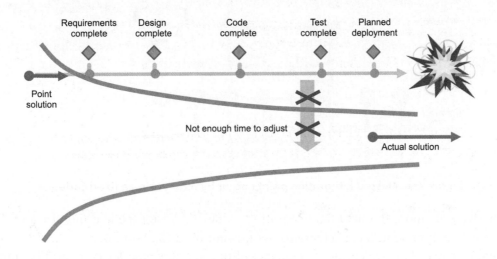

Figure 4-7. The problem with phase-gate milestones

Base Milestones on Objective Evidence

Unlike the phase-gated model, development milestones in SAFe involve a portion of each step—requirements, design, development, testing—together producing an increment of value. Further, this is done routinely on a cadence, which provides the discipline needed to ensure periodic availability and evaluation, as well as predetermined time boundaries that can be used to collapse the field of less desirable options.

What is measured at these critical integration points is subject to the nature and the type of system being built. But the point is that the system can be objectively measured, assessed, and evaluated by the relevant stakeholders frequently throughout the solution development life cycle. This evaluation provides the financial, technical, and fitness-for-purpose governance needed to ensure that continued investment makes economic sense.

Principle #6: Visualize and Limit WIP, Reduce Batch Sizes, and Manage Queue Lengths

"Operating a product development process near full utilization is an economic disaster."
    —Donald Reinertsen

To achieve the shortest sustainable lead time, Lean enterprises strive for a state of continuous flow, which allows them to move new system features quickly from concept to cash. This flow requires a sufficient capacity of people and resources to respond to unforeseen events. In addition to capacity, there are three primary keys to implementing flow, each of which are described in the following sections.

Visualize and Limit WIP

Overloading teams and ARTs with more work than can be reasonably accomplished causes too much WIP, which confuses priorities, causes frequent context switching, and increases overhead and wait times. Like a crowded highway at rush hour, there is simply no upside to having more WIP than the system can handle. Experience shows that excess WIP drives high utilization, which results in the inability to respond to change, burnout, late product launches, reduced profits, and poor economic outcomes.

The first step to correct the problem is to make the current WIP visible to all stakeholders. The simple Kanban board in Figure 4-8 provides one example of how to do this.

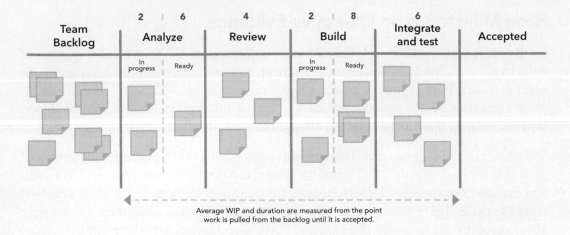

Figure 4-8. Example Kanban board

Kanban boards show the total amount of work for each development state and help identify bottlenecks. In some cases, simply visualizing the work helps address the problems of starting too much work and not finishing enough. When any state reaches its WIP limit, no new work is started until the bottleneck is addressed, which significantly increases flow. Establishing WIP limits balances the demand against the available capacity.

Reduce Batch Size

Another way to improve flow is to decrease the batch sizes of the work. Small batches flow through the system faster and with more predictability, which results in more rapid learning and value delivery. As Figure 4-9 illustrates, the economically optimal batch size depends upon both the holding cost (of inventory and of delaying feedback and value) and the transaction cost (of planning, implementing, and testing the batch).

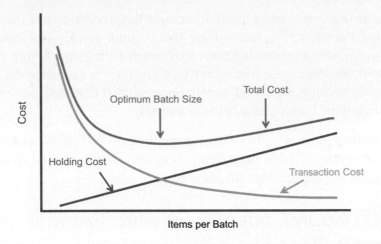

Figure 4-9. Total cost is the sum of the transaction and holding costs

To improve the economics of smaller batches and to increase throughput and reliability, it's essential to reduce the transaction costs. This cost reduction typically involves more investment in infrastructure and test automation, including practices such as continuous integration, test-driven development, and DevOps.

Manage Queue Lengths

The last insight to improve flow is to manage and reduce the length of the work queue. Long queues of work create all sorts of undesirable results.

- *Longer cycle times.* New work entering the queue takes longer to complete.

- *Increased risk.* The value of items in the queue, such as requirements, decays over time.

- *Increased variability.* Each item has some variability, and the more items, the more overall variability.

- *Lower motivation.* A large queue of work lowers the sense of urgency.

In contrast, reducing queue length decreases delays, reduces waste, and increases the quality and predictability of outcomes. Little's law—the fundamental law of queuing theory—tells us that the average wait time for an item in the queue is equal to the average queue length, divided by the average processing rate.

The line to buy coffee at Starbucks teaches us that the longer the queue, the longer the wait. It also tells us that there are only two options to decrease wait times: reduce the length of the queue (e.g., open more lines) or increase the processing rate (make coffee faster). Increasing the processing rate—doing things more quickly—is indeed beneficial, but improvements in processing rates may reach their limits before they truly impact throughput. So, the fastest way to reduce wait times is to reduce the length of the queue. Keeping backlogs short and largely uncommitted facilitates accomplishing this goal. Visualizing the backlog also helps immensely.

By combining the three elements of visualizing and limiting WIP, reducing batch sizes, and managing queues, measurable improvements in throughput, quality, customer satisfaction, and employee engagement are possible.

Principle #7: Apply Cadence; Synchronize with Cross-Domain Planning

"Cadence and synchronization limit the accumulation of variance."
  —Donald Reinertsen

Solution development is an inherently uncertain process. If it weren't, the solutions would already exist, and there would be no room for the next generation of innovations. This uncertainty conflicts with the need for businesses to manage investments, track progress, and have sufficient confidence in future outcomes to plan and commit to a reasonable course of action.

Agile development functions best in a 'safety zone,' where enough uncertainty provides the freedom to pursue innovation and react to events, while also giving confidence the business needs to operate. The primary means to achieve this balance is through the objective knowledge of the current state. This knowledge is gained by applying cadence and synchronization, coupled with cross-domain planning.

- *Cadence* makes routine everything that can be routine so teams can focus on managing the variable parts of solution development.

- *Synchronization* allows multiple solution perspectives to be understood, resolved, and integrated at the same time.

Figure 4-10 highlights many of the benefits of cadence and synchronization.

Cadence	Synchronization
▸ Converts unpredictable events into predictable ones and lowers cost	▸ Causes multiple events to happen at the same time
▸ Makes waiting times for new work predictable	▸ Facilitates cross-functional tradeoffs
▸ Supports regular planning and cross-functional coordination	▸ Provides routine dependency management
▸ Limits batch sizes to a single interval	▸ Supports full system and integration and assessment
▸ Controls injection of new work	▸ Provides multiple feedback perspectives
▸ Provides scheduled integration points	

Figure 4-10. Benefits of cadence and synchronization

Taken together, cadence and synchronization help development teams proceed confidently despite the inherent uncertainty.

Align Development Cadence

Figure 4-11 illustrates that each team is 'sprinting' on the same cadence, allowing multiple teams to evolve, integrate, and demo the solution on a predictable schedule. This improves alignment, communication, coordination, and integration.

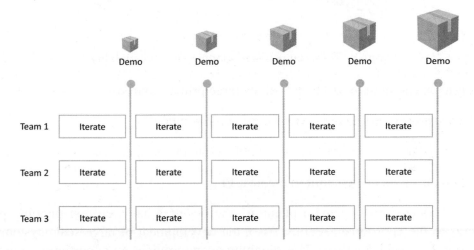

Figure 4-11. Common cadence supported by regular system demos

However, Reinertsen notes that 'delivering on cadence' is another matter entirely, one that requires scope or capacity margin (buffer). ARTs need to be careful about planning to meet date-based commitments, which requires some scope or capacity margin—something that you'll see in many elements of the SAFe PI planning and commitment processes.

Synchronize with Cross-Domain Planning

In addition to common cadence, periodic cross-domain planning (Program Increment [PI] planning) provides the opportunity for the various aspects of a solution—business and technical—to be integrated and evaluated together at one time. This helps teams manage variability by frequently revisiting and updating the plan. In other words, cadence-based planning limits variability to a single time interval (Figure 4-12).

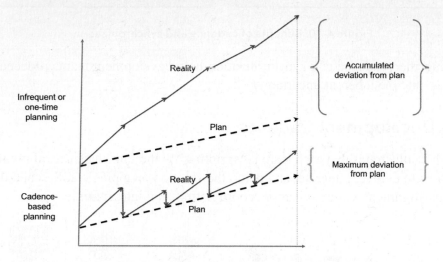

Figure 4-12. Cadence-based planning limits variability

PI planning is essential to SAFe and serves three primary purposes.

- A milestone to assess the current state of the solution

- Realigns all stakeholders to a shared technical and business vision

- The teams plan and commit to the next PI

With synchronized cross-domain planning, the business has a current ongoing plan that leads to the appropriate actions. Also, the development of large-scale systems is fundamentally a social activity. This planning event provides an opportunity to create and improve the social network that builds the solution. Taken together, cadence and synchronization—and the associated activities—help reduce uncertainty and manage the variability inherent in solution development.

Principle #8: Unlock the Intrinsic Motivation of Knowledge Workers

"Knowledge workers are people who know more about the work they perform than their bosses."
 —Peter Drucker[2]

Drucker's definition of a knowledge worker causes us to question how managers can seriously attempt to supervise, outthink, and coordinate the technical work of a large number of people who know more about the system than they do. Simply put, they can't. Instead, it's far more beneficial for management to focus on unlocking the intrinsic motivation of knowledge workers, as described by the examples in the next four sections.

Leverage Systems Thinking

Leveraging systems thinking allows knowledge workers to see the whole picture, communicate across functional boundaries, make decisions based on an understanding of solution economics, and receive fast feedback about the viability of their solutions. They can participate in continuous, incremental learning and mastery, and they can contribute to a more productive and fulfilling solution development process.

Understand the Role of Compensation

Many organizations still embrace outdated assumptions about human potential and individual work performance. Despite mounting evidence that short-term incentives and pay-for-performance plans don't work and often do harm, they continue to apply these and similar measures. Authors as varied as Pink[3] and Drucker[4] have highlighted the core paradox of compensation for knowledge workers: If you don't pay people enough, they won't be motivated. But after a certain point, adding incentive compensation can shift the focus to the money, rather than the work, resulting in worse employee performance. Lean-Agile leaders understand that neither money nor the reverse—threats, intimidation, or fear—inspires ideation, innovation, and deep workplace engagement. Specifically, monetary incentives based on individual objectives may cause harmful internal competition and destroy the cooperation needed to achieve the broader aim.

---

2. Peter F. Drucker, *The Essential Drucker* (Harper-Collins, 2001).

3. Daniel Pink, *Drive: The Surprising Truth About What Motivates Us* (Riverhead Books, 2011).

4. Peter F. Drucker, *The Essential Drucker* (Harper-Collins, 2001).

Create an Environment of Mutual Influence

An environment of mutual influence fosters motivation and empowerment. Leaders create an environment of mutual influence by giving honest feedback supportively, showing a willingness to become more vulnerable, and encouraging others to do the following:[5]

- Disagree when appropriate

- Advocate for the positions that represent their beliefs

- Make their needs clear and push to achieve them

- Enter into joint problem-solving, with management and peers

- Negotiate, compromise, agree, and commit

Provide Autonomy with Purpose, Mission, and Minimum Possible Constraints

Daniel Pink's work, and the work of many others, helps us understand that there are three primary factors in establishing deep workplace engagement.[6]

- *Autonomy* is the desire to self-direct or to manage one's own life. When it comes to knowledge work, self-direction is better.

- *Mastery* is the inherent need for people to grow in their careers and acquire new skills that allow them to provide ever higher levels of contribution.

- *Purpose* is the need to make a connection between the aim of the enterprise and the worker's daily activities. This makes the work more meaningful and links the worker's personal goals to the company mission.

Lean-Agile leaders need to understand these concepts and strive to continuously create an environment where knowledge workers can do their best work.

---

5. David L. Bradford and Allen Cohen, *Managing for Excellence: The Leadership Guide to Developing High Performance in Contemporary Organizations* (John Wiley and Sons, 1997).

6. Daniel Pink, *Drive: The Surprising Truth About What Motivates Us* (Riverhead Books, 2011).

Principle #9: Decentralize Decision-Making

"Knowledge workers themselves are best placed to make decisions about how to perform their work."
—Peter F. Drucker

Delivering value in the shortest sustainable lead time requires decentralized decision-making. Any decision escalated to higher levels of authority introduces a delay, which can decrease the effectiveness of the decision-making process. Decentralized decision-making, in contrast, has the benefit of local context and reduces delays and improves product development flow. It enables faster feedback, more innovative solutions, and higher levels of empowerment.

Centralize Strategic Decisions

Of course, not *every* decision should be decentralized. Some decisions are strategic, have far-reaching impact, and are largely outside of the team's areas of knowledge and responsibility. This leads us to conclude that some decisions should be centralized. Generally, these types of decisions have the following characteristics:

- *Infrequent*. These decisions aren't made often and typically aren't urgent. Thus, deeper consideration is appropriate.

- *Long-lasting*. Once reached, these decisions are unlikely to change.

- *Provide significant economies of scale*. These decisions provide large and broad economic benefits.

Leadership is charged with making these types of decisions, supported by the input of those impacted by the decisions.

Decentralize Everything Else

However, most decisions do not reach the threshold of strategic importance. Therefore, all other decisions should be decentralized. The people who have better local context and detailed knowledge of the technical complexities of the current situation should make these decisions. These types of decisions typically meet the following criteria:

- *Frequent*. These decisions are common and occur often.

- *Time critical*. A delay in these types of decisions comes at a high cost.

- *Require local information*. These decisions need specific local context.

Principle #10: Organize Around Value

"The world is now changing at a rate at which the basic systems, structures, and cultures built over the past century cannot keep up with the demands being placed on them. Incremental adjustments to how you manage and strategize, no matter how clever, are not up to the job."
—John Kotter

Many enterprises today are organized around principles developed during the last century, which worked to increase efficiency, predictability, profitability, and competitive advantage. But in today's digital economy, the only truly sustainable competitive advantage is the speed with which an organization can sense and respond to the needs of its customers. Its strength is its ability to deliver value in the shortest sustainable lead time. Traditional organizational structures "are just not up to the job." Instead, business agility demands that enterprises organize around value to deliver more quickly. And when market and customer demands change, as they inevitably will, the enterprise has to adapt rapidly and seamlessly to reorganize around that new value flow.

By organizing the enterprise around the flow of value instead of the traditional organizational silos, SAFe provides a second, networked operating system (Figure 4-13). This allows enterprises to focus on both the innovation and growth of new ideas as well as the execution, delivery, operation, and support of existing solutions.

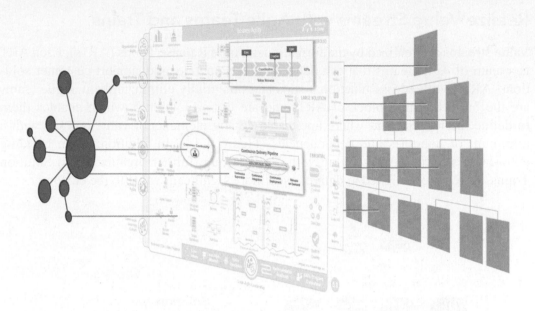

Figure 4-13. A view of SAFe as a second organizational operating system

Understand the Flow of Value

SAFe's networked operating system is intensely focused on continuous value delivery, requiring the enterprise to organize its portfolios around the flow of value, called 'value streams.' A SAFe portfolio is a collection of development value streams, which are connected to deliver more aligned value together. This allows the entire enterprise—from Agile teams to ARTs and from Solutions Trains to the portfolio—to deliver value to the customer in the shortest sustainable lead time. Organizing portfolios around value streams offers substantial benefits to the enterprise, including the following:

- Faster learning

- Shorter time to market

- Higher quality

- Higher productivity

- Leaner budgeting mechanisms

Furthermore, value stream mapping can be used to identify and address delivery delays, waste, and non-value-added activities.

Realize Value Streams with Agile Teams and Trains

Value streams are realized by the formation of Agile Release Trains (ARTs). Each ART is a team of Agile teams that can define, deliver, operate, and support customer solutions. ARTs work across functional silos and potentially eliminate them. Agile teams are the basic building block of ARTs and are cross-functional, which enables them to define, build, test, and where applicable deploy elements of value quickly with a minimum of handoffs and dependencies (Figure 4-14). In addition, when building extra-large systems, ARTs, along with suppliers, are further organized into Solution Trains, which are designed to deliver even more significant value to the customer.

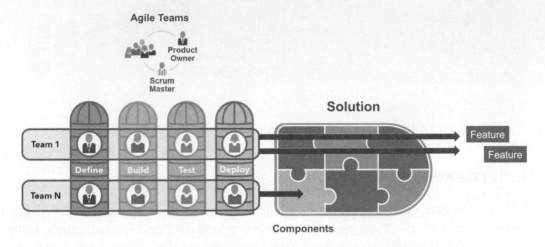

Figure 4-14. Agile teams are cross-functional

Reorganize around Value

While it's best to keep teams and trains together to foster high performance, the organization must be flexible and adapt when the market, customer needs, or strategy changes. After a while, some solutions may require more or less investment or need to be decommissioned entirely. In short, the solutions in a value stream evolve constantly, and the teams and trains need to evolve with them. The ability of organizations to organize around value, and to reorganize around new flows of value as needed, is a key driver for business agility.

Summary

Fortunately, as Deming notes, "our problems may be different," but the principles that we can use to address the problems of large-scale software and solution development are universal in nature. SAFe's ten Lean-Agile principles provide the core beliefs, truths, and economic values that inform the roles and practices of the framework. Before SAFe can be effectively applied, everyone—especially leadership—needs a deep understanding of the principles to know how and why SAFe works. That understanding will create the right knowledge and culture to implement SAFe effectively and, more importantly, to achieve the business benefits that SAFe can provide.

Part II
The Seven Core Competencies of the Lean Enterprise

"Success today requires the agility and drive to constantly rethink, reinvigorate, react, and reinvent."
—Bill Gates

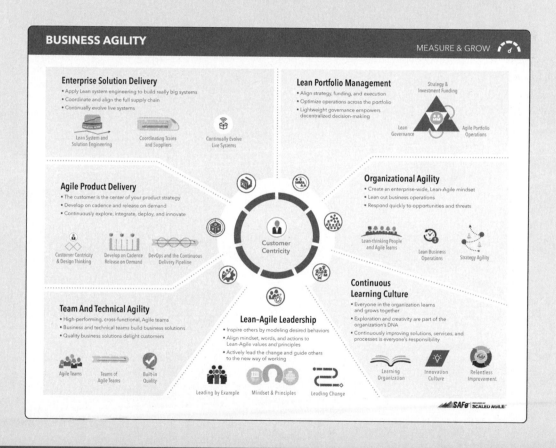

Introduction to the Seven Core Competencies

In this part of the book, we will describe the seven core competencies needed to achieve business agility. Each competency is a set of related knowledge, skills, and behaviors that is further described in three dimensions. They are independent, in that each can advance the outcomes of the enterprise. But they are interdependent, in that they build on each other and full business agility is achieved only when the enterprise masters them all. Together, they enable enterprises of all sizes to thrive in the age of software and digital.

Each competency is described in a subsequent chapter of the same name, starting with Lean-Agile leadership, which is the foundation for all the other competencies.

5

Lean-Agile Leadership

It is not enough that top management commit themselves for life to quality and productivity. They must know what it is that they are committed to—that is, what they must do. These obligations cannot be delegated. Support is not enough: action is required.
—W. Edwards Deming, *Out of Crisis*

The Lean-Agile leadership competency describes how Lean-Agile leaders drive and sustain organizational change and operational excellence by empowering individuals and teams to reach their highest potential. Leading by example, these leaders learn and model the Scaled Agile Framework (SAFe) Lean-Agile mindset, values, principles, and practices. They lead the change to the new way of working.

Why Lean-Agile Leaders?

An organization's managers and leaders are responsible for the adoption, success, and continuous improvement of Lean-Agile development and for fostering the competencies that lead to business agility. Only they have the authority to change and continuously improve the systems that govern how work is done. Only these leaders can create an environment that supports high-performing Agile teams that quickly produce value and improve continuously. Therefore, leaders need to internalize and model leaner ways of thinking and operating so teams will learn from their example.

Business agility requires a different approach to leadership. It starts with leaders exemplifying the Lean and Agile principles and behaviors that will inspire and motivate the organization to pursue a better way of working. Leaders set the example through coaching, empowering, and engaging individuals and teams to reach their highest potential.

In short, knowledge alone is not enough. Lean-Agile leaders need to do more than support the transformation. They actively lead the change and guide the activities necessary to understand and continuously optimize the flow of value through the enterprise.

By helping leaders develop their knowledge and skills based on the three dimensions shown in Figure 5-1, organizations can establish Lean-Agile leadership as the foundational core competency.

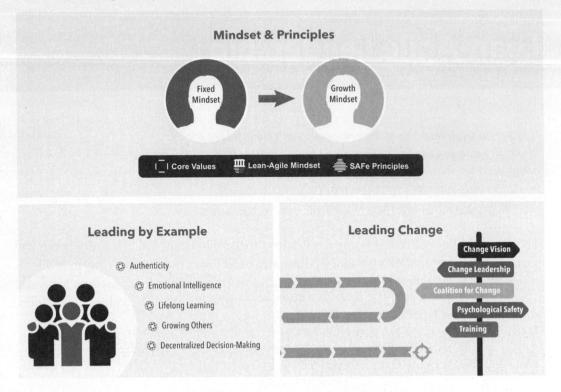

Figure 5-1. The dimensions of Lean-Agile leadership

These dimensions are as follows:

- *Mindset and principles.* By embedding the Lean-Agile way of working in their beliefs, decisions, responses, and actions, leaders model the expected norms throughout the organization.

- *Leading by example.* Leaders gain earned authority by modeling the desired behaviors for others to follow, inspiring them to incorporate the leader's example into their own personal development.

- *Leading change.* By creating the right environment, leaders are actively engaged in the transformation, rather than simply supporting it. They prepare the people and provide the necessary resources to realize the desired outcomes.

The following sections explore the three dimensions of Lean-Agile leadership.

Mindset and Principles

"The basic tenets of Lean challenge many of the aspects of traditional management theory and call for a mindset that is foreign to most executives."

—Jacob Stoller, author of *The Lean CEO: Leading the Way to World-Class Excellence*

Mindset and principles is the first dimension of Lean-Agile leadership competency. Stoller's quote reminds us that traditional management practices cannot accommodate the changes needed to achieve business agility. Instead, the Lean enterprise depends on what Toyota calls 'Lean-thinking manager-teachers.' These leaders understand Lean thinking and SAFe principles and teach them to others. It is integral to who they are and what they do.

When leaders routinely refer to these values and principles and make them part of their coaching and mentoring, it reinforces the new mindset as the way of thinking and behaving.

Chapter 3, Lean-Agile Mindset, described the criticality of the new mindset and how it provides the foundation for adopting and applying SAFe principles and practices and how it supports an enhanced company culture that enables business agility. Further, we noted the awareness and importance of a growth mindset, which requires a belief that new abilities can be developed with time and effort. In turn, this opens leaders to the possibility that existing mindsets can and need to evolve to guide the needed organizational change.

Chapter 4, SAFe Principles, described the 10 immutable, underlying Lean-Agile principles. These tenets and economic concepts inspire and inform the roles and practices of SAFe.

Leading the transformation needed to achieve business agility requires a mindset based on the core values and principles of Lean, Agile, and SAFe (Figure 5-2).

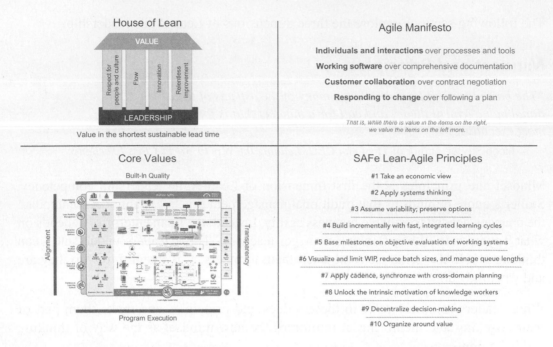

Figure 5-2. Lean-Agile mindset and the core values and principles of SAFe

Next, we will cover one last aspect of the mindset and principles dimension: the four core values of SAFe, which represent the fundamental beliefs that are key to SAFe's effectiveness.

SAFe Core Values

The four core values that define SAFe's essential ideals and beliefs are alignment, transparency, built-in quality, and program execution. Leaders play a critical role in communicating, exhibiting, and emphasizing them, which helps guide the organization on its mission.

The following are some tips leaders can use to reinforce these values:

- *Alignment.* Communicate the mission by establishing and expressing the portfolio strategy and solution vision. Help organize the value stream and coordinate dependencies. Provide relevant briefings and participate in Program Increment (PI) planning. Help with backlog visibility, review, and preparation; regularly check for understanding.

- *Built-in quality.* By refusing to accept or ship low-quality work, Lean-Agile leaders demonstrate their commitment to quality. They support investments in capacity planning for maintenance and to reduce technical debt. This ensures that the quality concerns of the entire organization are part of the regular flow of work, including design thinking, user experience, architecture, operations, security, and compliance.

- **Transparency.** Visualize all relevant work. Take ownership and responsibility for errors and mistakes. Admit missteps while supporting others who acknowledge and learn from theirs. Never punish the messenger. Instead, celebrate learning. Create an environment where the facts are always friendly and transparent.

- **Program execution.** Participate as Business Owners in PI execution and establish business value. Help adjust the scope to ensure demand matches capacity. Celebrate high-quality program increments while aggressively removing impediments and demotivators.

Each core value is critical to experiencing the personal and business benefits of SAFe. Moreover, the core values, mindset, and principles work together as a system. Lean-Agile leaders embrace these values and principles and routinely demonstrate and apply them as they carry out their responsibilities, as discussed in the next section.

Leading by Example

"Setting an example is not the main means of influencing others; it is the only means."
— Albert Einstein

The second dimension of the Lean-Agile leadership competency is leading by example. Through their words and actions, a leader's behavior greatly influences the organization's culture, for better or worse. The most effective way to transform into a Lean enterprise is for leaders to internalize and then model the right behaviors and mindsets of business agility so that others can learn and grow by example.

In his book *Leaders Eat Last*, author Simon Sinek underscores this concept with the following excerpt:

"The leaders of companies set the tone and direction for the people. Hypocrites, liars, and self-interested leaders create cultures filled with hypocrites, liars, and self-interested employees. The leaders of companies who tell the truth, in contrast, will create a culture of people who tell the truth. It is not rocket science. We follow the leader."[1]

---

1. Simon Sinek, *Leaders Eat Last*, Kindle edition (Penguin Random House, 2014)

Leaders set the tone for the company's culture and recognize that a positive culture is an important mechanism for attracting, motivating, and retaining talented employees; it may be the single best predictor of organizational excellence. It's more fun, too. One long-term study discovered that organizations with strong cultures outperform those with weak cultures two to one.[2]

Sociologist Ron Westrum believed that organizational culture was a predictor of safety and performance outcomes in the healthcare industry.[3] He classified cultures into three types of organizations.

- **Pathological (power-oriented).** These organizations are characterized by low cooperation across groups and a culture of blame. Information is often withheld for personal gain.

- **Bureaucratic (rule-oriented).** Bureaucratic cultures are overly preoccupied with rules and position, and responsibilities are compartmentalized by the department, with little concern for the overall mission of the organization.

- **Generative (performance-oriented).** The hallmarks of a generative organization are good information flow, high cooperation and trust, bridging between teams, and conscious inquiry.

So, it follows that by modeling the right behaviors, leaders can influence the organization's culture from pathological and bureaucratic to a generative culture, which enables the Lean-Agile mindset to flourish and spread.

Figure 5-3 provides a comparison of Westrum's cultural model and defines its three archetypes.[4]

2. Robert Daft, *The Leadership Experience,* 7th edition (Cengage Learning, 2017).
3. https://cloud.google.com/solutions/devops/devops-culture-westrum-organizational-culture.
4. Robert Daft, *The Leadership Experience,* 7th edition (Cengage Learning, 2017).

Pathological *Power-oriented*	Bureaucratic *Rule-oriented*	Generative *Performance-oriented*
Low cooperation	Modest cooperation	High cooperation
Messengers blamed	Messengers neglected	Messengers trained
Responsibilities shirked	Narrow responsibilities	Responsibilities shared
Collaboration discouraged	Collaboration tolerated	Collaboration encouraged
Failure leads to scapegoating	Failure leads to justice	Failure leads to improvement
Innovation crushed	Innovation leads to problems	Innovation implemented

Figure 5-3 Westrum's organizational culture model (adapted)[5]

This raises the next important question: what, then, are the behaviors for leaders to embrace to set the right example to build a generative culture? Although the list could be quite long, the following characteristics offer a good starting point to successfully guide the organization to a generative culture:

- *Authenticity* is when leaders act with honesty, integrity, and transparency, remaining true to themselves and their beliefs.

- *Emotional intelligence* is how leaders manage their emotions and those of others through self-awareness, self-regulation, motivation, empathy, and social skills.

- *Lifelong learning* enables leaders to engage in an ongoing, voluntary, and self-motivated pursuit of knowledge and growth, while encouraging and supporting others to do the same.

- *Growing others* helps leaders provide the personal, professional, and technical guidance and resources each employee needs to assume increasing levels of responsibility and decision-making.

- *Decentralized decision-making* takes decision authority and moves it down to the people with the information. This requires investing in the team's technical competence and providing organizational clarity with decision guardrails.[6]

These same behaviors also build *earned authority*—power gained through trust, respect, expertise, or act. This engenders greater engagement and commitment to organizational

---

5. Ron Westrum, "A topology of organisational cultures," BMJ Quality & Safety 2004; 13: ii22–ii27.
6. David Marquet. *Turn the Ship Around*, Kindle edition (Penguin Group, 2013).

aims than sheer positional authority. Such leaders inspire others to follow their direction and to incorporate the leader's example into their own personal development journey. This is a key element of Leading Change, which is described next.

Leading Change

"Nothing undermines change more than behavior by important individuals that is inconsistent with the verbal communication."
—John P. Kotter, *Leading Change*

Leading change is the third dimension of the Lean-Agile leadership competency. Becoming a Lean-thinking manager-teacher provides leaders with the thought processes and practical tools they'll need to start building the Lean enterprise and achieving business agility. The benefits of delivering value in the shortest sustainable lead time, creating flow, and producing customer delight all with happy, engaged employees— are clear. It's also clear that for many organizations, the new way of working represents a powerful shift in culture and practice from past paradigms.

Successful organizational change requires leaders to *lead* the transformation rather than simply support it. They create the environment, prepare the people, and provide the necessary resources to realize the desired outcomes.

In fact, research shows clear correlations between the leader behaviors described in the 'Leading by Example' section of this chapter and the success of organizational change driven by Agile, Lean, and DevOps initiatives. Other researchers found that these leader behaviors have a greater influence on an employee's commitment to support the change, rather than simply following a prescriptive change model.[7,8]

By developing and applying the following skills and techniques, Lean-Agile leaders drive the change process in the following ways:

- *Change vision* occurs when leaders communicate *why* change is needed and do so in ways that inspire, motivate, and engage people.

- *Change leadership* is the ability to positively influence and motivate others to engage in organizational change through the leader's personal advocacy and drive.

7. Stephen Mayner. *Transformational leadership and organizational change during Agile and DevOps initiatives* (ProQuest, 2017).
8. DM Herold, DB Fedor, S Caldwell, and Y Liu, "The effects of transformational and change leadership on employees' commitment to change: a multi-level study." *Journal of Applied Psychology*, vol. 93 (2008): pp. 346–357.

- *A powerful coalition for change* forms when individuals from multiple levels and across silos are empowered and have influence to effectively lead the change.

- *Psychological safety* occurs when leaders create an environment for risk-taking that supports change without fear of negative consequences to self-image, status, or career.

- *Training everyone in the new way of working* ensures that the whole company learns the values, principles, and practices of Lean and Agile, including a commitment by leaders so they can lead by example.

Clearly, these aspects require the active participation of the leaders driving the change. But even this is not enough. As Dan and Chip Heath note in their book on change,[9] leaders "need to script the critical moves" that are essential to accomplish the change.

Based in large part on Kotter's proven organizational change management strategies, the SAFe implementation roadmap describes the steps an enterprise can take to execute them in an orderly, reliable, and successful fashion. This roadmap helps leaders 'know the way,' as they drive for successful change. This is described further in Part III, Implementing SAFe: Measure and Grow.

Role of the SAFe Program Consultant

Even with Lean-Agile leaders and sound organizational change strategies in place, observations from many SAFe implementations indicate that a significant number of change agents and experienced coaches are also needed. Although every leader plays a part in producing the change, SAFe Program Consultants (SPCs) are trained and equipped for this task. SPCs' training, tools, courseware, and intrinsic motivation play a critical role in successfully implementing a SAFe transformation.

---

9. Chip Heath, Dan Heath, *Switch: How to Change Things When Change Is Hard*, Kindle edition (The Crown Publishing Group, 2010).

Summary

Implementing SAFe is not just any change; it's a shift to persistently and relentlessly improving business agility, all based on the fundamentals of Agile and Lean. It requires managers, executives, and other leaders who understand how to lead, sustain, and indeed accelerate the transformation to a new way of working.

Leaders alone have the authority to change and continuously improve the systems that govern how work is performed. Only they can create the environment that encourages high-performing Agile teams to flourish and produce value. Leaders, therefore, must internalize and model leaner ways of thinking and operating so the rest of the organization will learn from their example, coaching, and encouragement.

Effective leadership ultimately provides the foundation responsible for the adoption and success of Lean-Agile development and mastery of the competencies that lead to business agility.

6

Team and Technical Agility

"Continuous attention to technical excellence and good design enhances agility."

—Agile Manifesto

The *team and technical agility* competency describes the critical skills and Lean-Agile principles and practices that high-performing Agile teams and teams of Agile teams use to create innovative business solutions for their customers.

Why Team and Technical Agility?

Agile teams and Agile Release Trains (ARTs) create and support the business solutions that deliver value to customers. Consequently, an organization's ability to thrive in the digital age depends entirely on whether its teams can quickly deliver innovative solutions that reliably meet customer needs. The team and technical agility competency is the cornerstone of business agility and consists of three dimensions (Figure 6-1).

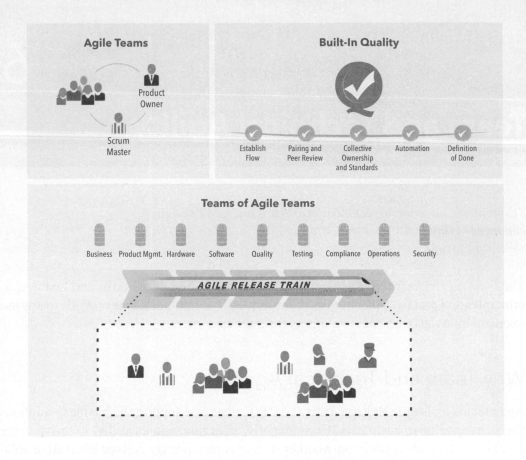

Figure 6-1. The three dimensions of team and technical agility

- *Agile teams.* High-performing, cross-functional teams anchor the competency by applying effective Agile principles and practices.

- *Teams of Agile teams.* Agile teams operate within the context of an ART, a long-lived team of Agile teams that provides a shared vision and direction and is ultimately responsible for delivering solutions.

- *Built-in quality.* All Agile teams apply practices to create high-quality, well-designed solutions that support current and future business needs.

These three dimensions are complementary and help shape the high-performing teams that power the Scaled Agile Framework (SAFe) and, ultimately, the entire enterprise. Each of these dimensions is further discussed next.

Agile Teams

The first dimension of the team and technical agility competency is *Agile teams*. The Agile team is the basic building block of Agile development—a cross-functional group of 5 to 11 individuals who can define, build, test, and deliver an increment of value in a short timebox. These teams have the authority and accountability to manage their own work, which increases productivity and reduces time to market. Agile teams commit to developing in small batches of work, which allows them to shorten feedback cycles and adjust to changing needs. They can be software, hardware, business, operations, or support teams. Or they can be a cross-cutting team of multiple disciplines.

Although organizations have traditionally been organized for functional excellence, value delivery spans across functional silos. Therefore, Agile teams are cross-functional, with all the people and skills needed to deliver value in short iterations, avoiding handoffs and delays (Figure 6-2). Each team member is dedicated to a single team. This reduces the overhead of multitasking and provides a single-minded purpose to achieve the team's goals.

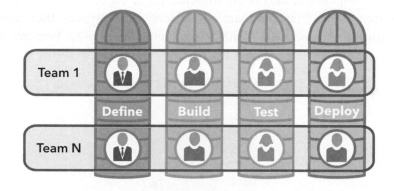

Figure 6-2. Agile teams are cross-functional

Agile teams in SAFe have two specialty roles:

- The **Product Owner (PO)** is responsible for managing the team backlog, ensuring it reflects the customer's needs. This includes prioritization and maintaining the conceptual and technical integrity of the solution's features and components.

- The **Scrum Master** is a servant leader and coach for the team, instilling the agreed-to Agile process, removing impediments, and fostering an environment for high performance, continuous flow, and relentless improvement.

Team Backlog

The *team backlog* contains user and enabler *stories*. It may include other work items as well, representing all the things a team needs to do to advance their portion of the system.

User stories are the primary means of expressing needed functionality. Because they focus on the user as the subject of interest, and not the system, user stories are *value-centric*. To support this, the recommended form of expression is the user-voice format, shown here:

> As a (user role),
>
> I want (activity) to,
>
> so that (business value)

This user-voice format guides teams to understand who is using the system, what they are doing with it, and why they are doing it. Applying this format tends to increase the team's domain competence; they begin to better grasp the real business needs of their user. Stories may come from the team's local context; however, they also typically result from splitting business and enabler features (Figure 6-3). Features are further described in Chapter 7, Agile Product Delivery.

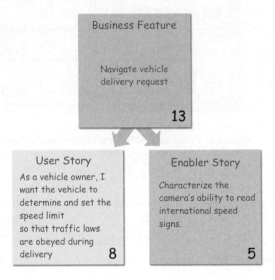

Figure 6-3. Stories typically originate from splitting business and enabler features

In addition, enabler stories describe the work needed to build the architectural runway, which supports the efficient development and delivery of future business features.

These may include items such as exploration, architecture, refactoring, infrastructure, and compliance concerns.

To achieve flow, the team backlog must always contain some stories that are ready to be implemented without significant risk or delay. This is accomplished by frequently refining the backlog. Backlog refinement looks at upcoming stories (and features, as appropriate) to discuss, estimate, and establish an initial understanding of acceptance criteria.

Also, as multiple teams refine their respective backlogs, new issues, dependencies, and stories are likely to emerge. In this way, backlog refinement helps surface problems of understanding or challenges with the current plan.

SAFe Teams Typically Blend Agile Methods

SAFe teams use Agile practices of choice based primarily on Scrum, Kanban, and quality practices derived, in part, from Extreme Programming (XP) (Figure 6-4).

Scrum is a lightweight, team-based process that fosters fast feedback and quick, iterative development of the solution. In Scrum, teams define, build, test (and where applicable, deploy) functionality in short sprints (iterations).

To assure throughput and continuous flow, most teams integrate the best practices of Kanban with Scrum to visualize their work, establish Work In Process (WIP) limits, and illustrate bottlenecks and opportunities for improving throughput. Teams whose work is more active and demand-based often choose Kanban as their primary practice. However, they still plan in cadence with other teams and typically apply the Scrum Master and Product Owner roles (or equivalents) for consistent operation within the ART.

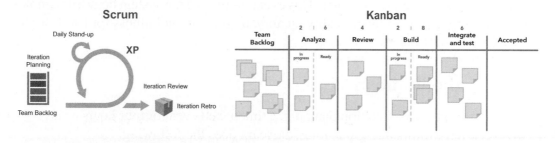

Figure 6-4. SAFe teams typically blend Agile methods

Estimating Work

Agile teams use story points to estimate their work. A story point is a single number that represents a combination of qualities.

- *Volume*. How much is there?

- *Complexity*. How hard is it?

- *Knowledge*. What's known?

- *Uncertainty*. What's unknown?

Story points are relative, without a connection to any specific unit of measure. The size (effort) of each story is estimated relative to other stories, with the smallest story assigned a size of one. A modified Fibonacci sequence (1, 2, 3, 5, 8, 13, 20, 40, 100) is applied to reflect the inherent uncertainty in estimating, as the size get larger. (e.g., 20, 40, 100).[1]

Iterating

Agile teams work in iterations, which provide a regular, predictable planning, development, and review cadence. This ensures that a full Plan–Do–Check–Adjust (PDCA) cycle is executed as quickly as possible. Each iteration is a standard, fixed timebox, which is typically one to two weeks.

These short time periods help the team and other stakeholders regularly test and evaluate the technical and business hypotheses in a working system. Teams integrate their code frequently throughout the iteration. Each iteration also anchors at least one significant, system-level integration point. This event, known as the system demo, assembles various system aspects—functionality, quality, alignment, and fitness for use—across all the teams' contributions.

Planning the Iteration

The iteration starts with iteration planning, a timeboxed event of four hours or less (for a two-week iteration). During planning, the team does the following:

- Reviews, refines, and estimates stories, which are typically presented by the PO

---

1. Mike Cohn, *User Stories Applied: For Agile Software Development* (Addison-Wesley, 2004).

- Defines the acceptance criteria

- Splits larger stories into smaller ones where necessary

- Determines what they can deliver in the upcoming iteration, based on their known velocity (story points per iteration), into iteration goals

- Commits to a short set of iteration goals

Some teams further divide stories into tasks, estimating them in hours to better refine their understanding of the work ahead.

Even before iteration planning starts, Agile teams prepare content by refining the team backlog. Their objective is to better understand the work to be delivered in the upcoming iteration.

Coordinating with Daily Stand-Up Events

Each day, the team has a Daily Stand-Up (DSU) to understand where they are, escalate problems, and get help from other team members. During this event, each team member describes what they did yesterday to advance the iteration goals, what they are going to work on today, and any blocks they are encountering. The DSU should take no more than 15 minutes and typically occurs standing before the team's Kanban board (or electronic equivalent for distributed teams).

But team communication does not end there, as team members interact continuously throughout the iteration. Facilitating such communication is the main reason why teams should be collocated whenever possible.

Delivering Value

During the iteration, each team collaborates to define, build, and test the stories they committed to during iteration planning, resulting in a high-quality, working, tested system increment. They deliver stories throughout the iteration and avoid 'waterfalling' the timebox. These completed stories are demoed throughout the iteration. Teams track the iteration's progress and improve the flow of value by using Kanban boards and the DSU.

To ensure they are solving the right problem, teams apply design thinking and customer centricity (see Chapter 7). To build the system right, teams also apply built-in quality practices, which are described later in this chapter.

Improving the Process

At the end of each iteration in Scrum, the team conducts an iteration review and an iteration retrospective. During the iteration review, the team's increment of stories is demoed for that iteration. This is not a formal status report; rather, it's a review of the tangible outcomes of the iteration. Teams also conduct brief retrospectives—a time to reflect on the iteration, the process, things that are working well, and current obstacles. Then the team comes up with improvement stories for the next iteration.

Teams of Agile Teams

The second dimension of the team and technical agility competency is *teams of Agile teams*. Even with good, local execution, building enterprise-class solutions typically requires more scope and breadth of skills than a single Agile team can provide. Therefore, Agile teams operate in the context of an ART, which is a long-lived team of Agile teams. The ART incrementally develops, delivers, and (where applicable) operates one or more solutions (Figure 6-5).

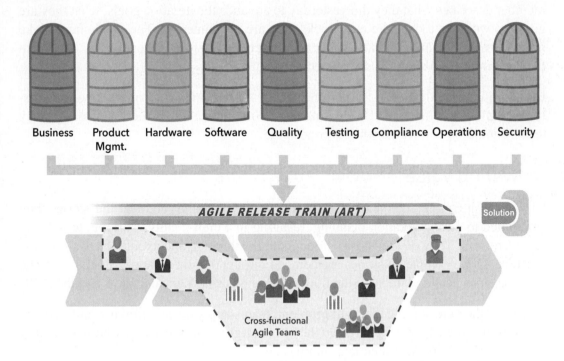

Figure 6-5. Agile Release Trains develop, deliver, and support one or more solutions

ARTs align teams to a common business and technology mission. Each is a virtual organization (typically 50 to 125 people) organized around the enterprise's significant value streams and existing solely to realize the promise of that value by building solutions that deliver benefit to the end user.

The ART applies systems thinking (SAFe Principle #2) and organizes around value (SAFe Principle #10) to build a cross-functional organization optimized to facilitate value flow from ideation through deployment and release and into operations. This creates a far leaner organization, one where traditional daily task and project management is no longer required. Value flows more quickly, with a minimum of overhead.

In addition to the Agile teams, the following roles help ensure successful ART execution:

- *Release Train Engineer (RTE)* is a servant leader who facilitates program execution, impediment removal, risk and dependency management, and continuous improvement.

- *Product Management* is responsible for 'what gets built,' as defined by the vision, roadmap, and new features in the program backlog. They are responsible for defining and supporting the building of desirable, feasible, viable, and sustainable products that meet customer needs over the product-market lifecycle.

- *System Architect/Engineering* is an individual or team that defines the overall architecture of the system. They work at a level of abstraction above the teams and components and define Non-Functional Requirements (NFRs), major system elements, subsystems, and interfaces.

- *Business Owners* are key stakeholders of the ART and have ultimate responsibility for the business outcomes of the train.

- *Customers* are the ultimate recipients of the solution's value.

In addition to these critical ART roles, the following functions can often play an essential part in ART success:

- *System Teams* typically assist in building and supporting DevOps infrastructure for development, continuous integration, automated testing, and deployment into the staging environment. In larger systems they may do end-to-end testing, which cannot be readily accomplished by individual Agile teams.

- *Shared Services* are specialists—for example, data security, information architects, Database Administrators (DBAs)—who are necessary for the success of an ART but cannot be dedicated to a specific train.

All the teams on the ART apply the same iteration cadence and duration to synchronize their work, so that they can plan, demo, and learn together, as illustrated in Figure 6-6. This provides the objective evidence that the whole system is iterating. This alignment also enables teams to *independently* explore, integrate, deploy, and release value, as further described in Chapter 7, Agile Product Delivery.

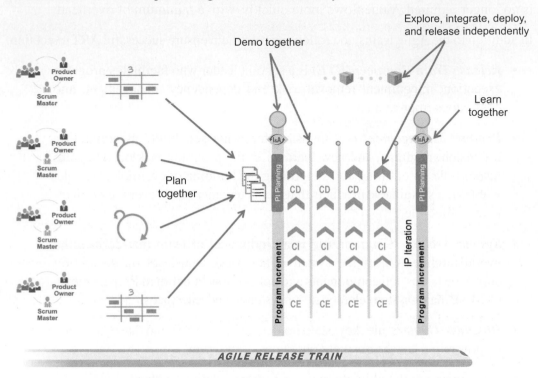

Figure 6-6. Agile Release Trains build, deliver, and support significant solutions

Built-in Quality

Built-in quality is one of the SAFe core values, as well as the third dimension of the team and technical agility competency. All Agile teams—software, hardware, business, and others—must create quality solutions and define their own built-in quality practices. These practices directly affect their ability to deliver predictably and meet commitments. The following quality practices apply to all types of Agile teams, both business and technical.

Establish Flow

To develop and release high-quality work products quickly, Agile teams operate in a fast, flow-based environment. Creating flow requires eliminating the traditional start-stop-start project initiation and development process, along with the phase gates that hinder progress. Instead, *teams visualize and limit WIP, reduce the batch sizes of work items, and manage queue lengths* (SAFe Principle #6). They also base milestones and measures on an *objective evaluation of working systems* (SAFe Principle #5).

Teams build a Continuous Delivery Pipeline (CDP) to guide new pieces of functionality from ideation to on-demand releases of value to the end user. Unlike traditional project management, where success is measured by completing an entire initiative, small features flow through the system quickly to provide feedback and allow course correction.

Peer Review and Pairing

Peer review and pairing help ensure built-in quality during development. Peer review provides feedback on another team member's work. Pairing is when two or more team members work on the same item simultaneously.

Some teams primarily use peer reviews for design-level feedback and pair during development when addressing a challenging problem or performing an activity that requires diverse skills; other teams pair work more frequently or even continuously. Each of these practices builds in quality by leveraging the knowledge, perspectives, and best practices from others. They also raise and broaden the skillset for the entire team, as people learn from each other. Regardless of the approach, all artifacts are subject to multiple sets of eyes and perspectives before being accepted or released.

Collective Ownership and Standards

Collective ownership means that anyone can change an artifact to enhance the system or improve its quality. This reduces dependencies between and within teams and ensures that a team member's absence doesn't block progress. But because the work is not 'owned' by one team or individual, standards are required to assure consistency, enabling everyone to understand and maintain the quality of each work product. Standard peer reviews and lightweight governance help assure that individuals don't make a local change that has an unintended, system-level consequence.

Automation

To increase speed, accuracy, and consistency, Agile teams automate repetitive, manual tasks. Teams typically automate in two ways.

- Automate the processes that build, deploy, and release the solution. This approach takes the teams' raw artifacts (e.g., code, models, images, content) and generates production-ready versions as necessary, integrates them across teams and ARTs, and makes them available in a production environment.

- Automate quality checks in the CDP to ensure standards are followed, and artifacts meet agreed upon quality levels (e.g., unit and integration tests, security, compliance, performance).

Definition of Done

Agile teams develop a Definition of Done (DoD), which is a standard way to ensure that artifacts and larger increments of value can be considered finished only when they demonstrate the agreed level of quality and completeness. For example, the following might be a few DoD conditions:

- Acceptance criteria have been met.

- Tests are automated.

- All tests have been passed.

- NFRs have been met.

- No must-fix defects.

- Relevant documentation updated.

These DoD agreements align teams around *what* quality means and *how* it's built into the solution.

Additional Technical Practices

To continually improve the solution under development, additional quality practices for software teams can also be applied. These are summarized here with links provided for further reading:

- *Agile architecture.*[2] This supports Agile development practices through collaboration, emergent design, intentional architecture, and design simplicity.

- *Agile testing.*[3] In Agile testing, everyone tests. Solutions are developed and tested in small increments, and teams apply test-first and test-automation practices.

- *Test-Driven Development (TDD).*[4] This philosophy and practice recommends building and executing tests before implementing the code or a component of a system.

- *Behavior-Driven Development (BDD).*[5] This test-first, Agile testing practice helps assure built-in quality by defining and automating the testing of the full functionality of the solution. It also serves as a method for determining, documenting, and maintaining requirements.

- *Refactoring.*[6] This activity updates and simplifies the design of the existing code or a component without changing its external behavior.

- *Spikes.*[7] This is a type of exploration enabler story in SAFe. Spikes are used to gain the knowledge necessary to reduce risk, better understand a requirement, or increase the reliability of a story estimate.

Summary

Although organizational hierarchies and organization by function provide time tested structures, practices, and policies, they simply can't provide the speed and quality needed for the digital age. In contrast, team and technical agility focuses on organizing cross-functional Agile teams, and teams of agile teams that apply the best of Agile methods and techniques, without being bound to any one specific Agile way of working. This approach creates long lived teams that apply built-in quality practices throughout the product lifecycle; they learn together and grow together.

2. https://www.scaledagileframework.com/agile-architecture/

3. https://www.scaledagileframework.com/agile-testing/

4. https://www.scaledagileframework.com/test-driven-development/

5. https://www.scaledagileframework.com/behavior-driven-development/

6. https://www.scaledagileframework.com/refactoring/

7. https://www.scaledagileframework.com/spikes/

Further, these teams form cross-functional teams of Agile teams (ARTs) that are aligned along the enterprise value streams and are thereby able to cover the full development lifecycle, from inception, to deployment and production.

These teaming constructs help instantiate the second operating system, which gives the enterprise the resiliency and adaptability it needs to deliver value directly, with far fewer dependencies, handoffs, and delays. The result is more innovative business solutions, delivered to the market more quickly than ever before.

7

Agile Product Delivery

"Specifically, you can take the time to develop and bring to the table an outside-in, market-centric perspective that is so compelling and so well informed that it can counterbalance the inside-out company-centric orientation of last year's operating plan."
—Geoffrey Moore, *Escape Velocity*

Agile product delivery is a customer-centric approach to defining, building, and releasing a continuous flow of valuable products and services to customers and users.

Why Agile Product Delivery?

Achieving business agility requires enterprises to improve their ability to deliver innovative products and services rapidly. Businesses, however, need to balance their execution focus with a customer focus to help assure that they are creating the right solutions, for the right customers, at the right time. These capabilities are mutually supportive and create opportunities to sustain market and service leadership. As illustrated in Figure 7-1, there are three dimensions to Agile product delivery.

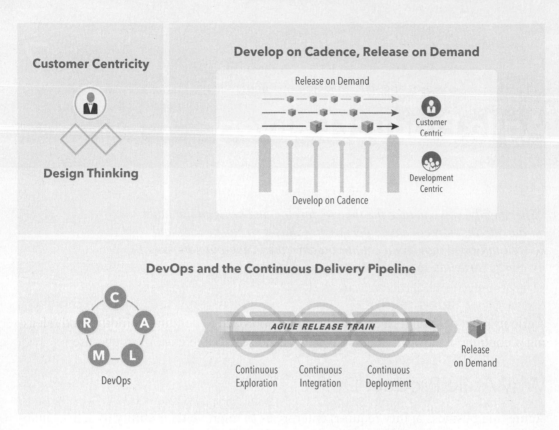

Figure 7-1. The three dimensions of Agile product delivery

- *Customer centricity and design thinking.* Customer centricity puts the customer at the center of every decision. Applying design thinking ensures the solution is desirable, feasible, viable, and sustainable.

- *Develop on cadence, release on demand.* Developing on cadence helps manage the variability inherent in product development. Decoupling the release of value from the development cadence ensures customers can get what they need when they need it.

- *DevOps and the continuous delivery pipeline.* DevOps and the Continuous Delivery Pipeline (CDP) create the foundation that enables enterprises to release value, in whole or in part, at any time to meet customer and market demand.

Each dimension of Agile product delivery is described in the following sections.

Customer Centricity and Design Thinking

Customer centricity and design thinking comprise the first dimension of Agile product delivery. This mindset and way of doing business puts the customer first, at the core of the enterprise, to provide positive customer experiences and to build long-term relationships. As a result, customer-centric businesses typically increase employee engagement and more thoroughly satisfy customer needs.

Teams apply design thinking to ensure products and services that Agile Release Trains (ARTs) create are desired by customers and users while confirming that the solution is feasible, economically viable, and sustainable throughout its life cycle.

Customer Centricity

Whenever a customer-centric enterprise makes a decision, it deeply considers the effect it will have on its end users.[1] This thinking motivates teams to do the following:

- *Focus on the customer.* Apply market and user segmentation to align and focus on specific, targeted groups based on common characteristics.

- *Understand the customer's needs.* Invest the time to identify and truly understand customer needs and build solutions that address those needs.

- *Think and feel like the customer.* Be empathetic and see the world from the customer's viewpoint.

- *Build whole-product solutions.* Design a complete solution for the user's needs, ensuring that the initial and long-term experiences of the customer are optimal and evolve as needed.

- *Create customer lifetime value.* Move beyond a transactional mindset, where customers do a one-time exchange of money for a product. Instead, focus on the lifetime value of a customer. The resulting long-term engagement from this approach enables businesses to create added customer value, often in ways that were not anticipated when the solution was first released.[2]

---

1. Don Norman, *The Design of Everyday Things* (Doubleday, 1990).
2. Alexander Osterwalder, Yves Pigneur, Gregory Bernarda, and Alan Smith, *Value Proposition Design: How to Create Products and Services Customers Want* (Wiley, 2014).

Design Thinking

Design thinking represents a profoundly different approach to product and solution development, in which divergent and convergent techniques are applied to understand a problem, design a solution, and deliver it to the market.

Design thinking simultaneously considers what is desirable from a human point of view, what is technologically feasible, and what is economically viable to create sustainable solutions.[3] It has three main activities, as shown in Figure 7-2.

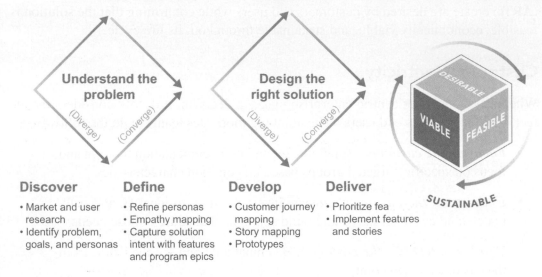

Figure 7-2. Design thinking activities

1. ***Understand the problem.*** The first diamond in Figure 7-2 helps teams truly understand, rather than simply assume, what problem they are trying to solve. It involves spending time with people who are affected by the problem, exploring different aspects of it, and, indeed, sometimes discovering other, more critical problems that can be addressed. This part of the process provides insight into the requirements and benefits of a desirable solution.

2. ***Design the right solution.*** The second diamond encourages the product team to explore different ways to address the problem, including seeking inspiration from elsewhere and co-designing with a range of different people while collaborating internally to build a technically feasible

---

3. https://designthinking.ideo.com/resources

solution. Delivery involves testing various alternatives on a small scale, rejecting those that will not work, and improving the ones that will.

3. **Validate that the solution is sustainable.** To better assure economic success (SAFe Principle #1), teams understand and manage solution economics to ensure that the product or solution will return more value or revenue than the cost to develop and maintain it.

Each diamond focuses on both divergent and convergent thinking. During divergence, *choices* are being *created* (understanding, exploring), while during convergence (evaluating options), *decisions* are being *made*.[4] While presented as a sequential flow, in practice design thinking is an iterative, nonlinear process. New insights and learnings may require returning to an earlier step in the process. Feedback from the actual use of products and services may also motivate a new cycle of design thinking.

Design thinking embraces the reality that the likelihood of creating a perfect product on the first release is slim. Instead, design thinking provides the tools to help teams navigate their path to success by focusing on the intersection of desirability, feasibility, and viability. And of course, the product must be sustainable by the business. In other words, design thinking measures success by these attributes:

- **Desirable**. Do customers want this?

- **Feasible**. Can we actually build it?

- **Viable**. Should we build it?

- **Sustainable**. Are we managing the product so that it returns profit or value to the business over its life cycle?

Moreover, design thinking is not a 'once-and-done' approach. In today's fast-moving digital world, no idea is ever truly complete. Successive applications of design thinking incrementally advance the solution over its product life cycle.

In the following sections, we'll explore some of the useful tools that teams use to apply customer centricity and design thinking.

Market and User Research

The foundation of customer centricity and design thinking consists of market and user research, which creates actionable insights into the problems customers face and the

---

4. https://designthinking.ideo.com/blog/what-does-design-thinking-feel-like

solution's functional and operational requirements. Market research tends to drive strategy (who we are serving), while user research primarily drives design (how we meet their needs) (Figure 7-3).

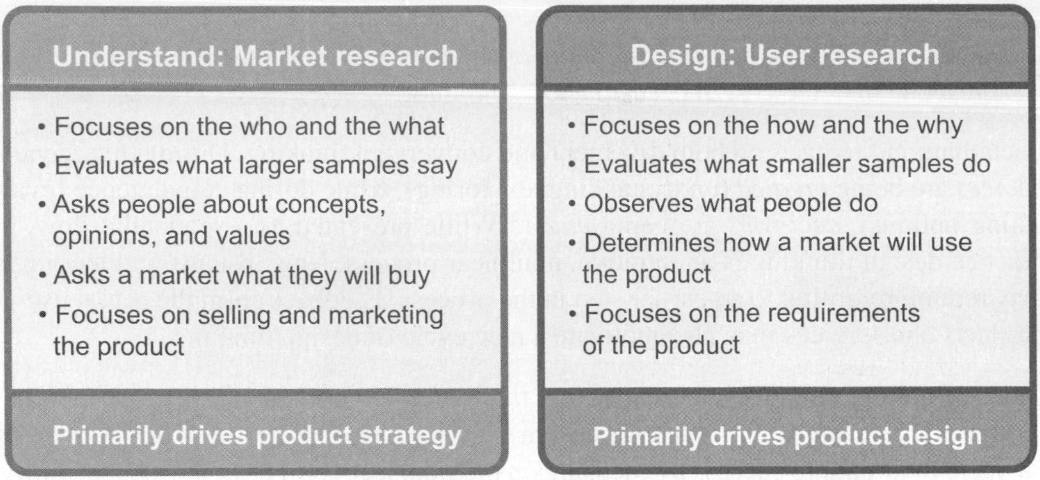

Understand: Market research	Design: User research
• Focuses on the who and the what • Evaluates what larger samples say • Asks people about concepts, opinions, and values • Asks a market what they will buy • Focuses on selling and marketing the product	• Focuses on the how and the why • Evaluates what smaller samples do • Observes what people do • Determines how a market will use the product • Focuses on the requirements of the product
Primarily drives product strategy	Primarily drives product design

Figure 7-3. Market and user research explore different aspects of the problem and solution space

Research activities occur continually and are supported through exploration in the CDP, product data analytics, and various feedback loops. Learning gained during market and user research also defines the solution context—the operational environment for a solution—which provides a basic understanding of requirements, usage, installation, operation, and support of the solution itself.

Conducting market research also helps determine the nature of the solution context. This context is primarily determined by whether the product is: 1) a *general* solution intended to be used by a significant group of customers or 2) a *custom-built* solution that is built and designed for a specific customer.

Understanding the solution context identifies external constraints that are often outside the organization's control. Some aspects of solution context are variable (undecided or negotiable), and some are fixed (decided), and finding ways to manage this balance is crucial to value delivery. It impacts development priorities, and solution intent such as features, and Non-Functional Requirements (NFRs).

Identify the Personas, Problems, and Goals

Supported by market research, the next critical aspect of design thinking is to understand who will benefit from the product's design. This information is captured by establishing *personas*, fictional characters (Figure 7-4) that represent different customer types that will similarly use the product. Personas help understand and empathize with the end users' problems, experiences, behaviors, and goals.

Cary the Consumer

Age:	36
Location:	Reno, Nevada, USA
Time in App:	10 minutes

"I'm a working dad with three children ages 3, 6, and 10. I'm also in a band, which means I want to spend as much time as possible with my kids and my band. I need my package delivered on time so that I can maximize time with my family."

I like technology! I have an iPhone, iPad, and nice home Wi-Fi setup	I'm not home on some weekends	I'd rather order online than dial the phone and talk to somebody
My wife also works during the week, so she doesn't have much spare time to help	Text is my favorite form of communication with suppliers	I don't own a computer, only tablets and phones

Figure 7-4. Personas drive key design activities

Refine Personas and Establish Empathy

To further enhance the development of desirable solutions, customer-centric enterprises use empathy throughout the design process. Empathy maps (Figure 7-5) are design thinking tools that help teams imagine what a specific customer is thinking, feeling, hearing, and seeing as they do their daily jobs and use the product. The higher the degree of empathy that a team has for its customers, the more likely the team will be able to design a desirable solution. In turn, empathy maps help refine the personas.

Figure 7-5. Empathy map canvas

Customer Journey Maps

Customer journey maps identify the process that a person goes through to accomplish a goal[5] (Figure 7-6). They illustrate the experiences that customers have as they navigate a product from first engagement to achieving their objectives and thereby establish a positive and long-term relationship with the brand.

___

5. https://www.nngroup.com/articles/journey-mapping-101/

Customer Journey Mapping (Mortgage Loan)

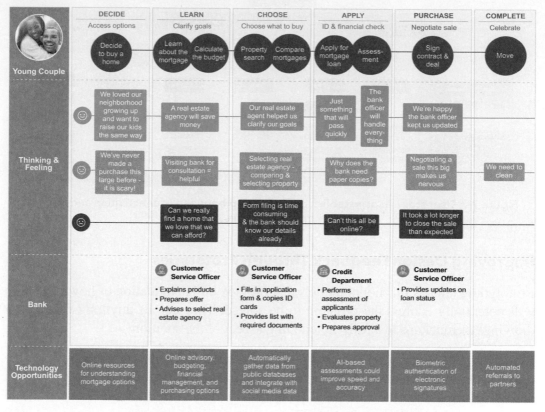

	DECIDE Access options	LEARN Clarify goals	CHOOSE Choose what to buy	APPLY ID & financial check	PURCHASE Negotiate sale	COMPLETE Celebrate
Young Couple	Decide to buy a home	Learn about the mortgage / Calculate the budget	Property search / Compare mortgages	Apply for mortgage loan / Assessment	Sign contract & deal	Move
Thinking & Feeling	We loved our neighborhood growing up and want to raise our kids the same way	A real estate agency will save money	Our real estate agent helped us clarify our goals	Just something that will pass quickly / The bank officer will handle everything	We're happy the bank officer kept us updated	
	We've never made a purchase this large before - it is scary!	Visiting bank for consultation = helpful	Selecting real estate agency - comparing & selecting property	Why does the bank need paper copies?	Negotiating a sale this big makes us nervous	We need to clean
		Can we really find a home that we love that we can afford?	Form filing is time consuming & the bank should know our details already	Can't this all be online?	It took a lot longer to close the sale than expected	
Bank		🏦 **Customer Service Officer** • Explains products • Prepares offer • Advises to select real estate agency	🏦 **Customer Service Officer** • Fills in application form & copies ID cards • Provides list with required documents	🏦 **Credit Department** • Performs assessment of applicants • Evaluates property • Prepares approval	🏦 **Customer Service Officer** • Provides updates on loan status	
Technology Opportunities	Online resources for understanding mortgage options	Online advisory, budgeting, financial management, and purchasing options	Automatically gather data from public databases and integrate with social media data	AI-based assessments could improve speed and accuracy	Biometric authentication of electronic signatures	Automated referrals to partners

Figure 7-6. Customer journey map for a consumer loan

Story Maps

Story maps are an approach to organizing and prioritizing stories (Figure 7-7). They make the users' workflow explicit and visible and show the relationships between user activities and the solution's features and stories required to implement them. Story maps also help prioritize a group of related stories and ensure a conceptually complete set of system behavior is released together.[6]

---

6. https://www.jpattonassociates.com/storymappingslides/

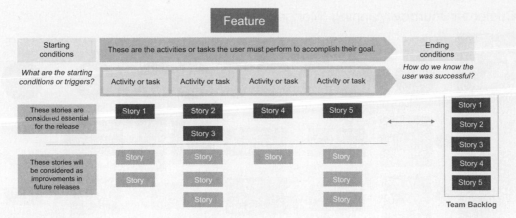

Figure 7-7. User story maps establish a relationship between user activities and features and user stories

Improving Design Feedback Through Prototypes

Prototyping creates functional models that provide initial validation of how a solution will potentially address the problem to be solved. They can be anything from paper drawings or mockups to a fully functioning aspect of the solution.

Prototyping helps the team clarify their understanding of the problem and reduces the risk of solution development. These mockups or models can be used for getting fast feedback or gaining clarity of the requirements for the desired feature or solution and new intellectual property and patent filing.

To gain actionable feedback, teams should strive to leverage the lowest-cost, fastest form of prototyping that best suits the learning in each situation.

Develop on Cadence, Release on Demand

The second dimension of Agile product delivery is to *develop on cadence but release on demand*. This dimension helps customer-centric enterprises offer a continuous flow of value to the market and customers (Figure 7-8).

As described in Principle #7, applying cadence to development makes routine what can be routine and increases predictability of the inherently uncertain nature of product development. However, the timing of releases is a different matter. Release timing and frequency are determined by market and customer needs and the economics of value delivery. Some enterprises may release frequently (continuously, hourly, daily, weekly), while others may be constrained by compliance requirements or other market rhythms that motivate less frequent releases. Collectively, the Scaled Agile Framework (SAFe) refers to these capabilities as *release on demand*.

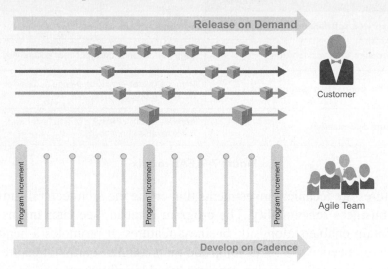

Figure 7-8. Develop on cadence and release on demand

The Program Increments (PIs) shown in Figure 7-8 are a larger timebox, a planning interval that consists of multiple iterations during which a team of Agile teams (an ART) delivers incremental value in the form of working, tested solutions. PIs are typically established as fixed 8- to 12-week periods, comprised of three to five development iterations, followed by one Innovation and Planning (IP) iteration. Shorter PIs are often employed when the market is more dynamic. Releasing can happen at any time during a PI, and at any frequency.

Program Backlog

The work of a train is defined by the program backlog, which consists of upcoming features intended to address user needs and deliver business benefits.

A feature is a distinctive characteristic of a product or service that fulfills a stakeholder need. Product Managers, in collaboration with Product Owners and other key stakeholders, define them in the local context of an ART. They are sized to be delivered in a single PI or less and are specified using a *Features And Benefits (FAB) matrix* (Figure 7-9).

- *Feature*. A short phrase giving a name with context.

- *Benefit hypothesis*. The proposed measurable benefit to the end-user or business.

Feature	Benefit Hypothesis
In-service software update	Significantly reduced planned downtime
Hardware VPN acceleration	High-performance encryption for secure WAN
Traffic congestion management	Improve overall quality of service across different protocols
Route optimization	Improve quality of service due to faster and more reliable connectivity

Figure 7-9. FAB matrix

Enabler features are technical investments that create the architectural runway to support future business functionality. The program Kanban (see later in this chapter) is used to maintain enablers alongside business features. It promotes a healthy balance with all the work needed to both develop and maintain the solution. Feature acceptance criteria are typically defined during program backlog refinement.

The backlog is 'anchored' by NFRs that help ensure the usability and effectiveness of the system. NFRs define system attributes such as security, reliability, and scalability, and they serve as constraints on system design. Failing to meet any of them can result in systems that do not meet business, user, or market needs, or other requirements that may be imposed by regulatory or standards bodies. Unlike features, they do not enter and leave the backlog when done; instead, they are persistent qualities and restrictions that govern all new development.

Prioritizing the Program Backlog

Product Management has the primary responsibility for developing and maintaining the backlog and for making decisions regarding the sequence in which to implement features. SAFe applies a comprehensive model called Weighted Shortest Job First (WSJF) to prioritize work based on the economics of product development flow.[7] WSJF is calculated by dividing the Cost of Delay (CoD) of a job by the duration. Jobs that can deliver the most value (or CoD) in the shortest period are typically selected first for implementation.

In SAFe, the 'jobs' are the features in the backlog. Since it's rarely possible to determine their duration before they are planned for implementation, SAFe typically uses

---

7. Don Reinertsen, *Principles of Product Development Flow: Second Generation Lean Product Development* (Celeritas Publishing, 2009).

relative job size as a proxy for the duration. Relative proxy measures are also applied for the CoD based on three components, as shown in Figure 7-10.

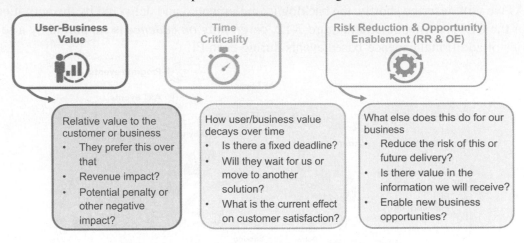

Figure 7-10. CoD has three primary components

Using a simple table to compare jobs, WSJF is calculated for each feature (Figure 7-11). Unless there are sequencing dependencies between the jobs, the features with the highest scores are implemented first.

Feature	User-business value	Time criticality	RR | OE value	CoD	Job size	WSJF
	+	+	=	÷	=	
	+	+	=	÷	=	
	+	+	=	÷	=	

- Scale for each parameter: 1, 2, 3, 5, 8, 13, 20
- Note: Do one column at a time, start by picking the smallest item and giving it a "1."
- There must be at least one "1" in each column!
- The highest priority is the highest WSJF.

Figure 7-11. A table for calculating WSJF

Each feature is estimated relative to the others for each of the three components of CoD and job size. The smallest item in each column is set to 'one,' and the others in that same column are estimated relative to that one. The CoD is the sum of the first three attributes for each item. WSJF is calculated as CoD divided by job size. The job with the highest WSJF is the next most important one to do.

Executing PI Events

As we will describe shortly, the backlog is implemented and delivered by the activities of the CDP. As illustrated in Figure 7-12, *developing on cadence* is supported by a series of additional cadence-based events during each PI.

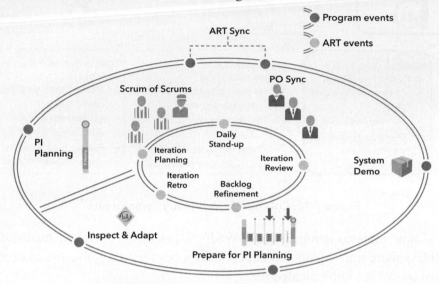

Figure 7-12. Events that support PI execution

The following sections describe each of these events.

PI Planning

"The people who do the work, plan the work."
   —A SAFe tenet

PI planning is a cadence-based event that serves as the heartbeat of the ART, aligning all the teams on the ART to a shared mission and vision (Figure 7-13). PI planning is held face-to-face whenever possible. For geographically distributed ARTs, PI planning may occur at multiple locations simultaneously by maintaining constant audio and video communication between all sites. In some circumstances, like the COVID-19 crisis that is ongoing at the time of this writing, PI planning is fully distributed. The advanced topic article "Distributed PI Planning with SAFe"[8] provides additional guidance and considerations for successfully managing this scenario.

---

8. https://www.scaledagileframework.com/distributed-pi-planning/

Facilitated by the Release Train Engineer (RTE), PI planning includes all members of the ART. It typically takes place over two days and occurs within the IP iteration, which avoids affecting the schedule and capacity of other iterations. PI planning is essential to SAFe: if you are not doing it, you are not doing SAFe.

Figure 7-13. Face-to-face PI planning. Remote teams are planning at the same time using video conferencing

Business Benefits of PI Planning

PI planning delivers many business benefits, including:

1. Aligning development to the business context and goals, vision, and team and ART PI objectives

2. Building the social network the ART depends upon

3. Identifying dependencies and fostering cross-team and cross-ART collaboration

4. Providing the opportunity for 'just in time' and 'just the right amount' of requirements, design, architecture, and user experience guidance

5. Matching demand to capacity and eliminating excess Work in Process (WIP)

6. Faster decision-making. All the relevant parties are focused on the same objectives and can consider and make necessary tradeoffs in real time

Inputs and Outputs of PI Planning

Inputs to PI planning include the business context, roadmap and vision, and the top ten features of the program backlog. Outputs of PI planning include the following:

- *Committed PI objectives*. A set of SMART[9] objectives that are created by each team with a business value assigned by the Business Owners.

- *Program board*. It highlights feature delivery dates, dependencies between teams, and relevant milestones.

Conducting PI Planning

The RTE facilitates PI planning, and event attendees include Business Owners, Product Management, Agile teams, System Architecture and Engineering, the System Team, and other stakeholders, all of whom must be well prepared. The active participation of Business Owners in this event provides an essential guardrail for prioritization of business value. Figure 7-14 illustrates a typical standard two-day PI planning agenda.

Figure 7-14. Standard two-day PI planning agenda

Day 1 Agenda

- *Business context*. A Business Owner or senior executive describes the current state of the business, shares the portfolio vision, and presents a perspective on how effectively existing solutions are addressing current customer needs.

---

9. SMART is an acronym for Specific, Measurable, Achievable, Realistic, and Time-bound.

- ***Product vision***. Product Management presents the current vision (typically represented by the next top 10 upcoming features) and highlights any changes from the previous PI planning meeting, as well as any upcoming milestones.

- ***Architecture vision and development practices***. System Architecture and Engineering (typically a CTO, or Enterprise Architect) presents the vision for architectural changes and a senior development manager may introduce new or revised Agile development practices for the upcoming PI (e.g., such as introducing test-driven development or adjusting the CI/CD pipeline).

- ***Planning context and lunch***. The RTE presents the planning process and expected outcomes of the event.

- ***Team breakouts #1***. In the first breakout, teams estimate their capacity for each iteration and identify the backlog items they will likely need to realize the features. Each team creates their draft plans, visible to all, iteration by iteration.

During PI planning a program board (Figure 7-15) is used to visualize and track dependencies and to identify opportunities to eliminate or reduce them.

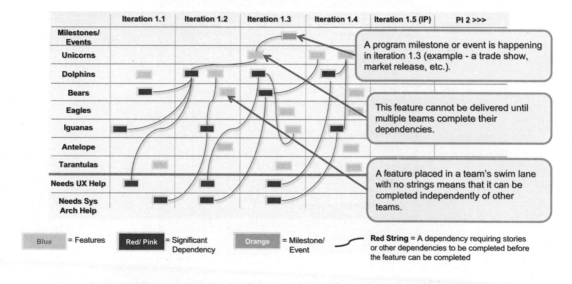

Figure 7-15. Program board showing features and dependencies

- ***Draft plan review.*** During the timeboxed draft plan review, teams present key planning outputs, which include capacity and load, draft PI objectives, potential risks, and dependencies. Business Owners, Product Management, and other teams and stakeholders review and provide input.

- *Management review and problem-solving.* It's almost certain that the draft plans have identified challenges associated with scope, people and resource constraints, and dependencies. During the problem-solving meeting, management may negotiate scope changes and resolve other problems by agreeing to various planning adjustments.

Day 2 Agenda

- *Planning adjustments.* The next day begins with management presenting any changes to prioritization, planning scope, people, and resources.

- *Team breakouts #2.* Next, teams continue planning based on their agenda from the previous day, making the appropriate adjustments. They finalize their objectives for the PI, to which the Business Owners assign business value, as shown in Figure 7-16.

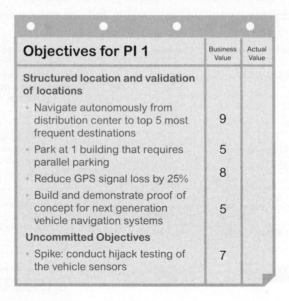

Objectives for PI 1	Business Value	Actual Value
Structured location and validation of locations		
Navigate autonomously from distribution center to top 5 most frequent destinations	9	
Park at 1 building that requires parallel parking	5	
Reduce GPS signal loss by 25%	8	
Build and demonstrate proof of concept for next generation vehicle navigation systems	5	
Uncommitted Objectives		
Spike: conduct hijack testing of the vehicle sensors	7	

Figure 7-16. A team's PI objectives sheet with assigned business value

- *Final plan review and lunch.* During this session, all teams present their plans to the group. The team then asks the Business Owners if the plan is acceptable. If the Business Owners have concerns, teams are given the opportunity to adjust the plan as needed to address the issues identified. The team then presents their revised plan.

- **Program risks**. During planning, teams have identified program risks and impediments that could impact their ability to meet their objectives. These are addressed in front of the whole train and categorized into one of the following ROAM categories:

  - **Resolved**—The teams agree that the risk is no longer a concern.

  - **Owned**—Someone on the train takes ownership of the risk since it cannot be resolved during PI planning.

  - **Accepted**—Some risks are just facts or potential problems that must be understood and accepted.

  - **Mitigated**—Teams identify a plan to reduce the impact of the risk.

- **Confidence vote**. Once program risks have been addressed, teams vote on their confidence in meeting their team PI objectives. Each team conducts a 'fist of five' confidence vote. If the average is three fingers or above, then management should accept the plan. Any person voting two or fewer should be given an opportunity to voice their concerns. This might add to the list of risks, require some re-planning, or simply be informative. Once each team has voted the process is repeated for the entire ART with everyone expressing their confidence in the collective plan.

- **Plan rework**. If necessary, teams rework their plans until a high confidence level can be reached. This is one occasion where alignment and commitment are valued more highly than adhering to a timebox.

- **Planning retrospective and moving forward**. Finally, the RTE leads a brief retrospective for the PI planning event to capture what went well, what didn't, and what can be done better next time.

Over the course of the program increment, the ART proceeds to execute the PI, track progress, and adjust plans as needed to adapt as new learning occurs. Execution of the PI begins with all the teams conducting planning for the first iteration, using their PI plans as a starting point.

Scrum of Scrums and Product Owner Sync (ART Sync)

After PI planning, the RTE typically facilitates weekly (or more frequently, as needed) SoS and Product Owner sync events. The SoS helps coordinate the dependencies of the ARTs and provides visibility into progress and impediments. The RTE, Scrum Masters, and others (where appropriate) meet to review their progress toward milestones and PI objectives, as well as dependencies among the teams. The event is timeboxed for 30–60 minutes and is followed by a 'meet after' where individuals who need to resolve specific problems or questions can remain behind. Figure 7-17 shows a suggested agenda for the SoS event.

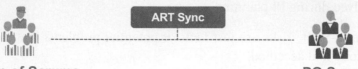

Scrum of Scrums

▶ Visibility into progress and impediments

▶ Facilitated by RTE

▶ Participants: Scrum Masters, other select team members, SMEs if necessary

▶ Weekly or more frequently, 30–60 minutes

▶ Timeboxed and followed by a 'Meet After'

PO Sync

▶ Visibility into progress, scope, and priority adjustments

▶ Facilitated by RTE or PM

▶ Participants: PMs, POs, other stakeholders, and SMEs as necessary

▶ Weekly or more frequently, 30–60 minutes

▶ Timeboxed and followed by a 'Meet After'

Figure 7-17. ART sync, Scrum of Scrums, and PO sync

Like the SoS, Product Owners and Product Management often hold a Product Owner sync. This event typically occurs weekly, or more frequently, as needed. The Product Owner sync is also timeboxed (30–60 minutes) and includes a meet after discussion. Sometimes the SoS and Product Owner sync are combined into one event, referred to as an 'ART sync' (Figure 7-17).

System Demo

A system demo is a significant event that occurs at the end of each iteration, which provides fast feedback about the effectiveness, usability, and releasability of the system (Figure 7-18). It offers an integrated view of the new features delivered by the ART over the past iteration, providing a fact-based measure of system-level progress and velocity within the PI.

This demo is done in a production-like environment (often staging) to receive feedback from stakeholders. It helps ensure that integration between teams on the same ART occurs regularly and that the emergent behavior of the full system can be evaluated. These stakeholders include the teams, Business Owners, executive sponsors, development management, and customers (or their proxies) who provide input on the fitness for purpose for the solutions being developed. The feedback is critical, as only they can give the guidance the ART needs to stay on course or make adjustments.

Figure 7-18. The system demo

Prepare for the Next PI Planning Event

While we note this activity as a PI event, in reality, preparing for the upcoming PI is an ongoing process, with three primary focus areas.

- Alignment and organizational readiness for planning

- Backlog and content readiness

- Facility readiness—the actual logistics for the event

Since any one of these items can interfere with the potential outcome—a committed PI plan—careful consideration and planning is required for all three focus areas.

Inspect and Adapt

The I&A is a significant event held at the end of each PI, just prior to the next planning. It consists of three parts.

1. **PI system demo.** This demo is a little different from the regular system demos because it shows all the features that the ART has developed throughout the PI. During this demo, Business Owners collaborate with each team to agree on the actual business value achieved for their specific PI objectives.

2. **Quantitative and qualitative measurement.** Teams collectively review any quantitative and qualitative metrics they have decided to collect and then discuss the data and trends. One primary measure is the *program predictability measure*. The RTE summarizes the planned versus actual business value for each team's PI objectives to create the overall program predictability measure.

3. **Retrospective and problem-solving workshop.** The ART runs a brief retrospective, the goal of which is to identify a few significant issues they would like to resolve. For addressing systemic problems, a structured, root-cause *problem-solving workshop* is then used to determine the actual root causes of a problem. The result is a set of improvement backlog items that go into the program backlog to be addressed during PI planning.

DevOps and the Continuous Delivery Pipeline

The third dimension of Agile product delivery is *DevOps and the CDP*. The capability to release reliably and with high quality, whenever the market or customer demands, requires embracing the DevOps mindset and culture and creating an automated CDP.

Embracing DevOps Mindset, Culture, and Practices

As digital disruption continues to change the world and as software plays a more significant role in every company's ability to deliver and support its products and services, enterprises need to react faster to customer demands with digital solutions.

Popularized by *The Phoenix Project*[10] and *The DevOps Handbook*,[11] the DevOps movement seeks to better align development, operations, the business, information security, and other areas by sharing the work and responsibility for accelerating delivery.

---

10. Gene Kim, *The Phoenix Project: A Novel about IT, DevOps, and Helping Your Business Win*, Kindle Edition (IT Revolution Press, 2018).

11. Gene Kim, Jez Humble, Patrick Debois, and John Willis, *The DevOps Handbook: How to Create World-Class Agility, Reliability, and Security in Technology Organizations* (IT Revolution Press, 2016).

DevOps is the adoption of a mindset, culture, and set of practices that provide solution elements to the customer without handoffs and without requiring excessive production or operations support.

SAFe's CALMR approach (Figure 7-19) to DevOps is grounded in five concepts: Culture, Automation, Lean flow, Measurement, and Recovery.

Figure 7-19. A CALMR approach to DevOps

- **Culture** represents the philosophy of shared responsibility for fast value delivery across the entire value stream.

- **Automation** represents the need to remove as much human intervention from the pipeline as possible to decrease errors and reduce the cycle time of the release process.

- **Lean flow** identifies the practices of limiting WIP, reducing batch size, and managing queue lengths (SAFe Principle #6).

- **Measurement** fosters learning and continuous improvement by understanding and quantifying the flow of value through the pipeline.

- **Recovery** builds systems that allow fast fixes of production issues through automatic rollback and fix-forward (in production) capabilities.

DevSecOps

DevOps, however, isn't merely about development and operations. In the past, a specific group was dedicated to security testing toward the end of implementation. This practice was less of an issue when phase-gated development cycles lasted months or years. Today, outdated security practices can undo even the most efficient DevOps initiatives and have unacceptably high social and financial costs. It has become so critical that many use the phrase 'DevSecOps' to emphasize how essential it is to integrate security into the CDP.

The Continuous Delivery Pipeline

The CDP represents the workflows, activities, and automation needed to guide a new piece of functionality from ideation to an on-demand release of value to the end-user. As illustrated in Figure 7-20, the pipeline consists of four aspects: Continuous Exploration (CE), Continuous Integration (CI), Continuous Deployment (CD), and Release on Demand (RoD).

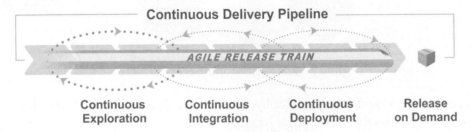

Figure 7-20. The SAFe continuous delivery pipeline

Each ART builds and maintains, or shares with other ARTs, a pipeline with the assets and technologies needed to deliver solution value as independently as possible. The first three elements of the pipeline (CE, CI, and CD) work together to support the delivery of small batches of new functionality, which are then released to meet market demand.

Continuous Exploration

CE fosters continuing research and alignment on what should be built. Design thinking continually explores market and customer needs and defines a vision, roadmap, and a set of features that meets those needs. During this period, new ideas are raised, refined, and prepared as a list of prioritized features in the program backlog. During CE planning, features are pulled into implementation, which begins the continuous integration process.

There are four main CE activities described in SAFe (Figure 7-21):

- *Hypothesize* describes the practices necessary to identify ideas and the measurements needed to validate them with customers.

- *Collaborate and research* describes the practices required to work with customers and stakeholders to refine the understanding of potential needs.

- *Architect* describes the practices necessary to envision a technical approach that enables quick implementation, delivery, and support of ongoing operations.

- *Synthesize* describes the practices that organize the ideas into a holistic vision, a roadmap, and a prioritized program backlog, and it supports final alignment during PI planning.

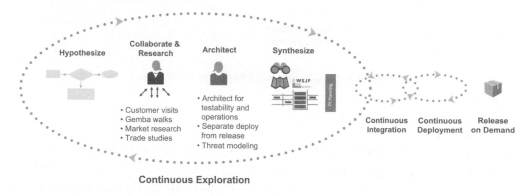

Figure 7-21. Continuous exploration activities

Continuous Integration

CI builds quality into the development process by continuously integrating the ongoing work of many Agile teams. All work is version controlled, and new functionality is developed and integrated into a full system or solution. It's then validated in a suitable staging environment that ranges from cloud-based software systems to physical devices and device simulators.

SAFe describes four activities associated with continuous integration (Figure 7-22):

- *Develop* describes the practices necessary to implement stories and commit the code and components into the trunk.

- **Build** describes the activities needed to create deployable binaries and merge the development branches into the trunk.

- **Test end-to-end** describes the methods necessary to validate the solution.

- **Stage** describes the required practices to host and verify the system in a staging environment before production.

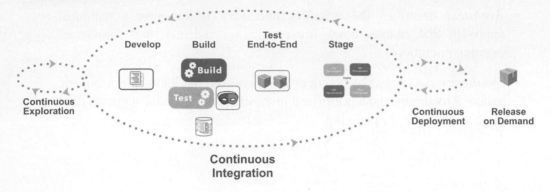

Figure 7-22. Continuous integration activities

Continuous Deployment

CD captures the processes associated with moving solutions through staging into production environments. As with continuous integration, this varies substantially based on the kinds of solutions created and their solution context. Ensuring solutions are ready for customers requires deployment and monitoring to provide flexibility in controlling releases, rolling back a version, or installing incremental updates and patches.

CD consists of four key activities in SAFe (Figure 7-23):

- **Deploy** to production describes the practices necessary to deploy a solution to a production environment.

- **Verify** the system represents the practices needed to make sure the changes operate in production as intended before they are made available to customers.

- **Monitor** for problems describes the practices to monitor and report on any issues that may arise in production.

- **Respond and recover** describes the activities to rapidly remedy any problems that happened during deployment.

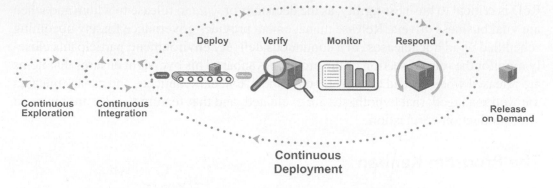

Figure 7-23. Continuous deployment activities

Release on Demand

As we described, RoD is the ability to make new functionality available to customers all at once or incrementally based on market and business needs. SAFe describes four RoD practices (Figure 7-24):

- **Release** describes how to deliver the solution to end users all at once or incrementally.

- **Stabilize and operate** describes the process needed to make sure the system is working well from a functional and nonfunctional perspective.

- **Measure** describes the practices necessary to quantify whether the newly released functionality provides the intended value.

- **Learn** describes how to decide what should be done with the information gathered and prepare for the next loop through the CDP.

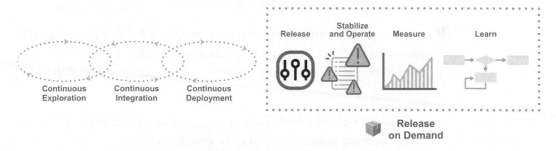

Figure 7-24. Four activities of RoD

RoD is critical to business agility, as the decisions of *what* to release to whom and when are vital business drivers. Release management provides governance for any upcoming scheduled or ad hoc releases. In a continuous delivery environment, participants closely monitor the release section of the program Kanban. This oversight ensures that items are released when needed to the right customers, that dark launches and canary releases are well managed, that hypotheses are evaluated, and that feature toggles are removed after production verification.

The Program Kanban

The program Kanban facilitates the flow of features through the CDP. Figure 7-25 illustrates a typical program Kanban with Work In Process (WIP) limits governing each state.

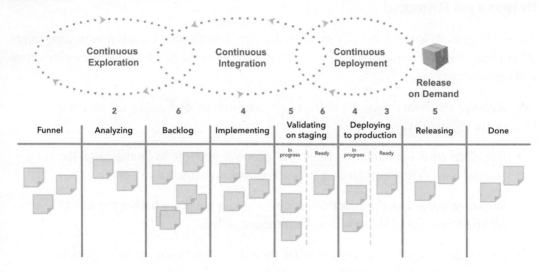

Figure 7-25. A typical program Kanban

New ideas begin with continuous exploration and may originate locally from the ART or an upstream Kanban system (e.g., solution or portfolio Kanban). Product Management and System Architects and Engineering manage this Kanban. The following states describe its flow:

- *Funnel.* All new ideas are welcome here. They may include new functionality, enhancement of the existing system functions, or enabler work.

- *Analyzing.* New ideas that align with the vision and support the strategic themes are further explored by Agile teams when they have available capacity. Analysis and refinement include the collaboration to turn an idea into one or more features with descriptions, business benefit hypotheses, acceptance criteria, and estimated story points.

- **Program backlog.** The highest-priority features analyzed and approved advance to this state and await implementation. Feature estimates and acceptance criteria are also refined here.

- **Implementing.** At every PI boundary, the ART pulls the top features from the program backlog and moves them into the implementing state. Through the PI planning process, they get split into stories, planned into iterations, and subsequently implemented by teams during the PI.

- **Validating on staging.** During each iteration, features are integrated and tested with the rest of the system in a staging environment. Approved features move to the 'ready' part of this state, where they are prioritized again using WSJF and await deployment.

- **Deploying to production.** When capacity becomes available for deployment activities (or immediately in a fully automated continuous delivery environment), the feature is moved to production. In systems that separate deployment from release, they are placed in the 'ready' part of this state. This state is WIP limited to avoid the buildup of features that are deployed but not yet released.

- **Releasing.** When there is sufficient value, market needs, and opportunity, features are released to some or all the customers, where the benefit hypothesis can then be evaluated. Although the feature moves to the 'done' state, new work items may be created based on the learning gathered.

The Kanban system described here is a good starting point for most ARTs. However, it should be customized to fit the ART's process, including the definition of WIP limits and the policies for each process state.

Program Epic Kanban System

ART initiatives that are simply too big to be completed in a single PI are called *program epics*. Also, some portfolio epics may need to be split into program epics to facilitate incremental implementation. Program epics may affect financial, human, and other resources that might be large enough to warrant a Lean business case, discussion, and financial approval from Lean Portfolio Management (LPM). Epics whose estimates exceed the established epic threshold will require review and approval.

Approving significant initiatives is one of the four critical Lean budget guardrails (see Chapter 9, Lean Portfolio Management, for more details).

Program Increment Roadmap

A PI roadmap is used to forecast the flow of work from the backlog (Figure 7-26). It consists of a series of planned PIs with identified milestones and releases. Each element on the roadmap is a feature scheduled to be completed within a particular PI. The PI roadmap may also reflect fixed-date and learning milestones occurring during that period. Releasing functionality can occur at any time during the PI.

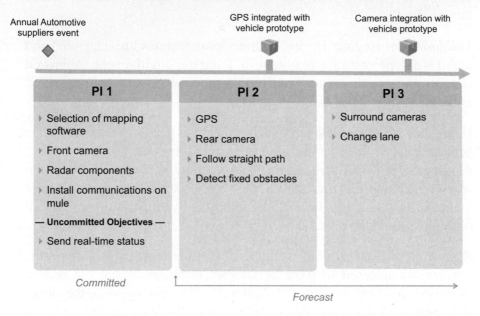

Figure 7-26. An example PI roadmap for an autonomous delivery vehicle

The roadmap in Figure 7-26 covers three PIs, which is typically sufficient to communicate a forecast to stakeholders, including the business and partners.

Market Rhythm and Events Inform the Roadmap

To create the highest value for all stakeholders, customer-centric organizations leverage market rhythms and market events to inform the roadmap.[12] Simply put, the benefits of a solution can vary significantly based on when it's released.

---

12. Luke Hohmann, *Beyond Software Architecture: Creating and Sustaining Winning Solutions* (Addison-Wesley, 2003).

- A *market rhythm* is a set of events that repeatedly occur on a predictable cadence. For example, retailers routinely prepare for the holiday shopping season by upgrading their systems to gain a competitive edge and to support significantly higher transaction volumes.

- A *market event* is a one-time future event, which has a high probability of materially affecting one or more solutions. They can be external, such as the launch of government regulations, or they can be internally created, such as a company's annual user conference.

Summary

Businesses need to balance their execution focus with a customer focus to help assure that they are creating the right solutions, for the right customers, at the right time. Agile product delivery is grounded in customer centricity, which puts the customer at the center of every decision. It uses design thinking to ensure the solution is desirable, feasible, viable, and sustainable.

Developing on cadence helps manage the variability inherent in product development. Release on demand decouples the release and development cadence to ensure customers can get what they need when they need it. DevOps and the CDP create the foundation that enables enterprises to release value, in whole or in part, at any time to meet customer and market demand.

The result of Agile product delivery is enhanced business agility with superior outcomes for the enterprise and the customers it serves.

8

Enterprise Solution Delivery

"I am an Engineer. I serve mankind by making dreams come true."
— Anonymous

The *enterprise solution delivery competency* describes how to apply Lean-Agile principles and practices to build and deploy the world's largest and most sophisticated systems.

Why Enterprise Solution Delivery?

Humanity has always dreamed big. Scientists, engineers, and software developers turn those big dreams into reality. They bring these innovations to life by defining and coordinating all the activities to successfully build and operate large and complex solutions. But these are large systems and the following challenges make their development unique:

- Their failure creates unacceptable social and economic consequences.

- They require innovation, experimentation, knowledge, and cooperation from hundreds or thousands of individuals across many disciplines and organizations.

- They require specification, design, and procurement of long lead-time components, many of which are provided by external suppliers.

- They are subject to significant regulatory and compliance constraints.

- They are exceedingly complex to test and validate.

Moreover, during the decades when these systems are operational, their purpose and mission evolve. That calls for new capabilities, technology upgrades, security patches, and other enhancements. As true 'living systems,' these activities are never really done because the system itself is never complete.

Due to the complexity and criticality of these large systems, does Agile development even apply? Or are we forever stuck with stage-gated models of development, proxy milestones, and risk that is largely deferred until the end? Will we always be slow to market?

Fortunately, not. As we have already seen in this book for software-only systems, advanced Agile and DevOps practices offer guidance for supporting frequent, and even continuous, system upgrades through a Continuous Delivery Pipeline (CDP). We have all learned from those experiences. Today, a range of innovations allows us to leverage these and similar practices to provide faster and more continuous delivery of value of these largest of all systems, including cyber-physical systems,[1] programmable hardware, the Internet of Things (IoT), and additive manufacturing. These innovations are changing the definition, and even the goal, of becoming operational. Systems are not simply deployed once and then merely supported. Instead, they are released early and updated continuously, allowing their development to evolve over time.

The enterprise solution delivery competency directly addresses this challenge by providing guidance on applying advanced Lean, Agile, and DevOps practices to define, build, deploy, and advance these systems. Figure 8-1 illustrates the three dimensions of enterprise solution delivery.

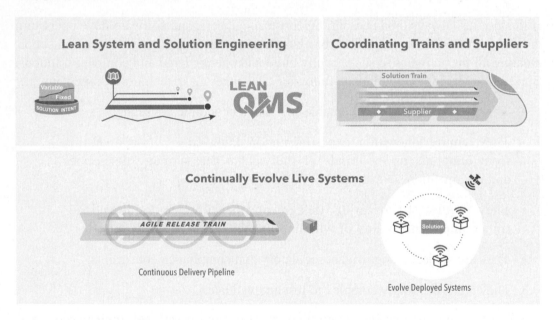

Figure 8-1. The three dimensions of Enterprise Solution Delivery

---

1. Cyber-physical systems are engineered systems that are built from, and depend upon, the seamless integration of computation and physical components (source: National Science Foundation. https://www.nsf.gov/funding/pgm_summ.jsp?pims_id=503286).

- ***Lean system and solution engineering***. Applies Lean-Agile practices to align and coordinate all the product life-cycle activities from specification to decommission for the world's largest and most complex systems.

- ***Coordinating trains and suppliers***. Coordinates and aligns the extended, often complex set of value streams to a shared business and technology mission. It uses a common vision, and aligns backlogs, roadmaps, Program Increments (PIs), and synchronization points.

- ***Continually evolve live systems***. Large systems must be architected to support continuous deployment and release on demand. This allows enterprises to quickly learn, deliver value, and get to market before the competition with less investment and better outcomes.

These three dimensions are complementary and help shape how high-performing Agile teams and teams of teams enable the entire enterprise to better build and deploy these systems. Each of these dimensions is described further in the next sections.

Lean Systems and Solution Engineering

Lean systems and solution engineering is the first dimension of the enterprise solution delivery competency. It applies Lean-Agile practices to align and coordinate all the activities necessary to specify, build, deploy, and operate these systems. Practices of this dimension follow.

Continually Refine Fixed and Variable Solution Intent

The systems engineering discipline has traditionally applied the familiar 'V' life-cycle model.[2] This model describes the critical activities for building large systems from inception through retirement. Flow-based systems like the Scaled Agile Framework (SAFe) describe these same activities, but they occur in smaller batches and continuously throughout the life cycle, as shown in Figure 8-2.

---

2. https://www.sebokwiki.org/wiki/System_Life_Cycle_Process_Models:_Vee

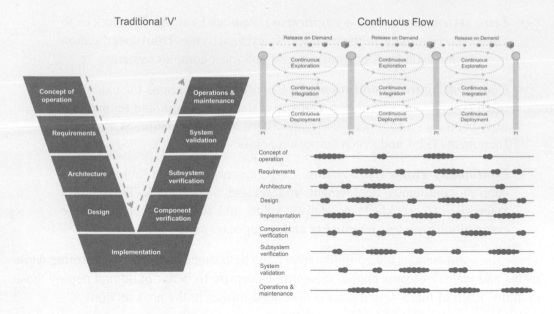

Figure 8-2. Perform systems engineering activities continuously

SAFe's flow-based model (Figure 8-2 right) enables engineers to continually perform the following types of activities simultaneously for each increment: explore innovative ideas, refine features, integrate and deploy features, and release value on demand.

Solution Intent

Due to the complexity of the systems being built, *solution intent* (Figure 8-3), a central knowledge repository, is used to store, manage, and communicate *what is being built* and *how it will be built*. Solution intent provides many benefits to the systems engineering process.

- Maintains a single source of truth regarding the intended and actual solution behavior

- Records and communicates requirements, designs, and system architecture decisions

- Facilitates further continuous exploration and analysis activities

- Aligns the customer, Agile teams, and suppliers to a common mission and purpose

- Supports compliance and contractual obligations

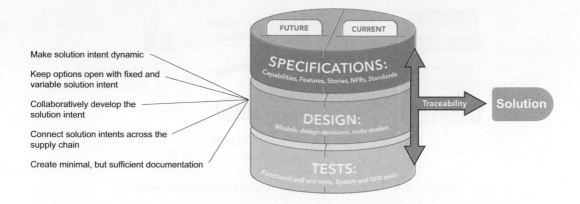

Figure 8-3. Solution intent is a central knowledge repository

Developers of complex systems must constantly know two things: what the system currently does now and what changes are intended for the future. Knowledge of both the current and future states can be captured in any form suitable and includes three primary elements: specifications, designs, and tests. As the future intent is implemented and evolved, it then gets recorded as the current system state.

Traceability helps confirm that life- and mission-critical systems (and others governed by regulation) are built in exact agreement with intended behavior. It connects all the solution intent elements and the system components that realize its full behavior. The solution intent is created collaboratively and evolves based on learning.

Solution Context

Every solution operates within the context of its environment (e.g., cloud, factory, home, on-premise servers, system of systems). Since a system is often installed and maintained in a different environment than it was developed, the solution context is needed to understand the requirements, usage, installation, operation, and support of a solution. As a result, understanding the solution context is critical to reducing risk and achieving fitness for purpose. Aligning the solution intent with the solution context (Figure 8-4) requires a customer-centric mindset and collaboration.

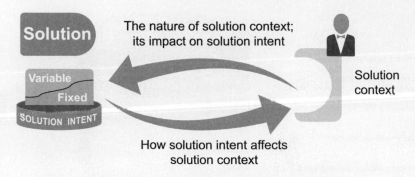

Figure 8-4. Solution intent and context inform each other

For example, customers participate in PI planning and solution demo events as frequently as possible to assure alignment. As solutions increase in size and complexity, the customer frequently integrates them into their specific solution context. Ideally, these integration cycles are aligned with the cadence of the train, so solution increments can be built, integrated, and deployed based on correct assumptions, allowing frequent validation of the solution under development.

Create Minimal but Sufficient Documentation

Document-based approaches to managing solution intent and context do not scale. Indeed, they quickly become obsolete and inconsistent with one another. The alternative is a set of related digital models that define, design, analyze, and document the system under development. Some models specify system requirements and design, while others are domain-specific (e.g., electrical, mechanical, or some systems property).

Connecting models ensures system completeness and coverage (Figure 8-5). For example, engineers can see whether all requirements are implemented by components and covered by tests. They can identify the impact of replacing a component, including what requirements and tests are affected. Together, these models record and communicate what the system does and how it does it to a diverse set of key stakeholders.

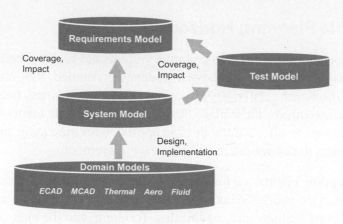

Figure 8-5. Linking cross-domain models

By using a more flexible approach to managing and communicating the specifications, solution intent aligns everyone to a shared direction. Its companion, solution context, defines the system's constraints—deployment, environmental, and operational.

Because solution intent and context for large solutions flow down into components and subsystems, they offer teams the implementation flexibility needed to make local requirements and design decisions. For example, Figure 8-6 shows that as downstream teams (system, subsystem, and component) implement decisions, the knowledge gained from continuous exploration, integration, and deployment returns feedback upstream and moves decisions from variable (undecided) to fixed (decided).

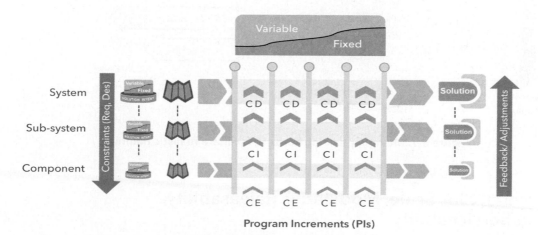

Figure 8-6. Incremental feedback evolves solution intent from variable to fixed

Apply Multiple Planning Horizons

Building massive, technology-based, innovative systems has high uncertainty and risk. The traditional way to reduce risk has been to develop detailed, long-range plans up front. In practice, however, gaps in specifications, evolving business needs, and technical issues can quickly make these plans obsolete. Instead, Agile teams and trains use backlogs and roadmaps to offer a more flexible approach for managing and forecasting work, enabling teams to deliver the most value each increment.

Effective road mapping efforts require an understanding of the appropriate time horizon. If the horizon is too short, the enterprise may jeopardize alignment and the ability to communicate future features and capabilities. Too long, and the enterprise is basing assumptions and commitments on an uncertain future. Multiple planning horizons provide a balance (Figure 8-7) between short- and longer-term planning. The outer levels of the planning horizon are longer-term and describe behavior that is less defined and less committed, while the inner levels are nearer term, defining better understood and more committed solution behavior (Figure 8-7).

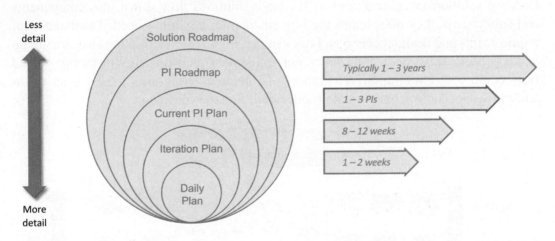

Figure 8-7. Multiple planning horizons facilitate realistic planning

Architect for Scale, Modularity, Releasability, and Serviceability

Architectural choices determine the effort and cost required for future changes and are critical economic decisions. Software development can leverage frameworks and infrastructure that provides proven architecture components out of the box. Conversely, builders of large, cyber-physical systems need to define their own components, applying intentional architecture and emergent design. This encourages collaboration between architects and teams to create a resilient system that enables teams and trains to independently build, test, deploy—and even release—parts of large solutions.

Developers and engineers apply *set-based design* (Principle #3) to keep requirements and design options flexible for as long as possible during the development process. Instead of choosing a single point solution up front, they identify and simultaneously explore multiple options, eliminating poorer choices over time. This enhances flexibility by committing to technical solutions only after validating assumptions, which produces better economic results.

With the right architecture, elements of the system may be released independently. Figure 8-8 illustrates an autonomous delivery system that was architected to enable system elements to be released independently. Here are some examples:

- A software application running in the cloud deploys continuously and releases frequently.

- Embedded code running in a vehicle is updated over the air and deployed and released less frequently.

- Hardware updates (e.g., sensors, CPUs) often require taking vehicles out of service and possible recertification, so they are updated less frequently.

Although design choices that enable continuous value delivery may lead to higher unit costs for more adaptable hardware and vehicle communications, they can significantly lower the *total cost of ownership* and the product's lifetime value as they support more frequent updates and enhance future flexibility.

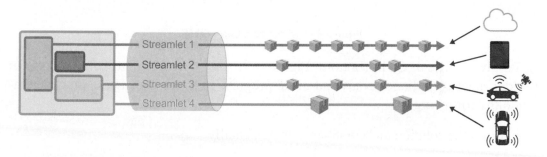

Figure 8-8. Architecture impacts the ability to release system elements independently

Continually Address Compliance Concerns

The failure of a large system can have unacceptable social and economic consequences. To protect the public safety, these systems are typically subject to significant regulatory oversight and compliance requirements. Quality Management Systems (QMS) help system builders ensure quality, reduce risk, and define practices that confirm safety and appropriate solution behavior.

However, most quality management systems were created based on traditional, sequential development approaches that often assumed (or mandated) up-front commitment to specifications and design, detailed work breakdown structures, and document-centric, phase-gate milestones (top, Figure 8-9).

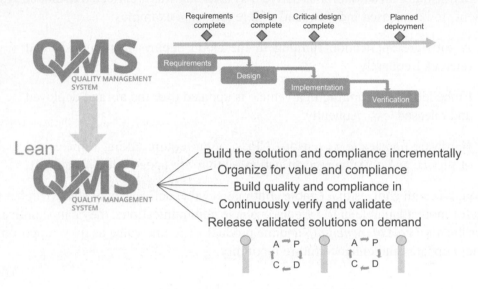

Figure 8-9. Move to a Lean QMS

In its place, a Lean QMS (bottom, Figure 8-9) is implemented to help the system builder meet compliance goals and make progress more visible. These practices include the following:

- Build the solution and compliance incrementally

- Organize for value *and* compliance

- Build quality and compliance in the daily work

- Continuously verify and validate the work

- Release continuously validated solutions on demand

These practices assure that compliance occurs throughout the product development process, instead of only during inspection at the end, which often causes significant rework and delays.

Coordinating Trains and Suppliers

Coordinating trains and suppliers is the second dimension of enterprise solution delivery. This dimension helps manage and align the complex value stream network required to build these systems to a shared business and technology mission. It coordinates the vision, backlogs, and roadmaps with a common set of PIs and synchronization points. Aspects of this dimension are described in the following sections.

Build and Integrate Components and Capabilities with Solution Trains

Solution Trains coordinate multiple ARTs and suppliers to build complex solutions that require hundreds or even thousands of people to build (Figure 8-10).

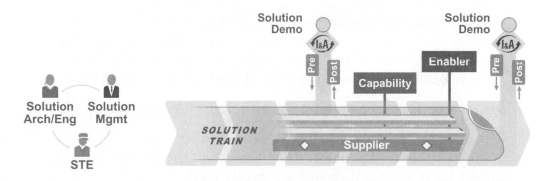

Figure 8-10. Solution Trains align ARTs and suppliers

As systems scale, alignment becomes more critical. To plan, demo, learn, and improve together, Solution Trains align all of their ARTs to a common cadence. They integrate their solutions at least every PI to validate that they are building the right thing and verify technical assumptions.

More frequent integration is possible for teams building software solutions (see the "Apply Continuish Integration" section below). ARTs that have longer lead times for components (e.g., hardware) deliver and demo incrementally through proxies (e.g., mockups, stubs, prototypes), which can integrate with the overall solution and support early validation and learning.

Solution Train Roles

Solution Trains require roles in addition to ART personnel. These include the following:

- *Solution Train Engineer (STE)* is the servant leader and coach for the Solution Train. They facilitate Solution Train events and coordinate delivery across ARTs and suppliers in collaboration with Release Train Engineers (RTEs).

- *Solution Management* has responsibility for the vision, roadmap, and backlog to deliver the overall solution. They collaborate across ARTs with Product Management to align the ARTs' roadmaps and define capabilities and split them into features within the ARTs' backlogs.

- *Solution Architects and Engineers* collaborate across ARTs to define the technology and architecture with System Architects and Engineers from each train.

Also, the following roles play an essential part in the Solution Train's success:

- *Customers* are the ultimate buyers of the solution, and are involved at every level of SAFe. They work closely with Solution Management, Product Managers, and other key stakeholders to shape the solution intent, the vision, and the economic framework in which development occurs.

- *System teams* are often formed for the Solution Train to address the integration issues across ARTs.

- *Shared services* are specialists that are necessary for the success of a solution but may not be dedicated to a specific train.

- *Suppliers* provide unique expertise and systems components, which can reduce the lead time and cost of solution delivery. SAFe coaches enterprises to embrace suppliers as long-term business partners, actively involving them in solution delivery and the adoption of Lean-Agile mindsets and practices to their mutual benefit.

Solution Backlog

The solution backlog is the holding area for upcoming capabilities and enablers, each of which can span multiple ARTs and is intended to advance the solution and build its architectural runway.

A capability is similar to a feature; however, it is a higher-level solution behavior that typically spans multiple ARTs. Capabilities are sized and split into multiple features to facilitate their implementation in a single PI.

Capabilities exhibit the same characteristics and practices as features. For example, they:

- Are described using a phrase and benefit hypothesis, and have acceptance criteria.

- Are sized to fit within a PI; however, they often take multiple ARTs to implement.

- Are made visible and analyzed using the solution Kanban.

- Have associated enablers to describe and bring visibility to all the technical work necessary to support efficient development and delivery of capabilities.

- Are defined by Solution Managers, who use the acceptance criteria to determine whether the functionality is fit for purpose.

- Are prioritized using Weighted Shortest Job First (WSJF).

Capabilities may originate in the local context of a Solution Train or occur as a result of splitting portfolio epics that may cut across more than one value stream. Another potential source of capabilities is the solution context, where some aspect of the environment may require new solution functionality.

Solution Kanban

The solution Kanban follows the same structure and process used for the program Kanban. However, Solution Management and Solution Architects manage this Kanban, which operates with capabilities instead of features. Also, where useful, Solution Trains implement a solution epic Kanban system for solution epics, which operates similarly to the program epic Kanban.

Solution Train Planning

Solution Train planning provides a way for ARTs and suppliers to collaboratively build a unified plan for the next PI. It also fosters team-building across the Solution Train, which helps create the social network necessary to achieve high performance. Solution Trains introduce two additional events (pre- and post-PI planning) to coordinate their ART's PI planning as shown in Figure 8-11.

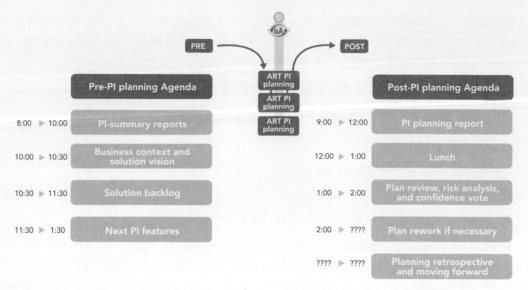

Figure 8-11. Solution Train pre- and post-PI planning agendas

The pre-PI planning event brings together stakeholders from all parts of the Solution Train to create a clear vision and context for the upcoming increments. Inputs include the current solution roadmap, vision, solution intent, and the top capabilities from the solution backlog. Attendees include the following:

- **Solution Train leaders**. This includes the Solution Train Engineer (STE), Solution Management, Solution Architects and Engineers, solution system team, and possibly customer representatives, particularly for bespoke systems.

- **Representatives from ARTs, suppliers**. Typically, this includes RTEs, Product Management, System Architects and Engineers, and other key stakeholders.

The post-PI planning event summarizes the results of each ART's PI plans to ensure alignment for the upcoming increment. It creates agreement on the solution PI objectives to be implemented and presented at the next solution demo.

Pre- and post-PI planning occur as close to the ART planning events as reasonable. While not always feasible, it is desirable to have all the ARTs plan at the same time. This allows for a joint solution-level context and vision briefing. And it enables a solution-level management review for any adjustments before the second day of planning as shown in Figure 8-12.

Figure 8-12. Solution Trains align ART PI planning

The practical logistics of Solution Train planning may limit solution stakeholders from participating in each ART's planning events. However, it's critical that key stakeholders participate in as many of the ART PI planning events as possible—particularly Solution Management, the STE, and Solution Architecture and Engineering. Typically, these solution stakeholders may attend by circulating among the different ART PI planning sessions. Suppliers and customers play a critical role here as well, and they should be represented.

The Solution Train planning events deliver similar benefits as PI planning for a single ART. Further, the post PI planning event assures demand matches capacity and removes potential excess Work In Process (WIP). A successful event delivers three essential artifacts:

- A set of 'SMART' Solution Train PI objectives, which includes any planned but uncommitted goals, and the business value set by Business Owners

- A solution planning board (Figure 8-13), which highlights the capabilities and their dependencies, anticipated delivery dates, and any other relevant milestones

- A commitment based on the confidence vote for meeting the Solution Train PI objectives

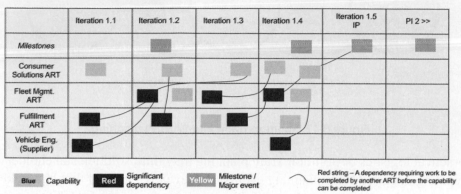

Autonomous Delivery Program Solution Planning Board

	Iteration 1.1	Iteration 1.2	Iteration 1.3	Iteration 1.4	Iteration 1.5 IP	PI 2 >>
Milestones		■			■	■
Consumer Solutions ART	■	■	■	■		
Fleet Mgmt. ART		■	■	■		
Fulfillment ART	■	■	■	■		
Vehicle Eng. (Supplier)	■			■		

Blue Capability	**Red** Significant dependency	**Yellow** Milestone / Major event	Red string – A dependency requiring work to be completed by another ART before the capability can be completed

Figure 8-13. Example solution planning board

Apply 'Continuish Integration'

In the software domain, continuous integration is the heartbeat of continuous delivery. It verifies changes and validates assumptions across the entire solution. Development teams invest in automation and infrastructure that builds, integrates, and tests every developer change, providing near-immediate feedback on errors.

Large, cyber-physical systems are far more difficult to integrate continuously: long lead-time items may not be available, integration spans organizational boundaries, and end-to-end automation is difficult to accomplish.

Instead, 'continuish integration' addresses the economic tradeoffs of frequent integration versus delayed knowledge and feedback. The goal is constant, partial integration with at least one full solution integration during each PI (Figure 8-14).

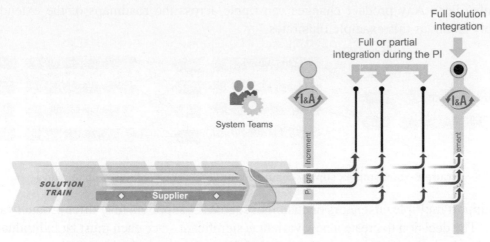

Figure 8-14. Integrate the entire solution at least every increment

When full integration is impractical, partial integration significantly reduces risks. Agile teams and trains integrate and test in a smaller context and rely on the system team for more extensive end-to-end tests with authentic production environments. This allows testing a partial scenario or use case, or testing with virtual and emulated environments, test doubles,[3] mocks, and other prototypes. These practices reduce the testing time and costs for teams and trains.

Manage the Supply Chain with Systems of Systems Thinking

Building large and complex systems requires integrating solutions across a substantial supply chain. Clearly, supplier alignment and coordination are critical to solution delivery. As a result, strategic suppliers participate in SAFe events (PI planning, system demos, I&A), use backlogs and roadmaps, and adapt to change. Agile contracts[4] encourage this behavior. The supplier's Product Manager and System Architect or Engineer continuously align the backlog, roadmap, and architectural runway with those of the overall solutions. Similarly, customer and supplier system teams have to share builds and tests to ensure that integration handoffs are smooth and free of delays.

Figure 8-15 shows a complex integration example for a large supply chain. The Product Manager of the Flight Controls component needs to continually align the backlog and roadmap to balance the needs of multiple customers (e.g., Boeing, Airbus, and

---

3. "A test double is a stand-in for a real object in a test, similar to how a stunt double stands in for an actor in a movie" (source: https://testing.googleblog.com/2013/07/testing-on-toilet-know-your-test-doubles.html).

4. For more information on Agile contracts, see https://www.scaledagileframework.com/agile-contracts/.

Bombardier). Any product changes can ripple across the roadmaps of the extended supply chain, as this example illustrates.

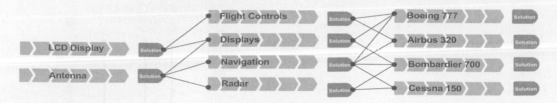

Figure 8-15. Complex supply chains depend on system-of-systems thinking

To support multiple customers or customer segments, suppliers may offer product variants.[5] The decision to create a new variant is significant since each must be individually tested, released, maintained, and supported. Due to the complexity, it's easy to create a new customer variant without having a strategy for coordination and understanding the entire life-cycle costs. There are two common patterns for coordinating customers and suppliers (Figure 8-16).

- *Clone-and-own model.* This is a common reuse practice that creates a product variant for each new customer based on assets from existing products. New variants are copied and adapted from existing products. This approach limits economies of scale since enhancements and defect fixes in one variant do not automatically propagate to the others and must be manually repeated. Over the long term, this often results in overall higher costs and lower quality.

- *Product line (or platform) model.* In this model, all developers work on a common architecture that creates a group of related product variants, which can be adapted for individual customers or customer segments. This approach necessitates a shared vision and roadmap that satisfies the needs of multiple customers. The supplier continually aligns backlogs with their customers and delivers new versions incrementally. While this approach may struggle to balance the needs of all customers, it provides opportunities for quality and technology investment that typically do not exist in clone-and-own.

---

5. A product variant is a version of a product that has different features or that operates in a different solution context.

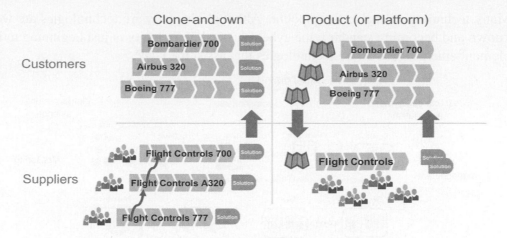

Figure 8-16. Patterns for coordinating dependent supply chains

'Internal open source' is a growing supplier collaboration practice where changes made to a customer variant are pulled back into the main product. This practice reduces delays to make changes while balancing support for multiple customers. The supplier is responsible for overall product quality and ensuring appropriate governance practices are followed, including who can make and contribute changes.

Continually Evolve Live Systems

Continually evolve live systems is the third dimension of enterprise solution delivery. This dimension ensures that systems are able to continuously deliver current value and can be evolved to deliver future value. Aspects of this dimension follow.

Build a Continuous Delivery Pipeline

Traditional large system development focuses on building the system right the first time and minimizing changes once the system is operational. After all, innovations and enhancements require a significant system upgrade effort. However, today's system must always evolve.

Figure 8-17 shows a typical CDP where every small developer change automatically runs a build process to create packages that are deployable and tested, giving feedback to developers within a few minutes. Packages that pass these tests then undergo more comprehensive automated acceptance testing. Once these packages pass all the automated tests, they become available for self-service deployment to other environments that support exploratory testing, usability testing, and ultimately release.

Many technologies enable the pipeline. Although the software technologies are well-known and becoming standard, the cyber-physical community is just beginning to implement emerging hardware technologies that assist the CDP.

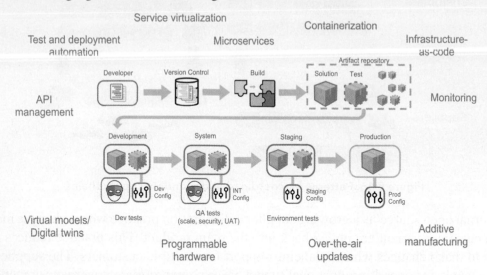

Figure 8-17. Software and hardware technologies enable the continuous delivery pipeline

Significant cyber-physical systems must also use CDPs to support continuous releases of new functionality. This requires investing in automation and infrastructure that can build, test, integrate, and validate small developer changes on an end-to-end staging environment or a close proxy. It also requires an architecture that can leverage technologies such as over-the-air updates and programmable hardware to enable faster deployment and release in the operational environment.

Development of the system and the CDP should start and evolve together. The following additional practices support the creation and use of the CDP:

- System engineering activities for analysis and design are performed in small batches to flow through the pipeline quickly.

- Planning includes building the pipeline as well as the system.

- 'Continuish' integration creates the automation and environments that can flow changes through the pipeline.

Evolve Deployed Systems

Investment in the CDP changes the economics for going live. A fast, cost-effective pipeline means a minimum viable system can often be released early and evolve. This delivers feedback and insights much earlier with less investment, possibly generating revenue sooner. Updating live systems is not new. For example, satellites have been launched before the software was fully ready. For businesses, the goal is to deploy the solution, quickly gain feedback and insights, deliver value, and reach the market before the competition.

Systems should be architected to support continuous deployment and release on demand. To create components more quickly and economically, hardware modeling languages, additive manufacturing, and robotic assembly can enable 'hardware as code.' Certain design decisions simplify system evolution, such as programmable versus application-specific integrated circuits, non-permanent fasteners, and allocation of system functions to upgradeable components.

Engineers are also exploring ways to adopt well-known software DevOps practices. For example, the blue-green deployment technique reduces downtime and risk by running two identical production environments—one for staging and one for live operations. This approach is being used on large systems like Navy ships, where the cost of redundant hardware is offset by releasing new capabilities into the operational system years earlier.

Applying Large Solution SAFe Elements to Other Configurations

The SAFe large solution level introduces a number of new concepts. These same concepts may be applied to other SAFe configurations. For example, a single ART developing a medical device will likely have one or more suppliers and use solution intent to manage compliance. Similarly, a Solution Train building a LIDAR system for autonomous vehicles will likely need to apply DevOps (Figure 8-18).

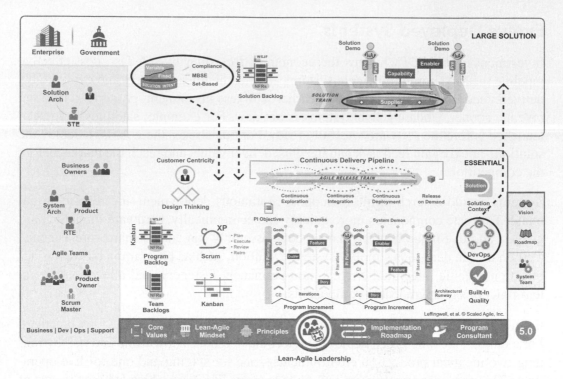

Figure 8-18. Applying SAFe elements to other configurations

Summary

For a long time now, Agile has shown the benefits of delivering early and updated often to generate frequent feedback and develop solutions that delight customers. To stay competitive, organizations need to apply the same approach to larger and more complex systems, which often includes both cyber-physical and software components. Enterprise solution delivery builds on the advances that have been made in Lean systems engineering and the technologies that have emerged to provide a more flexible approach to the development, deployment, and operation of such systems.

Alignment and coordination of ARTs and suppliers is maintained by continually refining solution intent, aligning everyone to a shared direction, alongside roadmaps that cover multiple planning horizons. 'Continuish integration' balances the economic tradeoffs between frequent systems integration and delaying feedback.

Enterprise solution delivery also describes the necessary adaptations to create a CDP in a cyber-physical environment by leveraging simulation and virtualization. This competency also provides strategies for maintaining and updating these true 'living systems' to continually extend their life and thereby deliver higher value to end-users.

9

Lean Portfolio Management

*"Most strategy dialogues end up with executives talking at
cross-purposes because nobody knows exactly what is meant by
vision and strategy, and no two people ever quite agree on which
topics belong where. We just don't have a good business discipline
for converging on issues this abstract."*
—Geoffrey Moore, *Escape Velocity*

The Lean Portfolio Management (LPM) competency aligns strategy and execution by
applying Lean and systems thinking approaches to strategy and investment funding,
Agile portfolio operations, and governance.

Why Lean Portfolio Management?

As Moore's quote reminds us, the supposedly simple act of defining and communicating an aligned strategy for the enterprise is not so simple after all. And yet nothing
could be more critical to improving overall business outcomes.

Strategy is typically the responsibility of those executives who are ultimately accountable for business outcomes. In most organizations, a portfolio management function is
used to organize the development of products and solutions to fulfill the strategy and
shepherd them to market.

However, traditional approaches to portfolio management were not designed for a
global economy or today's rapid pace of digital disruption. Businesses must work
with more uncertainty while delivering innovative solutions faster. As a result, portfolio management approaches must quickly evolve to the Lean-Agile way of working (Figure 9-1).

Traditional Approach	Lean-Agile Approach
People organized in functional silos and temporary project teams	People organized in value streams/ARTs; continuous value flow
Fund projects and project-cost accounting	Fund value streams, Lean budgets, and guardrails
Big up-front, top-down, annual planning and budgeting	Value stream budgets adjusted dynamically; participatory budgeting
Centralized, unlimited work intake; project overload	Strategic demand managed by portfolio Kanban; decentralized intake by value streams and ARTs
Overly detailed business cases based on speculative ROI	Lean business cases with MVP, business outcome hypothesis, Agile forecasting and estimating
Projects governed by phase gates; waterfall milestones, progress measured by task completion	Products and services governed by self-managing ARTS; objective measures and milestones based on working solutions

Figure 9-1. Evolving traditional portfolio mindsets and practices to a Lean-Agile approach

Figure 9-2 illustrates the three dimensions of the Lean Portfolio Management competency, followed by a brief description of each.

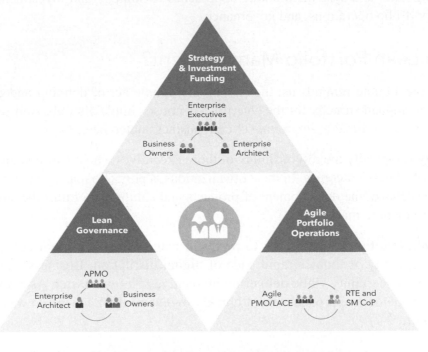

Figure 9-2. The three dimensions of Lean Portfolio Management

- ***Strategy and investment funding*** ensures that the entire portfolio is aligned and funded to create and maintain the solutions needed to meet business targets.

- ***Agile portfolio operations*** coordinate and support decentralized program execution and foster operational excellence.

- ***Lean governance*** oversees and manages spending, audit and compliance, forecasting expenses, and measurement.

However, before we describe these dimensions in greater detail, it's important to understand that each Scaled Agile Framework (SAFe) portfolio exists within the broader context of an *enterprise*, the source of the business strategy that it must address.

Portfolios Exist Within the Context of the Enterprise

A SAFe portfolio contains a set of *development* value streams for a specific part of the enterprise. Each development value stream delivers one or more solutions that help the enterprise meet its business mission. These can be products or solutions for customers or internal operational value streams. The enterprise funds portfolios and therefore has the highest level of governance authority.

Companies often organize the technology department to develop solutions that support various lines of business, internal departments, customer segments, or other business capabilities. Large enterprises will need several portfolios, each having a budget and a set of strategic themes for its part of the business strategy (Figure 9-3).

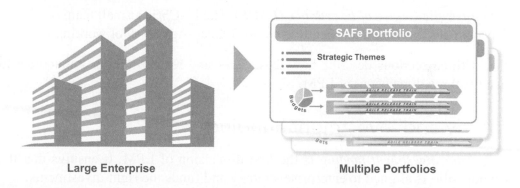

Large Enterprise   **Multiple Portfolios**

Figure 9-3. Large enterprises or government agencies may have several SAFe portfolios

Portfolio Roles and Responsibilities

The people in the LPM function have various titles and roles. Their responsibilities are held by business managers and executives who understand the enterprise's financial, technical, and business contexts and are ultimately accountable for the business outcomes.

The LPM roles include the following:

- *Enterprise Executives*. These senior-level leaders have financial, management, and compliance responsibilities for all or part of an enterprise.

- *Business Owners*. Stakeholders who have the primary business and technical responsibility for governance, compliance, and Return On Investment (ROI).

- *Enterprise Architect*. They work across value streams and Agile Release Trains (ARTs) to help provide the strategic technical direction that can optimize portfolio outcomes.

- *Epic Owners*. They are responsible for coordinating portfolio epics through the Kanban system.

- *Agile Program Management Office (APMO)*. They are responsible for supporting decentralized, efficient program execution and for supporting standard Lean metrics, shared best practices, and communication of knowledge.

- *Lean-Agile Center of Excellence (LACE)*. The LACE is a small team of people dedicated to implementing the SAFe Lean-Agile way of working.

The next three sections describe how these roles and responsibilities collaborate to realize the three dimensions of LPM.

Strategy and Investment Funding

Strategy and investment funding is the first dimension of LPM. It ensures that the entire portfolio is aligned to enterprise strategy and funds the right investments.

Each portfolio is responsible for achieving part of the enterprise strategy. Therefore, LPM needs to understand the portfolio's current state and have a plan to evolve it to the desired future state in accordance with that strategy.

This is achieved by a collaboration amongst enterprise executives, Business Owners, Enterprise Architects, and other portfolio stakeholders, as illustrated in Figure 9-4. This collaboration fulfills four important responsibilities, each of which is described next.

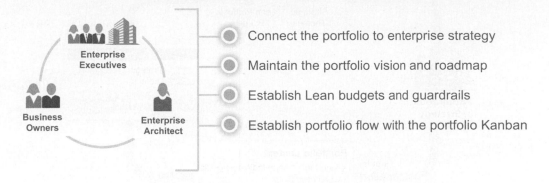

Figure 9-4. The strategy and investment funding collaboration and responsibilities

Connect the Portfolio to the Enterprise Strategy

"The way to get strategy executed is not by telling people what to do. It's by sharing the strategy in a way that everyone can understand and buy into it and see how their jobs relate to it. Then by putting the people processes in place to enable and encourage strategy execution."[1]

LPM accomplishes this communication primarily through *strategic themes*. The themes are a small set of business objectives that connect a portfolio to the enterprise strategy and guide the portfolio to the desired future state. Strategic themes influence the portfolio strategy and provide a business context for decision-making. They help drive innovation and competitive differentiation through a compelling portfolio of solutions.

Figure 9-5 illustrates that the portfolio is connected to the enterprise strategy by strategic themes and the *portfolio budget*. It provides feedback to the enterprise through the *portfolio context*.

---

1. Strategy Execution: Leadership to Align Your People to the Strategy,
   https://millian.nl/artikelen/strategy-execution-leadership-to-align-your-people-to-the-strategy

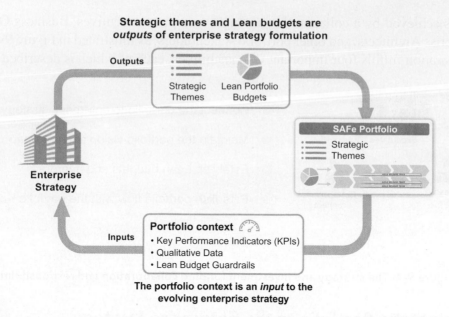

Strategic themes and Lean budgets are _outputs_ of enterprise strategy formulation

The portfolio context is an *input* to the evolving enterprise strategy

Figure 9-5. Strategy development is a bidirectional process between the enterprise and each solution portfolio

The *portfolio context* may include the following:

- **_Key Performance Indicators (KPIs)_**. KPIs consist of quantitative and financial measures, such as profitability, fitness for use, market share, ROI, customer net promoter score, and innovation accounting measures.[2]

- **_Qualitative data_**. This data may include a SWOT analysis and, most importantly, the solution, market, and business knowledge of the portfolio stakeholders.

- **_Lean budget guardrails_**. Lean budget guardrails describe the policies and practices for budgeting, spending, and governance for a specific portfolio.

Defining Strategic Themes

Strategic themes are elaborated by using a simple phrase or by using the Objectives and Key Results (OKRs) format (Figure 9-6). The following are a few examples of strategic themes described with a simple phrase:

---

2. Innovation accounting is a way of evaluating progress when all the metrics typically used in an established company (revenue, customers, ROI, market share) are effectively zero
(source: https://www.ideou.com/blogs/inspiration/innovation-accounting-what-it-is-and-how-to-get-started).

- Appeal to a younger demographic (clothing retailer)

- Cloud and mobile-first (a financial institution)

- Implement product support for trading foreign securities (a securities company)

- Implement single sign-on across applications (independent software vendor)

Figure 9-6 illustrates an example of a strategic theme described in OKR format. OKRs provide a simple approach to create alignment and engagement around measurable and ambitious goals.[3] They are frequently set, tracked, and re-evaluated each PI or so. "OKRs help ensure everyone is going in the same direction, with clear priorities, in a constant rhythm."[4]

Objective	Key Results
Increase customer engagement in our community platform	Reduce membership churn from 20% to 5%
	Increase Net Promoter Score (NPS) from 35 to 60
	Improve average weekly visits per active user from 5,000 to 20,000
	Increase non-paid (organic) traffic from 1,500 to 5,000
	Improve engagement from 30% to 60%

Figure 9-6. Example of a strategic theme in OKR format

Influence of Strategic Themes

Strategic themes identify what needs to be *new and different* from the current state. As such, these themes heavily influence many aspects of SAFe, such as the following:

- *Portfolio vision.* Strategic themes may affect elements of the portfolio vision maintained in the portfolio canvas (e.g., solutions, customer segments).

- *Value stream budgets and guardrails.* Strategic themes influence value stream budgets, which provide the funding, resources, and people necessary to accomplish the portfolio vision.

---

3. Felipe Castro, *The Beginner's Guide to OKRs*, https://felipecastro.com/en/okr/what-is-okr/
4. Ibid.

- *Portfolio Kanban and backlog*. Strategic themes act as decision-making filters in the portfolio Kanban system, influencing the content of the portfolio backlog and approval of epics.

- *ART and Solution Train vision and roadmap*. Strategic themes influence the ART and Solution Train vision and roadmap.

Maintain the Portfolio Vision and Roadmap

Maintaining the portfolio vision is the second responsibility of the strategy and investment funding collaboration. It describes how the development value streams will coordinate to achieve the portfolio's objectives and the broader enterprise goals. The vision offers a longer-term view for decision-making, helping Agile teams and trains make more informed choices about which features to implement now and in the future. In the book *Switch*,[5] authors Dan and Chip Heath liken this future vision to a 'destination postcard' (Figure 9-7).

A long view:

- How will our portfolio of future solutions solve the larger customer problems?

- How will these solutions differentiate us?

- What is the future context within which our solutions will operate?

- What is our current business context, and how must we evolve to meet this future state?

Vision: A postcard from the future

- Aspirational, yet realistic and achievable

- Motivational enough to engage others on the journey

Result: Everyone starts thinking about how to apply their strengths in order to get there.

Switch: How to Change Things When Change is Hard, Heath and Heath, Broadway Books, 2010

Figure 9-7. The portfolio vision is a 'postcard from the future'

Business Owners or senior leaders typically present the vision and business context during the Program Increment (PI) planning event. The vision helps leaders inspire and align the teams, increase engagement, and foster creativity to achieve the best results.

---

5. Chip Heath and Dan Heath, *Switch: How to Change Things When Change Is Hard* (Broadway Books, 2010)

Portfolio Canvas

The portfolio canvas (Figure 9-8) describes how a portfolio's value streams create and deliver value. It's an essential tool for developing and maintaining the portfolio vision in alignment with the enterprise. It contains the following information:

- The value propositions, the solutions they deliver, and the customers they serve

- The budgets and revenue allocated to each value stream

- The partners, activities, and resources needed to achieve the portfolio vision

It also describes the cost structure and how revenue or value is attained.

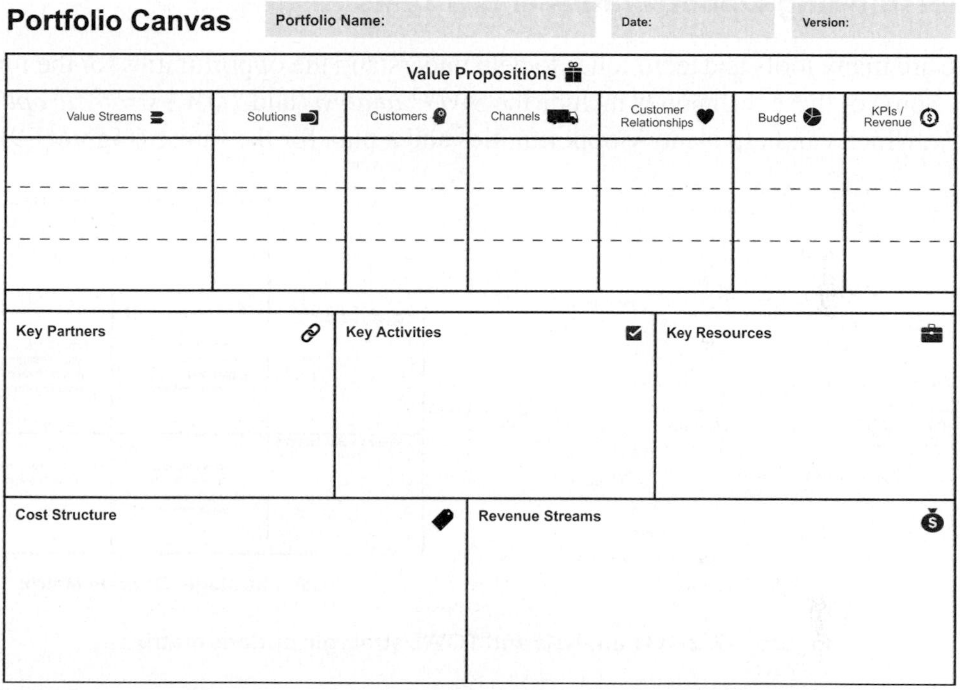

The portfolio canvas is adapted from the Business Model Canvas (http://www.businessmodelgeneration.com). This work is licensed under the Creative Commons Attribution-Share Alike 3.0 Unported License. To view a copy of this license visit: http://creative commons.org/licensed/by-sa/3.0.

Figure 9-8. Portfolio canvas

Capturing the Current State of the Portfolio

The current state canvas represents the as-is state for the portfolio, enabling alignment of the organization on its current structure, purpose, and status. It reflects the portfolio's current state on one page, providing a powerful visual baseline that can then be used to identify the future state.

Envision the Future State of the Portfolio

The next step is to envision the future state. The difference between the current and future state represents the portfolio vision, which guides the work that the value streams must accomplish.

Understanding Opportunities and Threats

There are many tools and techniques to help understand the opportunities for the future state. Some of these techniques include the *SWOT analysis* and *TOWS strategic options matrix*, which can help identify opportunities and a plan for the future (Figure 9-9).

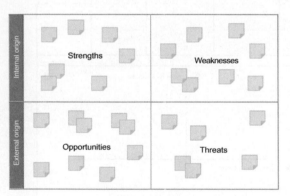

SWOT Analysis

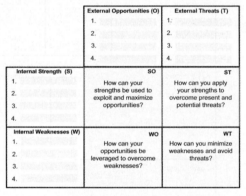

TOWS Strategic Options Matrix

Figure 9-9. SWOT analysis and TOWS strategic options matrix

The SWOT analysis identifies the Strengths, Weaknesses, Opportunities, and Threats related to the current business situation. Future opportunities are identified by answering the four questions in TOWS analysis using the information from the SWOT. The main difference between the SWOT and TOWS analysis is the outcomes that they create. A SWOT analysis is a great way to uncover the current situation of your value stream, product, or a portfolio. The TOWS analysis identifies strategic options to create a better future state.

Evaluating Alternatives to Determine a Future State

The portfolio's strategic themes and SWOT and TOWS analysis are critical inputs to exploring possibilities for the future state. LPM uses the current state portfolio canvas as a starting point to explore the different ways in which the portfolio could evolve in alignment with the strategic themes. An easy way to start is by selecting a specific block in the portfolio canvas, identifying a potential change or opportunity, and then exploring how it impacts the other parts of the canvas (Figure 9-10).

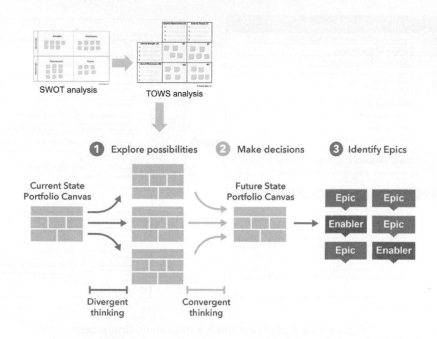

Figure 9-10. Process for envisioning the future state and identifying epics

Figure 9-10 also illustrates that divergent thinking is used to explore several different scenarios, while convergent thinking is applied to gain agreement and make decisions. The future state might be a blend of ideas from several different canvases, and some of the changes will require implementing new epics to achieve the desired business outcomes.

Defining Epics

Epics represent the most significant investments in a portfolio, which help evolve it to the desired future state. They are typically cross-cutting, spanning value streams and ARTs, and they usually take several PIs to implement. There are two types of portfolio epics: *business epics* deliver customer or end-user value, while *enabler epics* evolve the architectural runway to support upcoming business epics.

Epics are initially written as a *simple phrase* and then elaborated with an *epic hypothesis statement* to define and communicate critical information. Each is supported by a *Lean business case*, which supports the epic's technical and financial analysis. Figure 9-11 shows the templates for the epic hypothesis statement and Lean business case and how information flows between them.

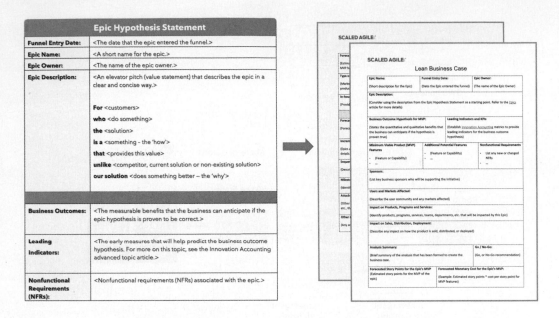

Figure 9-11. Epic hypothesis and Lean business case

SAFe Lean Startup Cycle

Traditionally, when new initiatives were defined to address marketplace challenges and opportunities, it was an all or nothing affair. These initiatives were described in deep business cases, with prospective and highly speculative ROI, and they were either funded in whole or not, based upon that business case. However, this creates funding commitments which can generally not be applied incrementally. This, in turn, tends to drive waterfall thinking and implementation for these, the most significant investments a company can make. So no matter how Agile the teams are, the net effect at the portfolio is still a big-bang, all-or-nothing investment approach.

Instead, the 'build-measure-learn' Lean startup cycle[6] (Figure 9-12) offers a far more incremental approach that better supports innovation and management of financial and business risk. The steps in this cycle are as follows:

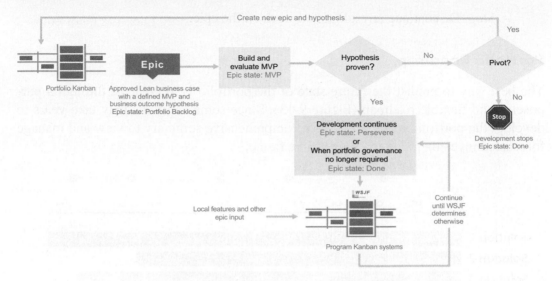

Figure 9-12. Epics in the Lean startup cycle

- *Hypothesize*. The Lean business case identifies the business outcomes hypothesis that describes the assumptions and potential measures that can assess whether an epic will deliver the appropriate level of value.

- *Build an MVP*. The next step is to implement a Minimum Viable Product (MVP)[6] to test the epic's hypothesis. In SAFe, this translates to the minimum feature set required to deliver the MVP.

- *Evaluate the MVP*. Once implemented, the MVP is evaluated against its hypothesis. Teams apply innovation accounting to provide fast feedback using leading indicators.

- *Pivot, persevere, or stop*. With the objective evidence in hand, teams and stakeholders can decide to do one of the following:

  - *Pivot*. Stop working on the epic but create a new epic hypothesis for review and approval.

---

6. Eric Ries, author of *The Lean Startup*, defines an MVP as that version of a new product that allows a team to collect the maximum amount of validated learning about customers with the least effort.

- **Persevere**. Continue working on the epic until its features cannot compete with others based on the Weighted Shortest Job First (WSJF) prioritization model.

- **Stop**. Discontinue any additional work on the epic.

Portfolio Roadmap

The best way to predict the future state of the portfolio is to create it through a purposeful and flexible roadmap (Figure 9-13). Since some solutions may take years to develop, the portfolio roadmap offers a comprehensive summary to view and manage forecasted investments over a longer time frame.

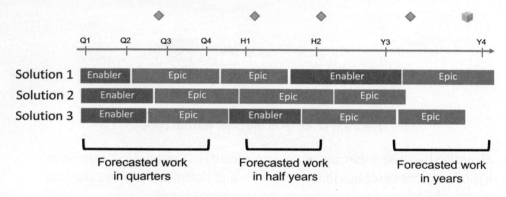

Figure 9-13. The portfolio roadmap communicates the longer-term picture

Because the portfolio roadmap may span several years, it requires estimating longer-term initiatives using Agile methods. It's critical to recognize that the roadmap represents uncommitted forecasts. While long-term predictability is indeed a worthy goal, Lean-Agile leaders know that *every long-term commitment decreases the organization's agility*. After all, you can't adapt to change if the organization is forced to follow an earlier plan.

The road to a better future state must be grounded in an architectural runway that enables the portfolio's technology to evolve. As a result, enterprise architecture is a critical component of strategy and investment funding. Enterprise Architects translate the business vision and strategy into effective technology plans and represent their initiatives on the portfolio roadmap as enabler epics. Enterprise Architects also promote adaptive design and engineering practices and facilitate the reuse of hardware and software components and proven design patterns across a portfolio.

Establish Lean Budgets and Guardrails

Establishing Lean budgets is the third responsibility of the strategy and investment funding collaboration. It defines a set of funding and governance practices that increase development throughput while maintaining financial and fitness-for-use governance. This funding model reduces friction, delays, and overhead related to traditional project-based funding and cost accounting.

Lean Budgets

Lean budgets provide funding for value streams that align with the business strategy and current strategic themes. As described in the next section, 'guardrails' provide Lean governance for budgets (Figure 9-14).

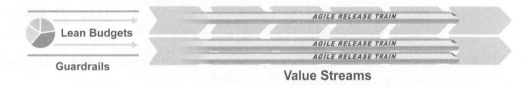

Figure 9-14. Each value stream has an operating budget for people and other resources

Funding value streams instead of projects allows the portfolio to plan, invest, and manage capacity based on a product delivery approach. This approach focuses the enterprise on delivering business results faster, validating benefits earlier, and creating a long-lived value stream network with stable Agile teams. Moreover, this funding approach eliminates the overhead of traditional project-based funding and cost-accounting with a process that is far more responsive to market needs and yet still provides fiscal responsibility.

Lean Budget Guardrails

Lean budget guardrails describe the policies and practices for budgeting, spending, and governance for a portfolio.

Figure 9-15 illustrates the four Lean budget guardrails.

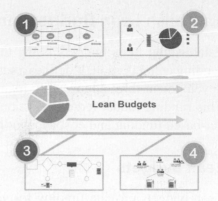

1. Guide investments by horizons

2. Apply capacity allocation to optimize value and solution integrity

3. Approve significant initiatives

4. Continuous business owner engagement

Figure 9-15. The four Lean budget guardrails

1. *Guiding investments by the horizon.* This ensures portfolio investments in solutions are aligned with the right allocations in SAFe's four investment horizons—evaluating, emerging, investing and extracting, and retiring.

2. *Applying capacity allocation to optimize value and solution integrity.* This helps value streams determine how much of the total capacity should be allocated for each type of activity (e.g., epics, features, enablers, tech debt, and maintenance).

3. *Approving significant initiatives.* Epics above a predefined threshold must be approved by LPM to provide appropriate financial oversight. Example thresholds include forecasted cost, forecasted number of PIs to implement an epic, strategic importance, or any combination of these factors.

4. *Continuous Business Owner engagement.* Business Owners are uniquely qualified to ensure that the funding allocated to value streams is going toward the right things. Therefore, their continued engagement in portfolio management serves as a critical guardrail that ensures that the priorities of the ARTs and Solution Trains are in alignment with LPM, customers, and Product Management.

Establish Portfolio Flow

Establishing portfolio flow is the fourth and final responsibility of strategy and investment funding. It facilitates the review, analysis, and approval of epics through the portfolio Kanban system.

The portfolio Kanban system visualizes and limits Work In Process (WIP), prevents long development queues, and assures that portfolio demand matches implementation capacity. The example in Figure 9-16 illustrates the steps and collaborations needed to move an epic from the intake funnel to done.

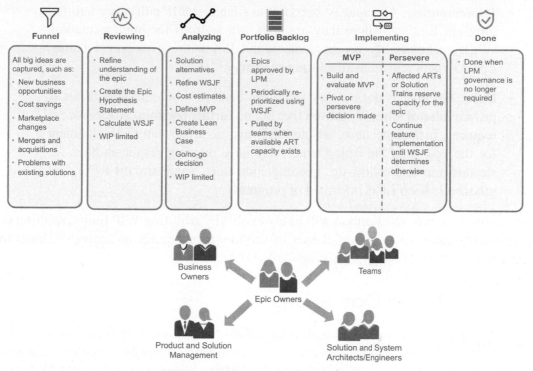

Figure 9-16. Portfolio Kanban system

- *Funnel*. This state captures all new big ideas. Epics that meet specific decision criteria are then moved to the next state, 'reviewing,' as WIP limits permit.

- *Reviewing*. Epics in reviewing are described with an epic hypothesis statement and are prioritized using the WSJF model. The ones with the highest score are pulled into the next state, 'analyzing,' as WIP limits permit.

- *Analyzing*. Epics in this state deserve more rigorous analysis and further investment. Alternatives for solution design and implementation are explored. A Lean business case is developed, and options for internal development and outsourcing are also considered. A Minimum Viable Product (MVP) is defined. Approved epics move to the 'portfolio backlog' state.

- **Portfolio backlog**. This state maintains epics that have been approved by LPM. They are reviewed and periodically prioritized using WSJF. When sufficient capacity from one or more ARTs is available, the highest priority item advances to 'implementing.'

- **Implementing**. As capacity becomes available, ARTs pull epics into the program Kanban, where they are split into features for implementation. While responsibility for implementation lies with development teams, Epic Owners remain available as necessary.

- **Done**. An epic is done either when the business outcome hypothesis is proven false or when it's proven true but no further portfolio governance is required. In the latter case, various ARTs may continue feature development for the epic; and the Epic Owner may have ongoing responsibilities for stewardship and follow-up. Leading indicators, value stream KPIs, and guardrails keep LPM informed of progress.

As learning occurs, the Kanban will likely evolve by adjusting WIP limits, splitting or combining states, or including classes of service (for example, an 'expedite' lane) to optimize the flow of epics.

Agile Portfolio Operations

The second dimension of LPM is *Agile portfolio operations*. This collaboration is responsible for coordinating and supporting decentralized program execution, and fostering operational excellence, while applying systems thinking to ensure that ARTs and Solution Trains are aligned and operate well in the broader portfolio context.

The Agile portfolio operations collaboration has three primary responsibilities (Figure 9-17):

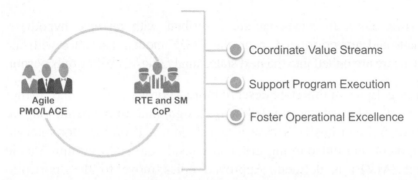

Agile PMO/LACE

RTE and SM CoP

Coordinate Value Streams

Support Program Execution

Foster Operational Excellence

Figure 9-17. Agile portfolio operations collaboration and responsibilities

Coordinate Value Streams

Although many value streams operate independently, cooperation among a set of solutions can provide some portfolio-level capabilities and benefits that competitors can't match. Lean-Agile leaders understand the challenges and opportunities of their value streams and strive to make them as independent as possible while connecting them to the enterprise's larger purpose.

Support Program Execution

Program execution support defines how to develop, harvest, and apply successful execution patterns and reporting across the portfolio.

Many enterprises have discovered that centralized decision-making and traditional mindsets can undermine the move to Lean-Agile practices. As a result, some enterprises have abandoned the traditional Program Management Office (PMO) approach, distributing all the responsibilities to ARTs and Solution Trains.

However, we've also observed a pattern where organizations evolve the traditional PMO to become an APMO (or Value Management Office [VMO] in some enterprises). After all, the people in the PMO have specialized skills, knowledge, and relationships with managers, executives, and other key stakeholders. They know how to get things done, and they can often help lead the change to the new way of working.

The APMO, operating as a group within the LPM function, can help cultivate and apply successful program execution patterns across the portfolio. The APMO also establishes objective metrics and reporting regarding business agility. It may also sponsor and support Communities of Practice for RTEs and Solution Train Engineers, as well as Scrum Masters. These role-based CoPs provide a forum for sharing effective Agile program execution practices and other institutional knowledge.

Foster Operational Excellence

Operational excellence focuses on continually improving efficiency, practices, and results to optimize business performance. LPM has a lead role in achieving operational excellence, helping the organization improve its ability to achieve business goals predictably. The LACE, which may be a standalone group or part of the APMO, is often responsible for leading operational excellence. In either case, the LACE becomes a continuous source of energy to power the enterprise through the necessary organizational changes.

In the course of a Lean-Agile transformation, the APMO often takes on additional responsibilities. In this expanded role, they may do the following:

- Lead the move to objective milestones and Lean-Agile budgeting

- Establish and maintain the systems and reporting capabilities

- Foster more Agile contracts and leaner supplier relationships and customer partnerships

- Establish KPIs for financial governance

- Advise as a communication liaison regarding the strategy to ensure smooth deployment and operation of value stream investments

The APMO also supports management and people operations (Human Resources) in Agile hiring and staff development.

Lean Governance

Lean governance is the third dimension of LPM. This function manages spending, audit and compliance, forecasting expenses, and measurement. The Lean governance collaboration and responsibilities require the active engagement of the APMO and LACE, Business Owners, and Enterprise Architects (Figure 9-18).

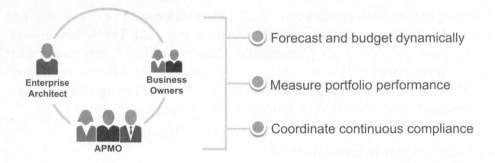

Figure 9-18. Lean governance collaboration and responsibilities

Forecast and Budget Dynamically

As described earlier, SAFe provides a Lean approach to budgeting—a lightweight, more flexible, Agile process that replaces traditional fixed, long-range budget cycles, financial commitments, and expectations. This new approach to planning and budgeting includes

Agile estimating and forecasting. It also adjusts value stream budgets over time using participatory budgeting. Each of these practices is described next.

Agile Estimating and Forecasting

LPM needs to understand the actual and forecasted costs of epics while maintaining a high-level view of when the potential new value can be delivered (see the portfolio roadmap described earlier).

Since epics often have lots of uncertainty, the best practice for *Agile estimation* is to decompose them into smaller pieces of functionality—such as business and enabler features. These items are then estimated in story points and totaled to forecast the epic's size and cost.

Agile forecasting is a way to estimate the delivery of large initiatives rapidly. It requires understanding these three data points:

- An epic's forecasted size in story points

- The historical velocity of the ARTs

- The percentage of capacity that each ART can potentially dedicate to working on an epic for the next several PIs

With these three data points, teams can formulate multiple 'what if' scenarios to forecast when each epic can be delivered.

Capital Expenses and Operating Expenses

Some enterprises capitalize a percentage of the labor involved in creating software for sale or internal use. Software capitalization practices are historically based on waterfall development, in which up-front requirements and design phase gates represent the events that trigger capital expense treatment. In Agile, however, these phase gates do not exist.

This may create a perceived inability to capitalize software expenses which may block the implementation of Agile development. The advanced topic article on the SAFe website[7] describes methods that can be used to classify capital (CapEx) and operating expenses (OpEx) in Agile development.

---

7. https://www.scaledagileframework.com/capex-and-opex/

Participatory Budgeting

Most organizations will generate more good ideas than they can fund, resulting in a portfolio prioritization challenge. As a result, LPM and participants from different value streams use 'participatory budgeting' to collaboratively determine value stream budgets.

Once established, value stream budgets can typically be adjusted twice annually. If adjusted less frequently, spending is fixed for too long, limiting agility. And while more frequent budget changes may seem to support increased agility, they may create too much uncertainty and an inability to commit to any near-term course of action.

Measure Portfolio Performance

Each portfolio establishes the minimum metrics needed to assure that strategy is implemented, spending aligns with the agreed guardrails, and business results are continually improving. These include value stream KPIs and a broader set of portfolio metrics.

KPIs are the quantifiable measures used to evaluate how a value stream is performing against its forecasted business outcomes. The type of value stream drives the KPIs that the business will need. Here are some examples:

- *New products, services, or solutions*. Some value streams create emerging new offerings. These value streams will need to rely on nonfinancial leading indicators known as *innovation accounting*. These KPIs offer faster feedback on the benefit hypothesis of features and epics.

- *Strategic themes*. Each value stream's contribution to strategic themes can be tracked and measured by assessing performance against the OKRs.

- *Cost centers*. Some development value streams serve internal operational value streams and are not independently monetized. In this case, value is measured through nonfinancial metrics such as customer satisfaction, net promoter score, and feature cycle time.

Also, experience has shown that the set of metrics shown in Figure 9-19 can be used to assess the internal and external progress for an entire portfolio.

Benefit	Expected Result	Metric Used
Employee engagement	Improved employee satisfaction; lower turnover	Employ survey; HR statistics
Customer satisfaction	Improved net promoter score (NPS)	Net promoter score survey
Productivity	Reduced average feature cycle time	Feature cycle time
Relentless improvement	Relentless improvement in team, program and portfolio performance	Self-assessments for each level of the Framework
Time-to-market	More frequent releases	Number of releases
Quality	Reduced defect counts and support call volume	Defect data and support call volume
Partner health	Improved ecosystem relationships	Partner and vendor surveys
Alignment	Improved progress against key results for strategic themes	Objectives and key results (OKRs)

Figure 9-19. Example of LPM portfolio metrics

Coordinate Continuous Compliance

As we described in Chapter 8, solutions are often subject to internal or external financial auditing requirements, and industry, legal, and regulatory standards. Traditional compliance practices tend to defer these activities to the end of the initiative. But as we also described in the last chapter that subjects the enterprise to the risk of late discovery and subsequent rework, as well as potential regulatory or legal exposure. The implementation of a Lean QMS system supports and enables continuous compliance while minimizing overhead and fostering continuous value flow (Figure 9-20).

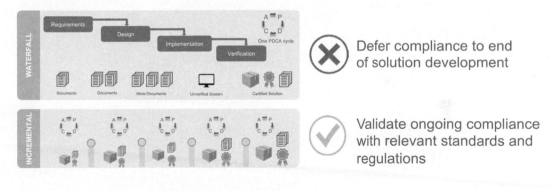

Figure 9-20. Rapid **Plan-Do-Check-Adjust** learning cycles include compliance concerns

This approach builds continuous compliance directly into the iterative development activities, leaving only final validation activities and official sign-offs to the end.

Summary

Successfully defining and executing a strategy in a world of increasing uncertainty is challenging. It requires that portfolio management practices are modernized through the application of Lean, Agile, and DevOps. What emerges is a more adaptable and responsive portfolio, organized around value streams, and motivated to support a continuous flow of value to the enterprise's customers.

Strategy and investment funding ensures the 'right work' is happening at the 'right time.' Continuous and early feedback on current initiatives, coupled with a Lean approach to funding, allows the portfolio to make the necessary adjustments to meet its business targets. Agile portfolio operations facilitates coordination across the value streams within the portfolio, maintaining alignment between strategy and execution, and fostering continued operational excellence. Lean governance closes the loop by measuring portfolio performance and supporting dynamic adjustments to budgets to maximize value.

When the right people work together and fulfill these responsibilities, the enterprise can better define and communicate strategy and thereby improve economic outcomes.

10

Organizational Agility

"Agility is the ability to adapt and respond to change ... agile organizations view change as an opportunity, not a threat."
—Jim Highsmith

The *organizational agility competency* describes how Lean-thinking people and Agile teams optimize their business processes, evolve strategy with clear and decisive new commitments, and quickly adapt the organization as needed to capitalize on new opportunities.

Why Organizational Agility?

In today's digital economy, the only truly sustainable competitive advantage is the speed at which an organization can sense and respond to the needs of its customers. Its strength is its ability to deliver value in the shortest sustainable lead time, to evolve and implement new strategies quickly, and to reorganize to better address emerging opportunities.

Organizational agility is critical to respond sufficiently to the challenges. "Unfortunately, the organizational structures, processes, and cultures of most businesses were developed more than a century ago. They were built for control and stability, not for innovation, speed, and agility. Small incremental changes to how businesses manage, strategize, and execute are insufficient to remain competitive. This requires a leaner and more agile approach which, in turn, requires sweeping changes that have a positive, long-lasting impact on the entire enterprise."[1]

As we described in Chapter 1, Business Agility, the SAFe approach to addressing the challenge of digital transformation is the 'dual operating system,' one that leverages

---

1. Richard Knaster and Dean Leffingwell, *SAFe 4.5 Distilled: Applying the Scaled Agile Framework for Lean Software and Systems Engineering* (Addison-Wesley, 2017).

the stability and resources of the existing organizational hierarchy while implementing a value stream network that leverages the entrepreneurial drive still present in every organization.

By organizing and reorganizing the enterprise around the flow of value instead of the traditional organizational silos, SAFe restores the second (network) operating system. It allows organizations to focus on both the innovation and growth of new ideas as well as the execution, delivery, operation, and support of existing solutions.

The organizational agility competency is instrumental in bringing the power of the second operating system to support the opportunities and threats of the digital age. This competency is expressed in three dimensions (Figure 10-1).

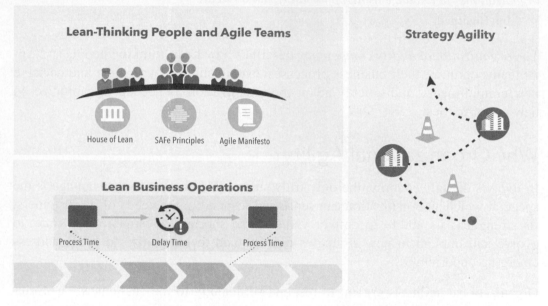

Figure 10-1. Three dimensions of organizational agility

- *Lean-thinking people and Agile teams*. Everyone involved in solution delivery is trained in Lean and Agile methods and embraces their values, principles, and practices.

- *Lean business operations*. Teams apply Lean principles to understand, map, and continuously improve the processes that deliver and support business solutions.

- *Strategy agility*. The enterprise is Agile enough to continuously sense the market and quickly change strategy when necessary.

Each of these dimensions is described in the sections that follow.

Lean-Thinking People and Agile Teams

Lean-thinking people and Agile teams is the first dimension of organizational agility. This dimension is critical to delivering *business solutions*— not just the software applications and digital systems, but all of the supporting activities (e.g., privacy, security, support, availability) necessary to continually address the business problem. Even the solution itself is not stand alone, it lives in the larger context of its environment—including other hardware, software, network systems, and more.

Figure 10-2 illustrates that everyone involved in the delivery of business solutions—operations, legal, marketing, people operations, finance, development, and others—can apply effective Lean and Agile methods and embrace the mindset, principles, and practices.

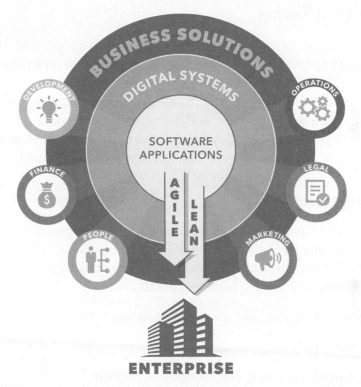

Figure 10-2. Extending Lean and Agile thinking to the enterprise

Extending the Mindset and Principles to the Enterprise

Extending the Lean-Agile mindset to the entire enterprise forms the cornerstone of a new management approach and results in an enhanced company culture that enables business agility. It provides leaders and practitioners throughout the enterprise with the thinking tools and behaviors needed to drive a successful SAFe transformation, helping individuals and the entire enterprise achieve their goals.

The Lean-Agile mindset establishes the right thinking, but as presented in Chapter 4, SAFe Principles, it's the ten underlying principles that guide effective roles, practices, and behaviors. These principles are fundamental to organizational agility and the Lean-thinking people and Agile teams who enable it. Everyone in the enterprise can apply these principles to their daily work, and thereby become part of the leaner, and more Agile, operating system.

Agile Technical Teams

As described in Chapter 6, Team and Technical Agility, the adoption of Agile development within software development is fairly advanced and well understood. Now, with the advent of the DevSecOps movement, IT operations and security are also rapidly adopting Agile. It's also making its way to other technical domains, such as networking, operations, hardware, electronics, and more. After all, Agile technical teams typically achieve a degree of unprecedented performance and personal satisfaction with their work. Who doesn't want to be on a high-performing Agile team?

Agile Business Teams

Once the business understands this new way of working, it begins to recognize that the same benefits apply and typically starts creating cross-functional Agile business teams. These teams may be involved in any of the functions necessary to support developing and delivering business solutions, including the following:

- Sales, product marketing, and corporate marketing
- Sourcing and supply chain management
- Operations, legal, contracts, finance, and compliance
- People (HR), training, and facilities
- Receiving, production, fulfillment, and shipping
- Customer service, support, and maintenance

We've often observed a 'three-step maturity cycle' which illustrates how Agile business teams typically form and mature (Figure 10-3).

Figure 10-3. Agile business team maturity cycle

Step 1: Be Agile

First, the teams adopt and master the Lean-Agile mindset and practices. This creates a universal value system and a shared understanding of what Agile is. But it goes beyond that. The SAFe Lean-Agile principles are equally important and, in some cases, even more so, guiding the right behaviors for business teams and their leaders. Just as the North Star guides people when they don't have a compass or a visible landmark to follow, the SAFe principles point the way to *being Agile*, even when specific Agile guidance doesn't exist for that function.

Step 2: Join the Value Stream

Step 1 is a great start to help business teams become Agile, in both the mindset and the execution. However, if they only optimize and improve their efficiencies locally, the larger, end-to-end system may not improve. To optimize the system as a whole (Principle #2, Apply systems thinking), most Agile business teams join the value stream by becoming part of an Agile Release Train (ART), which builds the business solutions they support.

How that works in practice depends on the scope and the nature of the work the teams do. For example, product marketing may be directly embedded in ARTs, as whole teams or inside other teams. In other cases, the marketing function may operate as a shared service, supporting several ARTs. Regardless, a common view of work, an alignment of terminology, a shared cadence, and synchronization across all of the teams all help the value streams deliver quickly and predictably with better quality.

In addition, system integration becomes broader and more impactful when business teams provide new policies and procedures (e.g., licensing, privacy, security) that become embedded in code, legal documents, operational workflows, and other artifacts which are part of the business solution.

Step 3: Specialize the Principles and Practices

The first two steps move the enterprise further on the path to business agility. However, as business teams mature, it becomes increasingly important for them to evolve their practices and as we described in Chapter 6, to define what Agile and built-in quality means in their context. In this way, they make it their own. Agile marketing is a good example. Since it is so tightly coupled to solution development, a set of Agile marketing principles has emerged that focuses on, among other things, validated learning, customer discovery, and iterative campaigns.[2]

Agile People Operations

All this new agility puts substantial pressure on how new employees are recruited and on changing policies and procedures for managing compensation and career growth. But addressing the needs of knowledge workers challenges many traditional human resources (HR) practices. In their place, 'Agile HR' brings the Lean-Agile mindset, values, and principles to hiring, engaging, and retaining people. Six themes for modernizing people operations are summarized here:[3]

- *Embrace the new talent contract*. This agreement recognizes the unique needs of knowledge workers and provides the engagement, empowerment, and autonomy they require to reach their full potential.

- *Foster continuous engagement*. Continuous employee engagement occurs when everyone in the enterprise understands the business mission, is engaged in meaningful work, and is fully empowered to do their part.

- *Hire for attitude and cultural fit*. Identify, attract, hire, and retain people who will be most successful in the dynamic team environment of an Agile culture.

- *Move to iterative performance flow*. Many Lean enterprises have eliminated the annual performance review. Instead, leaders and

2. https://agilemarketingmanifesto.org/
3. https://www.scaledagileframework.com/wp-content/uploads/delightful-downloads/2017/09/Agile-HR-with-SAFe.pdf

managers offer fast, continuous feedback and also solicit and receive feedback in return.

- ***Take the issue of money off the table***. Replacing traditional, individual incentives with the right shared incentives helps tailor compensation and motivation to the differing needs of individuals in the next-generation workforce.

- ***Support impactful learning and growth***. Modern careers are fueled more by personal choices and meaningful growth than by climbing a hierarchical ladder. Successful employers need to respond by providing rewarding work, more fluid roles, and individual growth paths.

Agile Working Environments

In addition to more contemporary HR practices, experience and research have shown that working environments and physical spaces are vital to highly productive Agile teams.[4]

For example, Figure 10-4 illustrates an Agile working environment for teams. In this design, individual teams work in a 'pod' of semi-private cubicles. Walls within the pod are low, allowing for informal discussions. Their personal focus space is inside their cubicle, yet it allows informal communication and knowledge sharing within the team. However, the higher outside walls of the pod prevent distractions from the noise and conversations of other teams or people who pass by. In addition, the gathering spaces in the middle provide an area for hoteling team members, spontaneous pairing, and quick, informal sessions. The pod is supported by whiteboards, a large monitor for video conferencing, and solution and process information radiators.

---

4. Jorgen Hesselberg. *Unlocking Agility: An Insider's Guide to Agile Enterprise Transformation*, Kindle edition (Pearson, 2018).

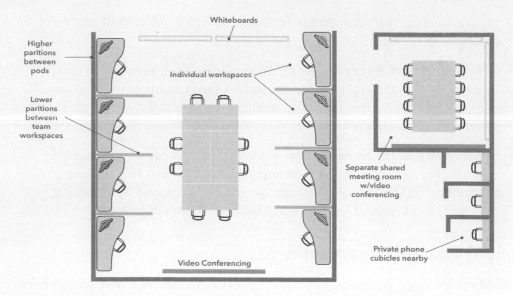

Figure 10-4. An Agile working environment for teams

Ideally, there's a dedicated meeting room nearby that provides space for the team to post their information on the walls and collaborate with remote team members and other teams. Where feasible, a few private phone cubicles support the need for individual privacy.

Workspaces for Remote Workers

Agile development is designed and optimized for collocated teams—it's a key principle of the Agile Manifesto ("The most efficient and effective method of conveying information to and within a development team is face-to-face conversation"[5]). To this end, enterprises often spend significant time and energy establishing collocation. The Agile pod design in Figure 10-4 is a reflection of that. However, collocation is not always feasible. Simply, some of the people who can contribute the most are not available to be located—or relocated—on site. The fact is that many Agile teams are distributed across geographies, sometimes with significant time zone differences.

We have both witnessed and participated in high performing teams with a significant degree of distribution. While being distributed does not change the basic Agile ways of working, it does impose some requirements on the business and the remote workers. These may include:

---

5. https://agilemanifesto.org/principles.html

- High bandwidth video and audio connectivity

- Tooling for team and program Kanban boards and backlogs

- A wiki or intranet site providing access to strategic themes, portfolio vision, and other critical information

- Collaboration tools for communication, visualization, and ideation

- Overlapping core hours for DSU, iteration planning, demos, and other events

- Commitment to routinely travel to PI planning events

Cross-Team Collaboration Spaces

The physical environment also plays an important role in supporting collaboration and innovation by providing spaces away from the daily work. Success patterns for these spaces include the following:

- *Ease of booking*. Make it easy to book rooms for innovation by avoiding blocking them with recurring meetings.

- *Facilitation kits*. Provide kits that include pens, stickies, scissors, and tape to support any innovation process.

- *Moveable whiteboards*. Whiteboards on wheels ensure that the output is not lost and can be worked on elsewhere in future sessions.

- *Rearrangeable furniture*. As the purpose of collaboration changes, the layout of the room will also need to adapt. Avoiding fixed furniture will allow people to set up these spaces for a variety of different scenarios.

- *Video conferencing*. Always-on video conferencing ensures that everyone, including remote workers, can participate.

- *Cross-team collaboration spaces*. Larger rooms support critical events such as Program Increment (PI) planning, system demos, Inspect and Adapt (I&A), as well as other cross-team activities.

PI Planning and ART Collaboration Space

PI planning is the most critical event in SAFe. As such, a semi-dedicated physical space for planning is a wise investment that will pay for itself over time. In addition to the physical space, adequate communication channels must be established for attendees who cannot be present in person. For many enterprises, room for a single ART or two is about all that can be allocated permanently. Figure 10-5 provides a typical room layout for a PI planning event.

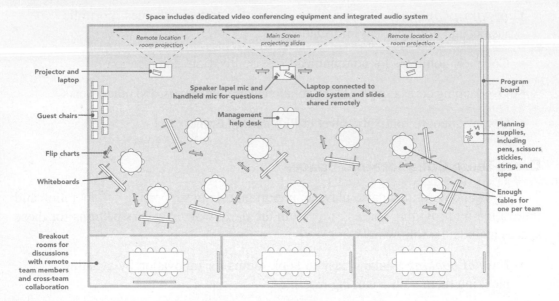

Figure 10-5. A typical room layout for a PI planning event

In larger enterprises with multiple ARTs, it may be impractical to provide a dedicated space for all the ARTs. In this case, a single on-site ART planning location becomes the centerpiece, but other internal or external venues may be needed. Of course, this space won't be used just for the regular PI planning schedule. It will also host the system demo and the I&A, as well as additional team-sharing spaces during the PI. A permanent location adds predictability, minimizes uncertainty, and reduces the transaction cost of organizing these events. In our experience, this space adds to the collaborative workspace strategy that benefits the Agile enterprise.

Visualizing Work

Frequently, during various SAFe training forums, attendees ask, "But if I was to leave here and do only one thing to start implementing Lean-Agile development at scale, what would it be?" Our answer is always the same: *visualize the work*. That is why when you visit an Agile enterprise, you *see* work everywhere—on walls, whiteboards, monitors, hallways, and wherever you look. Visualization converts the abstract to tangible; flushes out unnecessary, unplanned, unapproved, or duplicate work; and aligns everyone to the actual current state.

The common thread across all these approaches is that the information is always available: no effort is needed to go and discover it. Based on our experiences, we've recommended some starting points:

- *Visualize customers*. Agile teams use personas to bring the customer to life and post their representations on the walls of their team area, so they are always top of mind.

- *Visualize the flow of work*. Making the current work visible using Kanban systems exposes the amount of Work In Process (WIP), bottlenecks, and what people are really doing as opposed to what others think they are doing.

- *Visualize solution health*. Customer support teams have long seen the value in displaying the number of waiting calls, daily closed and open tickets, and current Service Level Agreements performance prominently on monitors close to the teams who rely on that information. This approach has been adopted by Agile teams to include metrics on the state of the current solution.

- *Visualize strategy*. Another example of visualizing work is an 'investment corridor' (Figure 10-6) that identifies all current and potential epics in flight at one large enterprise. Rather than confining the portfolio visualizations to a room, information in the corridor is outside, making it easy for people to walk up and add their thoughts and suggestions.

Figure 10-6. The investment corridor for a portfolio prioritization workshop (Courtesy of Travelport International LTD)

Tooling and Automation

Lean-thinking people and Agile teams have specific training and insights on how work flows through the system. They understand that optimizing one activity does not optimize the whole, and that delays in the process (see the 'Mapping Value Streams' section) exert more influence throughout than the efficiency of any one step. To combat this, they implement the tooling necessary to *see* the work as it flows through the system to identify bottlenecks and opportunities for improvement. This tooling typically includes the following:

- *Application lifecycle management (ALM)* tools demonstrate and connect the various backlogs and Kanban systems that teams use to manage their local work and provide enterprise-wide visibility.

- *Integrated development environments* provide the tools developers need to author, edit, compile, and debug software.

- *Continuous delivery pipeline* tools support the large number of artifacts—primarily code, tests, scripts, metadata—and provide the automation needed to efficiently integrate, test, build, and deploy the solution.

- *Collaboration tools* support local and distributed development and the intense degree of interaction required.

- *Systems engineering tools* support the modeling and requirements of large systems and establish traceability across the elements, administering quality assurance and compliance.

Most of these tools are available in both open source and commercial products at a relatively advanced and mature state. Applying them comprehensively is yet another critical factor in achieving business agility.

Lean Business Operations

Lean business operations is the second dimension of organizational agility. Organizational agility requires enterprises to understand both the operational value streams that deliver business solutions to their customers, as well as the development value streams (which are the primary focus of SAFe) that develop those solutions.

- *Operational value streams* contain the steps and the people who provide end-user value using the business solutions created by the development value streams.

- ***Development value streams*** contain the steps and the people who develop the business solutions used by operational value streams.

Figure 10-7 illustrates the relationship between operational and development value streams.

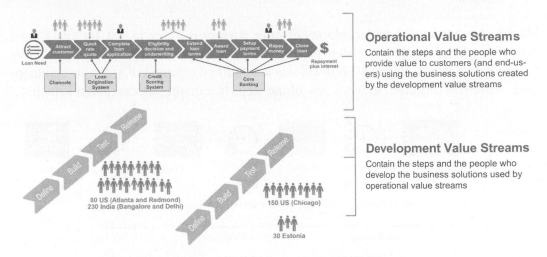

Operational Value Streams

Contain the steps and the people who provide value to customers (and end-users) using the business solutions created by the development value streams

Development Value Streams

Contain the steps and the people who develop the business solutions used by operational value streams

Figure 10-7. Operational and development value streams

A trigger (e.g., product order or new feature request) starts the flow of value, and there's some form of value delivered at the end. The steps in the middle are the activities used to develop or deliver the value.

For most developers, the people who run the operational value streams are the customers of the development value streams. They directly use and operate the solutions that support the flow of value to the end user. This requires that developers do the following:

- Understand (and often help analyze and map) the operational value streams they support

- Apply customer-centricity and design thinking

- Include the business teams that support the solution in the development process

These responsibilities help assure that the business solutions developed provide a 'whole-product solution' to satisfy the needs of both internal and external customers.

Mapping Value Streams

"Lean companies focus on value streams to eliminate non-value-creating activities."

—Alan Ward

Identifying operational and development value streams is a critical task for every Lean enterprise. Once identified, value stream mapping[6] is used to analyze and improve business operations. Figure 10-8 illustrates a simplified example of value stream mapping, which, in this case, shows a few of the steps in a marketing campaign launch.

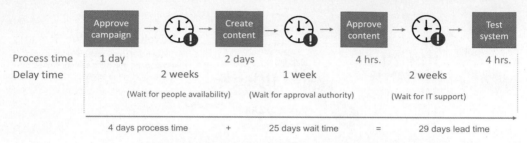

Figure 10-8. Value stream mapping showing total lead time, total processing time, and time efficiency

Teams look for the opportunity to improve the efficiency of each step, consequently reducing the total lead time. This includes reducing process time, as well as improving the quality of each step measured by the percent complete and accurate.[7]

As is the case in Figure 10-8, the delay time (the waiting time between steps) is often the biggest source of waste. If the team above wanted to deliver a marketing campaign faster, they would need to reduce the delay times, as the processing steps are only a small part of the total lead time. Reducing delays is typically the fastest and easiest way to shorten the total lead time and improve time to market.

---

6. Karen Martin, *Value Stream Mapping: How to Visualize Work and Align Leadership for Organizational Transformation*, Kindle edition (McGraw-Hill Education, 2013).

7. The percent complete and accurate represents the percentage of work that the next step can process without it needing to go back for rework.

Implementing Flow

In addition to mapping the value stream, the entire process can then be visualized with a Kanban system as a means to continuously improve performance and identify bottlenecks. SAFe Principle #6, Visualize and limit Work In Process (WIP), reduce batch sizes, and manage queue lengths, is then applied to optimize flow. Figure 10-9 illustrates a simplified Kanban system for a set of marketing campaigns associated with a major product launch.

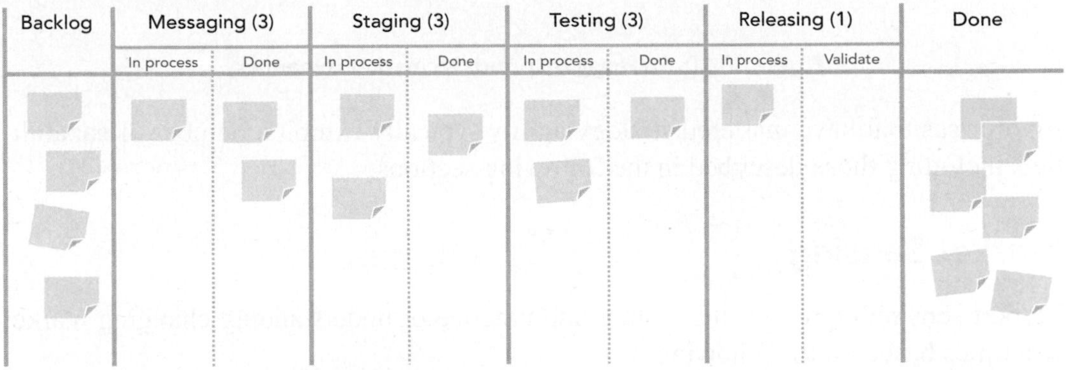

Backlog	Messaging (3)		Staging (3)		Testing (3)		Releasing (1)		Done
	In process	Done	In process	Done	In process	Done	In process	Validate	

Figure 10-9. A simple Kanban system for marketing campaigns for a new product launch

Each marketing campaign, represented by a card, works its way through the system from the backlog to done. WIP limits (the numbers in parentheses in Figure 10-9) help control the amount of work in the system.

Strategy Agility

Strategy agility is the third dimension of the organizational agility competency. Strategy agility is the ability to sense changes in market conditions and implement new strategies quickly and decisively when necessary. It also includes the good sense to persevere on the things that are working—or will work—if given sufficient time and focus. Figure 10-10 illustrates how strategy must respond to market dynamics to successfully realize the enterprise's mission.

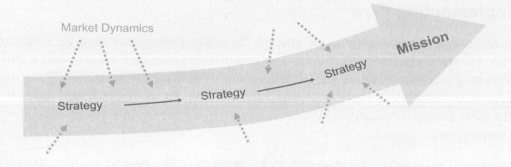

Figure 10-10. Strategy responds to market dynamics

Enterprises that have mastered strategy agility typically exhibit a number of capabilities, including those described in the following sections.

Market Sensing

Market sensing represents the culture and practice of understanding changing market dynamics based on the following:

- Market research

- Analysis of quantitative and qualitative data

- Direct and indirect customer feedback

- Direct observation of the customers in the marketplace

Savvy, Lean-thinking leaders 'go see' and spend significant time in the place where the customer's work is actually performed. They return with current, relevant, and specific information about the realities of their products and services, instead of opinions filtered through other perspectives.

Innovating Like a Lean Startup

After sensing opportunities, the Lean enterprise visualizes and manages the flow of new initiatives and investment by adopting a 'build-measure-learn' Lean startup cycle (Chapter 9). These are often new business solutions, but they may also be new business processes and capabilities that use existing solutions. Testing the outcome hypothesis with a Minimum Viable Product (MVP) before committing to a more significant investment reduces risk while generating fast and useful feedback.

Implementing Changes in Strategy

Identifying and defining a new strategy is only the first step. Once determined, the strategy must be communicated to all stakeholders in a new vision and roadmap and then, of course, be implemented. After all, significant changes to strategy often affect multiple solutions in the portfolio and require coordination and alignment. Consequently, most *large* strategy changes require new epics to implement the change across value streams.

Figure 10-11 illustrates how new epics go through the various Kanban systems and backlogs that manage the flow of work. During the normal course of work all backlogs are continuously reprioritized. Kanban systems help changes in strategy move quickly across value streams to the teams who do the implementation. This way, execution is aligned—and constantly realigned—to the evolving business strategy.

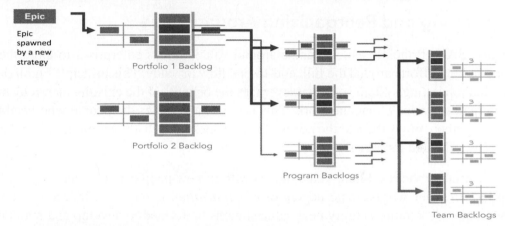

Figure 10-11. Strategy change makes its way quickly through the network of dynamic backlogs

However, other *smaller*, local changes may require only new stories or features and will go directly in the team or program backlogs.

Innovation Accounting

It can take a long time to evaluate the benefits of a change in strategy. Traditional financial and accounting metrics Profit and Loss (P&L) and Return On Investment (ROI) are lagging economic indicators that occur too late in the life cycle to inform the evolving strategy. In their place, **innovation accounting** (see Applied Innovation Accounting on the SAFe website[8]) applies leading indicators—*actionable metrics*

8. https://www.scaledagileframework.com/guidance-applied-innovation-accounting-in-safe/

focused on measuring specific early outcomes using objective data. They are an essential part of the economic framework that drives business agility.

Ignoring Sunk Costs

A key factor in strategy agility is *ignoring sunk costs*, the expenses that have already occurred in the course of solution development. Sunk costs cannot be recovered or changed and are independent of any future costs a company may incur.[9] Because strategic decision-making affects only the future course of business, sunk costs are absolutely irrelevant when evaluating a change in strategy. Instead, decision-makers should base all strategy decisions solely on the future costs of the initiatives necessary to achieve the change. When stakeholders do not have to waste energy to defend past spending, the organization can pivot more quickly to a new strategy.

Organizing and Reorganizing Around Value

Finally, SAFe Principle #10, organize around value, guides enterprises to align their development efforts around the full, end-to-end flow of value. This principle highlights the 'dual operating system,' one that leverages the benefits of the existing hierarchy but also creates a value stream network. This network assembles the people who need to work together, aligns them to the needs of the business and customer, minimizes delays and handoffs, and increases quality.

But as strategy moves, future value moves with it; new people and resources must be applied. In other words, some degree of *reorganization* is required. Indeed, in some cases, this will require entirely new value streams be formed to develop and maintain new solutions. Other value streams may need to be adjusted, and some will be eliminated entirely as solutions are decommissioned. Fortunately, the people and teams of an increasingly Agile enterprise see those changes coming through the portfolio. They can then use their new knowledge and skills to reorganize Agile teams and ARTs around value whenever it makes sense.

Agile Contracts

No portfolio is an island. Instead, each typically depends on other portfolios, suppliers, partners, operational support, and more, all of which require implicit or explicit contracts for the value to be delivered. Traditionally, these contracts are based on the

---

9. https://www.investopedia.com/ask/answers/042115/why-should-sunk-costs-be-ignored-future-decision-making.asp

assumption that requirements, deliverables, and service levels are known up front and will remain stable. We know from experience that is just not true. As strategy changes, these traditional contracts can become enormous impediments that lock the business into assumptions of a former strategy. Although the business would like to change strategy, it is blocked by existing contracts.

Achieving business agility requires a more flexible approach to all types of contracts. How this is achieved depends on the nature and type of contract, but each must be considered in terms of the adaptability that may be required as strategy evolves. Contracts for suppliers that provide components, subsystems, or services for enterprise solutions are particularly critical as they may tend to lock solution elements into requirements that were fixed long before. The 'SAFe managed-investment contract' describes an Agile approach to contracts and can be found on the SAFe website.[10]

Summary

Without organizational agility, enterprises can't react fast when things happen. To be fully responsive to threats and opportunities requires Lean and Agile ways of working to spread throughout the entire organization. This change demands a workforce that is not only trained in Lean-Agile practices, but one that understands and embodies the culture, values, and principles.

Lean business operations recognize that delighting customers goes further than purely solution development. The entire customer journey, which includes delivering, operating, and supporting business solutions, needs to be continually optimized to reduce time to market and increase customer satisfaction. Strategy agility provides the ability to sense and respond to changes in the market, to evolve and implement new strategies quickly, and to reorganize when necessary to address emerging opportunities. As a result, 'change becomes an opportunity, not a threat.'

---

10. https://www.scaledagileframework.com/agile-contracts/

11

Continuous Learning Culture

"Real learning gets to the heart of what it means to be human. Through learning, we recreate ourselves. Through learning, we become able to do something we never were able to do. Through learning, we re-perceive the world and our relationship to it. Through learning, we extend our capacity to create, to be part of the generative process of life. There is within each of us a deep hunger for this type of learning."

—Peter M. Senge, *The Fifth Discipline*

The *continuous learning culture* competency describes a set of values and practices that encourage individuals—and the entire enterprise—to continually increase knowledge, competence, performance, and innovation. This is achieved by becoming a learning organization, committing to relentless improvement, and promoting a culture of innovation.

Why a Continuous Learning Culture?

The pace of technology innovation in the 21st century is unprecedented. Organizations today are facing complex, turbulent forces that are creating both uncertainty and opportunity. Startup companies commonly challenge the status quo by transforming, disrupting, and even taking over entire markets. Tech giants are entering entirely new markets such as banking and healthcare. Expectations from a new generation of workers, customers, and society as a whole challenge companies to think and act beyond balance sheets and quarterly earnings reports. Due to all of these factors and more, one thing is certain: organizations in the digital age need to adapt rapidly or face decline—and potentially extinction.

What's the solution? Organizations have to evolve their way of thinking and working so they can constantly learn and adapt faster than the competition. Put simply, enterprises must have a *continuous learning culture* that applies the collective knowledge, experience, and creativity of their workforce, as well as customers, supply chain, and the broader ecosystem. Learning organizations manage the powerful forces of change to their advantage and are characterized by curiosity, invention, entrepreneurship, and informed risk-taking. Such organizations replace commitment to the status quo with a mindset of relentless improvement, while providing stability and predictability. Moreover, decentralized decision-making (Principle #9) becomes the new way of working, as leaders turn their focus to developing the vision and strategy, and to helping people achieve their full potential.

Any organization can begin the journey to a continuous learning culture by focusing its transformation along the three dimensions listed below and shown in Figure 11-1.

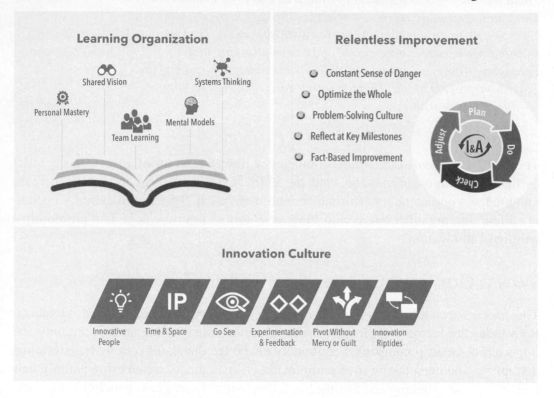

Figure 11-1. The three dimensions of a continuous learning culture

- *Learning organization*. Employees at every level are learning and growing so that the organization can transform and adapt to an ever-changing world.

- *Innovation culture*. Employees are encouraged and empowered to explore and implement creative ideas that enable future value delivery.

- **Relentless improvement.** Every part of the enterprise focuses on continuously improving its solutions, products, and processes.

Each dimension is described next.

Learning Organization

Developing a *learning organization* is the first dimension of a continuous learning culture. Learning organizations invest in and facilitate ongoing employee growth. When everyone in the organization is continuously learning, it fuels the enterprise's ability to dynamically transform itself as needed to anticipate and take advantage of opportunities that create a competitive edge. Learning organizations excel at creating, acquiring, and transferring knowledge while modifying practices to integrate the new insights.[1,2] These organizations understand and nurture the intrinsic motivation of people to learn and gain mastery for the benefit of the enterprise.[3]

Learning organizations are distinguished from those focused on simply improving *efficiency* using the earlier management methods promoted by Frederick Taylor. In Taylor's model, learning is focused on management, everyone else is expected to follow the policies and practices that management creates. Becoming a learning organization breaks this model and challenges the status-quo thinking that has led many former market leaders to bankruptcy. Learning drives innovation, leads to greater sharing of information, enhances problem-solving, increases the sense of community, and surfaces opportunities for more efficiency.[4]

As described by Peter Senge in *The Fifth Discipline*, transforming into a learning organization requires the following distinct disciplines.

- **Personal mastery.** Employees develop as 'T-shaped' people. They build a breadth of knowledge in multiple disciplines for efficient collaboration and deep expertise aligned with their interests and skills. T-shaped employees are a critical foundation of Agile teams and ARTs.

- **Shared vision.** Forward-looking leaders envision, align with, and open up exciting possibilities. They invite others to share and contribute to a

---

1. David A. Garvin, "Building a Learning Organization." Harvard Business Review, July-August 1993, https://hbr.org/1993/07/building-a-learning-organization.
2. Peter Senge. *The Fifth Discipline: The Art and Practice of the Learning Organization*, Kindle edition (Penguin Random House, 2010).
3. Daniel H. Pink, *Drive: The Surprising Truth About What Motivates Us,* Kindle edition (Penguin Group, 2009).
4. Michael Marquardt, *Building the Learning Organization*, Kindle edition (Nicholas Brealey Publishing, 2011).

common view of the future. Such leaders offer a compelling vision that inspires and motivates people to bring it about.

- **Team learning.** Teams work collectively to achieve common objectives by sharing knowledge, suspending assumptions, and learning together. Agile teams are cross-functional and apply their diverse skills to group problem-solving and learning. This practice is routine in high-performing teams.

- **Mental models.** Teams make their existing assumptions and hypotheses visible while working with an open mind to create new models of thinking based on the Lean-Agile mindset and deep customer knowledge. Mental models take complex concepts and make them easy to understand and apply.

- **Systems thinking.** The organization sees the larger picture, and applies a systems thinking approach (Principle #2) to learning, problem-solving, and solution development. In the Scaled Agile Framework (SAFe), this approach extends to the business through Lean Portfolio Management (LPM), which ensures that the enterprise is investing in experimentation and learning to drive better business outcomes.

In addition to the above, SAFe promotes a learning organization in the following ways:

- Lean-Agile leaders promote, support, and continually exhibit personal mastery of the new way of working.

- A shared vision is iteratively refined during each Program Increment (PI) planning event. This influences Business Owners, the teams on each Agile Release Train (ART), and the entire organization.

- Teams learn continuously through daily collaboration and problem-solving, supported by events such as team retrospectives and the Inspect and Adapt (I&A) event.

- *Design thinking* and the *team and technical agility* competency provide a set of powerful practices and tools that promote continuous learning as part of the team's regular work.

- Leaders exhibit and teach systems thinking, actively engage in solving problems, and eliminate impediments and ineffective internal systems. They collaborate with the teams to reflect at key milestones and help them identify and address shortcomings.

- Many SAFe principles support a learning culture (e.g., Principle #4, Base milestones on objective evaluation of working systems; Principle #5, Building incrementally with fast integrated learning cycles; Principle #8, Unlock the intrinsic motivation of knowledge workers, Principle #9; Decentralized decision-making; and more).

Innovation Culture

Developing an *innovation culture* is the second dimension of a continuous learning culture. As described in Chapter 3, Lean-Agile Mindset, innovation is one of the four pillars of the SAFe House of Lean. But the kind of innovation needed to compete in the digital age cannot be infrequent or random. It requires an *innovation culture*, which exists when leaders create a work environment that supports creative thinking, curiosity, and challenging the status quo. When an organization has an innovation culture, employees are encouraged and enabled to do the following:

- Explore ideas for enhancements to existing products

- Experiment with ideas for new products

- Pursue fixes to chronic defects

- Create improvements to processes that reduce waste

- Remove waste and improve productivity

Some organizations support innovation by allowing people to explore and experiment through intrapreneurship programs, innovation labs, hackathons, and other means. SAFe takes this a step further by providing a regular, consistent time during each PI for all members of the ART to pursue innovation activities during the IP iteration. Innovation is a key element of Agile product delivery and the continuous delivery pipeline. In Chapter 7, Agile Product Delivery, we illustrated that teams do continuous exploration during each iteration as well.

The following sections provide practical guidance for initiating and continuously improving an innovation culture.

Innovative People

The foundation of an innovation culture is the recognition that systems and cultures don't innovate; people do. Fostering innovation as an enterprise capability requires a commitment to encourage creativity, experimentation, and risk-taking. Acquiring this capability may necessitate coaching, mentoring, and formal training in the skills and behaviors of entrepreneurs and innovation. Individual goals and learning plans should enable and empower people to innovate. Rewards and recognition that balance intrinsic and extrinsic motivation reinforce the importance of everyone being an innovator. Criteria for hiring new employees should include evaluating whether candidates are a good fit within an innovation culture. Opportunities and paths for advancement should be clear and available for people who demonstrate exceptional talent and performance as innovation agents and champions.[5]

Time and Space for Innovation

Building time and space for innovation includes offering work areas that promote creative activities (see Chapter 10, Organizational Agility), as well as setting aside dedicated time from routine work to explore and experiment. Innovation space can also include the following:

- Frequent interactions with customers, the supply chain, and local communities connected to the organization

- Temporary and limited suspension of norms, policies, and systems (within legal, ethical, and safety boundaries) to challenge existing assumptions and explore what's possible

- Cadenced-based (IP iteration, hackathons, dojos, etc.) and ad hoc innovation activities

- Communities of Practice (CoPs) that collaborate regularly to share information, improve their skills, and actively work on advancing the general knowledge of a domain

Go See (Gemba)

Often, the best innovation ideas are sparked by seeing the problems to be solved firsthand—witnessing how customers interact with products or the challenges they face using existing processes and systems. *Gemba* is a Japanese term and Lean practice, meaning 'the real place,' the place where the customer's work is actually performed.

SAFe explicitly supports gemba through continuous exploration. Making firsthand observations and hypotheses visibly shifts the creative energy of the entire organization

---

5. Cris Beswick, Derek Bishop, and Jo Geraghty, *Building a Culture of Innovation*, Kindle edition (Kogan Page, 2015).

toward developing innovative solutions. Leaders should also openly share their views on the opportunities and challenges the organization faces to focus innovation efforts on the things that matter the most.

Experimentation and Feedback

Organizations with an innovation culture frequently conduct experiments to progress iteratively toward a goal. This scientific approach is the most effective way to generate insights that lead to breakthrough results. Regarding his many unsuccessful experiments to create an incandescent light bulb, Thomas Edison famously said, "I have not failed. I've just found 10,000 ways that won't work." The thinking behind the scientific method is that experiments don't fail; they simply produce the learning needed to accept or reject a hypothesis. Cultures that promote a fear of failure significantly inhibit innovation.

In contrast, innovation cultures depend on learning from experiments and incorporate those findings into future exploration. When leaders create the psychological safety described in Chapter 5, Lean-Agile Leadership, people are encouraged to experiment. They feel empowered to solve big problems, to seize opportunities, and to do so without fear of blame, even when the results of the experiments suggest going in a different direction.

Pivot Without Mercy or Guilt

Every innovation begins as a hypothesis: a set of assumptions and beliefs regarding how a new or improved product will delight customers and help the organization achieve its business objectives. However, until they're validated by feedback from customers, hypotheses are just informed guesses. As we described in Chapter 9, Lean Portfolio Mangaement, the fastest way to accept or reject a product development hypothesis is to experiment by building a Minimum Viable Product (MVP).[6] An MVP is a version of a new product that allows a team to collect, with the least effort, the maximum amount of validated learning from customers.

Target users test MVPs and provide fast feedback. In many cases, the feedback is positive and warrants further investment to bring the innovation to market or into production. In other instances, the results may cause a change in direction. This could be as simple as a set of modifications to the product followed by additional experiments for feedback, or it could prompt a pivot to a different product or strategy. When the fact-based evidence indicates that a pivot is required, the shift in direction

---

6. Eric Ries, *The Startup Way*, Kindle edition (Currency, 2017).

should occur as quickly as possible, without blame or consideration of sunk costs in the initial experiments.

Innovation Riptides

To create an innovation culture, organizations have to go beyond catchy slogans, innovation teams, and popular techniques such as hackathons and coding dojos. A fundamental rewiring of the enterprise's DNA is needed to fully leverage the innovation mindset and create the processes and systems that promote innovation. As shown in Figure 11-2, SAFe provides the bidirectional flow needed to foster innovation throughout a portfolio.

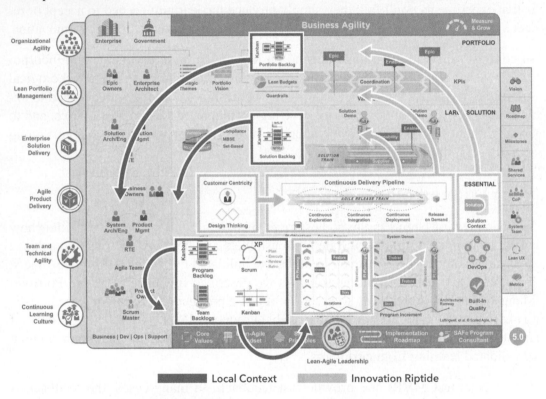

Figure 11-2. SAFe includes critical elements to support a consistent, continuous flow of innovation

The continuous flow of innovation is built on the foundation of SAFe Principle #9, Decentralized decision-making. Some innovation starts as strategic initiatives that are realized through portfolio epics and Lean budgets for value streams. During the implementation of these epics, additional opportunities for improving the solution are often identified by teams, suppliers, customers, and business leaders.

Other potential innovations come from many different directions (teams, ARTs, and portfolio) and flow into each other, creating an 'innovation riptide' that results in a tidal wave of new ideas flowing into the various backlogs that support innovation and solution development.

Some innovations flow directly into the program Kanban as features, while larger innovations may result in the creation of an epic that flows into the portfolio Kanban. It's this repeating cycle of innovation occurring at all levels that creates the innovation riptide, illustrated by the swirling arrows on the Big Picture in Figure 11-2. Moreover, SAFe provides the structure, principles, and practices to ensure alignment so that all teams progress toward the larger aim of the portfolio.

Relentless Improvement

Relentless improvement is the third dimension of a continuous learning culture and is also the fourth pillar in the SAFe House of Lean (Chapter 3).

Kaizen, the relentless pursuit of perfection, is a core belief of Lean. Although perfection is unattainable, the act of striving for perfection leads to relentless improvements to products and services. In the process, companies create more and better products for less money, with happier customers, all leading to higher revenues and greater profitability. Taiichi Ohno, the creator of what became Lean, emphasized that the only way to achieve relentless improvement is for everyone at all times to have a kaizen mindset. The entire enterprise—which is also a system, made up of executives, product development, accounting, finance, and sales—is continuously challenged to improve.[7]

But improvement requires learning. And the root causes and solutions to the problems that organizations face are rarely so easily identified. The Lean model for continuous improvement is based on a series of small iterative and incremental improvements, problem-solving tools, and experiments that enable the organization to learn its way to the most promising answers.

The sections that follow further describe how relentless improvement is a critical component of a continuous learning culture.

---

7. Jeffery K. Liker, *Developing Lean Leaders at All Levels*, Kindle edition (Lean Leadership Institute Publications, 2011).

Constant Sense of Danger

SAFe uses the term *relentless improvement* in its House of Lean to convey that improvement activities are essential to the very survival of an organization and should be given priority, visibility, and attention. This closely aligns with another core belief of Lean: focus intensely on delivering value to customers by providing products and services that solve their problems in ways they will prefer over your competitors' solutions.

SAFe promotes both ongoing and planned improvement efforts through its core values, practices, and events. Continuous improvement is built into the way Agile teams and trains do their work; it's not added later.

Optimize the Whole

Optimizing the whole is another view of systems thinking, one that increases the effectiveness of the entire solution by producing a sustainable flow of value versus optimizing individual teams, silos, or subsystems. So, improvements made to one area, team, or domain should not be done if they will negatively affect the overall system.

Organizing around value in ARTs, Solution Trains, and value streams creates opportunities for people in all domains to have regular discussions and debates about how to enhance overall quality, the flow of value, and customer satisfaction.

Problem-Solving Culture

In Lean, root-cause analysis and problem-solving drive continuous improvement. Lean recognizes that a gap always exists between the current state and the desired state, requiring an iterative and scalable problem-solving process. The Plan–Do–Check–Adjust (PDCA) cycle provides that iterative and scalable process. Until the target state is achieved, the process is repeated. This PDCA improvement cycle can be applied to anything, from individual teams trying to optimize software response time, to enterprises attempting to overcome a steady decline in market share.

A problem-solving culture treats difficult issues as opportunities for improvement in a blameless environment, where employees at all levels are empowered and equipped with the time and resources to identify and overcome obstacles.

SAFe provides the processes and tools that teams, ARTs, and Solution Trains need to facilitate the PDCA cycle shown in Figure 11-3.

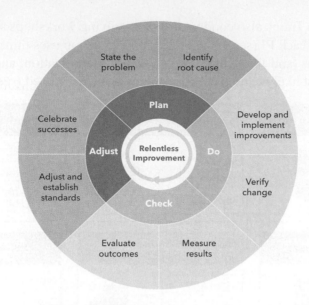

Figure 11-3. The PDCA problem-solving cycle scales from individual teams to entire organizations

As part of this, teams conduct *retrospectives* at the end of every iteration following one of the many techniques available such as the 'start-stop-continue' method, which is a simple and effective way for teams to reflect and determine the following (see Figure 11-4):

- What is the team *not* doing but should *start* doing?

- What is the team doing that's not working and should be *stopped*?

- What is the team doing that's working well and should *continue* doing?

Start	Stop	Continue
What should we start doing?	What should we stop doing?	What should we continue doing?
List ideas: • What things is the team not doing but should be doing? • What things can the team begin doing to improve? • What experiments should the team try to get better results?	List ideas: • What things is the team doing that aren't working and should be stopped? • What things are blocking the team? • What things are preventing the desired results?	List ideas: • What things is the team doing that are working well and should continue doing? • What team activities (or practices) do we want to keep doing? • What things should we continue to try?

Figure 11-4. Start-stop-continue retrospective method

ARTs and Solution Trains also conduct problem-solving workshops as part of the I&A event at the end of each PI (see Chapter 7). This workshop uses thinking tools such as 'fishbone' diagrams (and five whys) for root-cause identification, and Pareto analysis to identify the most likely causes of the problem being addressed (see Figure 11-5).

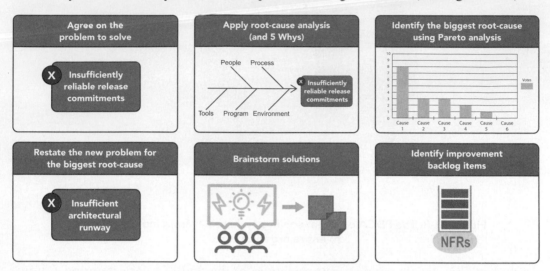

Figure 11-5. Fishbone (Ishikawa) diagram and Pareto analysis

Reflect at Key Milestones

It's easy to defer improvement activities in favor of more 'urgent work'—developing new features, fixing defects, responding to the latest outage. And yet it's often the case that this more urgent work is *less important* than the improvement activities, which would lead to faster value delivery, higher quality, and more delighted customers over time. As Stephen R. Covey would say, "We must never become too busy *sawing* to take time to *sharpen the saw.*"[8] To avoid neglecting this critical activity, relentless improvement is part of the workflow for Agile teams and trains, which is done on a regular cadence.

For individual teams, SAFe recommends retrospectives at iteration boundaries (at a minimum) and at the moment problems arise, when needed. ARTs and Solution Trains reflect every PI as part of the I&A event. In large product development efforts, this cadence-based milestone (event) provides predictability, consistency, and rigor to the process of relentless improvement (Figure 11-6).

---

8. Stephen R. Covey, *The 7 Habits of Highly Effective People: Restoring the Character Ethic*, revised edition (New York: Free Press, 2004).

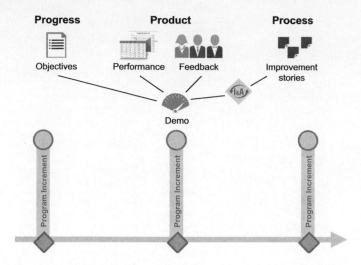

Figure 11-6. PI milestones provide a time to measure and reflect

Fact-Based Improvement

Fact-based improvement leads to changes guided by the data surrounding the problem and informed solutions, not by opinions and speculation. Improvement results are objectively measured, focusing on empirical evidence. This helps an organization concentrate more on the work needed to solve problems and less on assigning blame.

Summary

Too often organizations fall into the trap of assuming that the culture, processes, and products that led to today's success will also guarantee future results. That mindset increases the risk of decline and failure. The enterprises that will dominate their markets going forward will be adaptive learning organizations, with the ability to learn, innovate, and relentlessly improve more effectively and faster than their competition.

Competing in the digital age requires investment in both time and resources for innovation, built upon a culture of creative thinking and curiosity—an environment where norms can be challenged, and new products and processes emerge. Alongside this, relentless improvement acknowledges that the survival of an organization is never guaranteed. Everyone in the organization will be challenged to find and make incremental improvements, and priority and visibility is given to this work.

A continuous learning culture will likely be the most effective way for this next generation of workers to relentlessly improve, and the successful companies that employ them.

Part III
Implementing SAFe, Measure and Grow

"Many leaders pride themselves on setting the high-level direction and staying out of the details. It's true that a compelling vision is critical. But it's not enough. Big picture, hands-off leadership isn't likely to work in a change situation, because the hardest part of change—the paralyzing part—is in the details.

"Any successful change requires a translation of ambiguous goals into concrete behaviors. In short, to make a switch, you need to script the critical moves."

—Chip and Dan Heath, *Switch: How to Change Things When Change Is Hard*

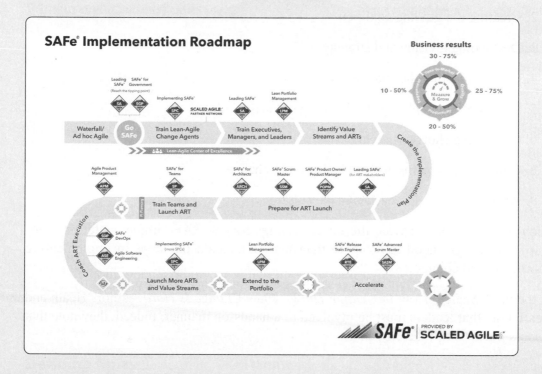

Introduction to the Implementation Roadmap

Throughout this book, we've described the values, principles, and practices of the Scaled Agile Framework (SAFe). Our goal was to show how a SAFe enterprise operates and achieves the business benefits that only Lean-Agile development at scale can provide. However, what we haven't done yet is describe *how* an enterprise implements SAFe to achieve business agility. That's where the real journey starts, and Part III—which comprises the final five chapters of this book—is dedicated to this purpose.

Recognizing that a SAFe implementation is a significant organizational change effort, we turned to Dr. John Kotter, Harvard professor of leadership, change leadership guru, and author of many books on this subject, for guidance on proven change practices to integrate into the roadmap. In his book *Leading Change*, Kotter discusses eight steps for guiding organizational transformation and what it takes to make it stick.[1]

1. Establishing a sense of urgency

2. Creating the guiding coalition

3. Developing a vision and strategy

4. Communicating the change vision

5. Empowering employees for broad-based action

6. Generating short-term wins

7. Consolidating gains and producing more change

8. Anchoring new approaches in the culture

Each of these steps provide the underpinnings for the SAFe implementation roadmap. But leaders need to do more than just understand the steps in implementing organizational change.

In the book *Switch, How To Change Things When Change Is Hard*, authors Heath and Heath note that leaders must be involved in a hands-on manner. Indeed, they note that leaders must "script the critical moves."[2]

---

1. John P. Kotter, *Leading Change*, Kindle edition (Harvard Business Review Press, 2012).
2. Chip Heath and Dan Health, *Switch: How To Change Things When Change Is Hard* (Crown Business, 2010).

Fortunately, hundreds of the world's largest enterprises have already gone down this path (see case studies[3] on the Scaled Agile website), revealing successful adoption patterns. While every transformation journey is unique and there is rarely a perfectly sequential step-by-step implementation, we know that enterprises get the best results by following a path similar to the *SAFe implementation roadmap*.

It consists of 12 main steps, which are described in the following five chapters:

Chapter 12
The Guiding Coalition
9. Reach the tipping point.
10. Train Lean-Agile change agents.
11. Train executives, managers, and leaders.
12. Create a Lean-Agile center of excellence.

Chapter 13
Designing the Implementation
13. Identify value streams and Agile Release Trains (ARTs).
14. Create the implementation plan.

Chapter 14
Implementing Agile Release Trains
15. Prepare for ART launch.
16. Train teams and launch the ART.
17. Coach ART execution.

Chapter 15
Launching More Agile Release Trains and Value Streams; Extending to the Portfolio
18. Launch more ARTs and value streams.
19. Extend to the portfolio.

Chapter 16
Measure, Grow, and Accelerate
20. Accelerate.

---

3. https://www.scaledagile.com/customer-stories/

12

The Guiding Coalition

"A strong guiding coalition is always needed. One with the right composition, level of trust, and shared objective."
—John Kotter

Introduction

Organizations arrive at the need for change from a wide range of starting points. Once the rationale and urgency for a significant change has been established, the difficult work begins, and the first critical move is to form what Kotter calls a 'sufficient powerful guiding collation.' This is accomplished by following the first four steps of the SAFe implementation roadmap.

1. Reach the tipping point.

2. Train Lean-Agile change agents.

3. Train executives, managers, and leaders.

4. Create a Lean-Agile center of excellence.

This chapter describes these first four steps of the journey.

Step 1: Reach the Tipping Point

"The tipping point is that magic moment when an idea, trend, or social behavior crosses a threshold, tips, and spreads like wildfire."
  —Malcolm Gladwell, *The Tipping Point: How Little Things Can Make a Big Difference*

Changing the way of working—including the habits and culture of a large organization—is hard. People naturally resist change. Accepting change means acknowledging the possibility that the organization and its people have some weaknesses. Even worse, it may challenge people's long-held beliefs or values. As a result, there must be a reason for change, one so compelling that maintaining the status quo becomes unacceptable.

In other words, the enterprise needs to reach its *tipping point*[4] — the crossroads at which the organization's imperative is to achieve the change rather than resist it, thus creating the sense of urgency needed to overcome inertia and the comfort of the status quo.

We've observed two forces that are the most common catalysts for tipping an organization to SAFe.

- *A burning platform*. Sometimes the need to change is obvious. The company is failing to compete, and the existing way of doing business is inadequate to achieve a new solution within a survivable time frame. People's jobs are at stake, driving a sense of urgency for mandatory change throughout the organization. This is the easier case for change. While there will always be those who resist, the energy that drives the need through the organization is overwhelming.

- *Proactive leadership*. In the absence of a burning platform, leadership is responsible for driving change proactively by 'taking a stand' for a better future state. This is the less obvious reason to drive change, as the people in the organization may not see or feel the urgency to do the additional hard work needed. After all, the organization is successful now. Why should people assume that won't continue in the future? Isn't change hard, and risky, too? In this case, leadership must continuously communicate the reasons for change, making it clear that maintaining the status quo is no longer acceptable.

In rare instances, organizations have both a burning platform and proactive leadership with the courage to direct the change. With SAFe as the transformation blueprint, such organizations can experience a rapid and dramatic turnaround from a bleak crisis to positive business results and a brighter future.

Reaching the tipping point, however, it not enough, by itself, to succeed. It requires a guiding coalition of practitioners, managers, and change agents who can implement specific process changes. Perhaps, even more important, it also requires leaders who can set the vision, show the way, and remove impediments to change. Such leaders

---

4. Malcom Gladwell, *The Tipping Point: How Little Things Can Make a Big Difference* (Little, Brown and Company, 2006).

must have sufficient organizational credibility to be taken seriously, and the expertise needed to make fast, intelligent decisions.

After the vision has been created, it's time to build a guiding coalition that is sufficiently powerful to implement SAFe. Achieving this requires organizations to take the steps described in the following three sections.

Step 2: Train Lean-Agile Change Agents

"Are you creating a critical mass of people to help you change?"[5]
  —W. Edwards Deming

Most enterprises source change agents from both inside and outside the organization. They may be business and technology leaders, Agile coaches, program and project managers, process leads, and more. In addition, scaling Agile across the enterprise requires training all the people who do the work. To make it practical and cost effective, SPCs are licensed to teach other SAFe courses. This affordable strategy supplies the trainers needed to initiate and implement the change. While attaining SPC certification provides the ability to teach, it's highly recommended that new SPCs who have limited hands-on SAFe experience pair with more experienced internal or external coaches.

The Scaled Agile course, Implementing SAFe with SPC certification, helps develop change agents and prepares them to lead the organizational transformation by adopting SAFe.

Step 3: Train Executives, Managers, and Leaders

"People are already doing their best. The problem is with the system. Only management can change the system. It is not enough that management commit themselves to quality and productivity, they must know what it is they must do... Such a responsibility cannot be delegated."
  —W. Edwards Deming

Some of these key leaders will provide ongoing executive sponsorship. Others will be directly involved in implementing SAFe, managing others who do, and participating directly in ART execution. All of these stakeholders need the knowledge and

---

5. Edwards Deming, W. *Out of the Crisis*. MIT Center for Advanced Educational Services. 1982..

skills to lead, rather than follow, the implementation. This training may include the following courses:

- **Leading SAFe.** This course is designed to teach the SAFe Lean-Agile mindset, principles, and practices, as well as the most effective leadership values in managing the new generation of knowledge workers. This course also helps the organization reach the tipping point for change and seeds the enterprise with the knowledgeable, active leaders prepared to guide it.

- **SAFe Lean Portfolio Management.** This is a course and workshop where attendees gain the practical tools and techniques necessary to implement the Lean Portfolio Management (LPM) functions of strategy and investment funding, Agile portfolio operations and Lean governance. While it's not initially necessary to train leaders in LPM, an increasing trend is to begin adopting it at the same time as the enterprise begins adopting SAFe. This provides leaders an opportunity to experience Lean-Agile practices in portfolio management, a domain that is familiar to them, which fosters better support for the transformation.

Step 4: Create a Lean-Agile Center of Excellence

"A guiding coalition that operates as an effective team can process more information, more quickly. It can also speed the implementation of new approaches because powerful people are truly informed and committed to key decisions."
—John Kotter

In Chapter 9, we noted how a Lean-Agile Center of Excellence (LACE) can be a powerful and persistent force in both achieving the transformation and fostering relentless improvement.

Indeed, experience has shown that the LACE is a significant differentiator between companies practicing Lean-Agile in name only and those truly committed to adopting Lean-Agile practices and thereby achieving the best business outcomes.

Establishing the Vision for Change

As the guiding coalition of leaders and change agents is being formed, they begin to craft a clear vision for the changes that will be enabled by the adoption of SAFe. The vision should start with a compelling and well-understood reason to change. Kotter notes that establishing a 'vision for change' is a primary responsibility of leadership.[6] The vision provides three vital benefits.

- *Purpose*. It clarifies the objective and direction for the change. It sets the mission for all to follow. It focuses everyone on the 'why,' not the 'how,' of the change.

- *Motivation*. The vision helps motivate people into action by giving them a compelling reason to make the change and start moving quickly in the new direction. After all, change is hard. People's roles and responsibilities will shift, and fear may even cause some people to leave. However, with a compelling vision, everyone will know that change must occur and that there is no job security in keeping things the same.

- *Alignment*. The power of alignment helps start the coordinated action needed to ensure that hundreds, perhaps even thousands, of people work together toward a new and more personally rewarding goal. With a clarity of vision, people are empowered to take the actions necessary to realize the vision without the need for constant management supervision.

In the case of a SAFe transformation, the vision for change must be rooted in the understanding of the Lean-Agile mindset (Chapter 3) and SAFe principles (Chapter 4). It's also critical that leaders understand that how they lead directly influences whether employees buy into the change and contribute to its success. The Lean-Agile leadership competency (Chapter 5) described the leader behaviors that create a positive environment for change.

---

6. John P. Kotter, *Leading Change* (Harvard Business Review Press, 1996).

LACE Mission Statement

Like any Agile team, the LACE needs to align itself with a common mission to achieve the vision for implementing SAFe. Figure 12-1 shows an example of a mission statement.

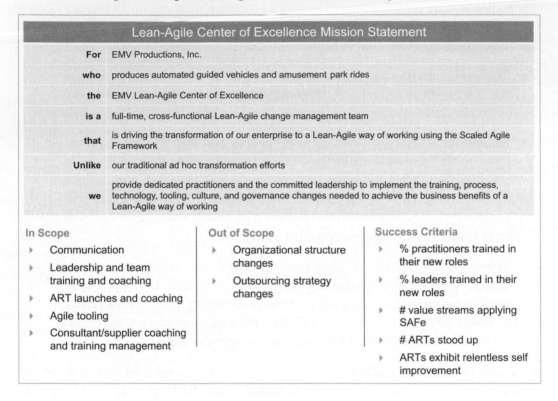

Lean-Agile Center of Excellence Mission Statement	
For	EMV Productions, Inc.
who	produces automated guided vehicles and amusement park rides
the	EMV Lean-Agile Center of Excellence
is a	full-time, cross-functional Lean-Agile change management team
that	is driving the transformation of our enterprise to a Lean-Agile way of working using the Scaled Agile Framework
Unlike	our traditional ad hoc transformation efforts
we	provide dedicated practitioners and the committed leadership to implement the training, process, technology, tooling, culture, and governance changes needed to achieve the business benefits of a Lean-Agile way of working

In Scope	Out of Scope	Success Criteria
▸ Communication	▸ Organizational structure changes	▸ % practitioners trained in their new roles
▸ Leadership and team training and coaching	▸ Outsourcing strategy changes	▸ % leaders trained in their new roles
▸ ART launches and coaching		▸ # value streams applying SAFe
▸ Agile tooling		▸ # ARTs stood up
▸ Consultant/supplier coaching and training management		▸ ARTs exhibit relentless self improvement

Figure 12-1. Sample LACE mission statement

As we noted in Chapter 9, the LACE may be part of an emerging Agile Program Management Office (APMO), or it may exist as a separate group. In either case, the LACE often serves as a focal point of knowledge and transformational activities that can power the enterprise through the changes. In addition, the LACE often evolves into a permanent organization for Lean-Agile education, communication, and relentless improvement.

Operation and Organization

The LACE typically operates as an Agile team (typically four to six people per business unit) and it applies the same iteration and Program Increment (PI) cadences as the ARTs. This allows the LACE to plan and Inspect and Adapt (I&A) in harmony with the ARTs, serving as an exemplar for Agile team behavior. As a result, similar roles are needed.

- A Product Owner works with stakeholders to prioritize the team's transformation backlog.

- A Scrum Master facilitates the process and helps remove roadblocks.

- The LACE team is cross-functional and has credible people from various functional organizations. That allows the team to address backlog items wherever they arise, whether they're related to the organization, culture, business, or technology.

- The team's Product Manager is typically a C-level leader (or one level below).

Typically, the LACE is responsible for the following types of activities:

- Communicating the business need for SAFe

- Integrating SAFe practices

- Fostering communities of practice

- Creating alignment around organizational changes

- Providing coaching and training to ART stakeholders and teams

- Establishing objective metrics

- Facilitating value stream identification workshops

Defining the LACE Team Size and Distribution

The size of the LACE must be in proportion to the size and distribution of the development enterprise. A small team of four to six dedicated people can support a few hundred, while a larger size team supports proportionally larger groups.

For smaller enterprises, a single centralized LACE can balance speed with economies of scale. However, in larger enterprises—typically those exceeding 500 to 1,000 practitioners—it's useful to consider employing either a decentralized or a hub-and-spoke model (Figure 12-2).

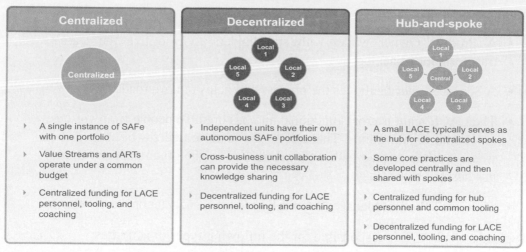

Figure 12-2. LACE team organizational models

The LACE has a tall order to fill: changing the behavior and culture of a large enterprise. Once a LACE has formed, there will be a natural desire to accelerate progress and work through its full backlog as quickly as possible. However, trying to remove all the major organizational impediments right at the start could bring the transformation to a halt. Instead, by defining and launching ARTs, the LACE empowers the organization to generate short-term wins with the support of the entire guiding coalition. It then consolidates those gains as additional ARTs are launched.

The LACE should work with Business Owners to identify the metrics that they care most about, determine how the business tracks the success of the transformation, get a baseline of these metrics before the first ART is launched, and remeasure with every PI and every new ART launch so that the business benefits over time can be tracked with hard numbers, even in the early stages of the transformation. This provides the positive momentum needed to tackle the broader organizational issues.

The business agility assessment (see Chapter 16, Measure, Grow, and Accelerate) can help the LACE understand where a portfolio is on the road to business agility. The LACE should offer a baseline assessment at the start of the transformation and then continuously measure progress and use the recommendations provided to drive the improvement backlog.

Communicating the Benefits

"If you can't communicate the vision to someone in five minutes or less and get a reaction that signifies both understanding and interest, you are not done."
—John Kotter

Whether the reason is a burning platform or proactive leadership, the goal is the same: realizing the business benefits that change is intended to deliver. SAFe's Principle #1 reminds us to 'take an economic view.' In this context, the leaders should communicate the goal of the change in terms that everyone can understand. Dozens of case studies[7] can help people understand the journey and its benefits, which are summarized in four major areas, as Figure 12-1 illustrates.

Figure 12-3. SAFe business benefits

Leaders should communicate these intended outcomes as part of the vision for the change. Also, they should describe any specific objectives and measures they hope to accomplish. This will provide the emotional fuel necessary to escape the inertia of the status quo.

Summary

Changing the habits and culture of a large organization is difficult. Some people naturally resist change. As a result, there must be a reason for such a move, one so compelling that maintaining the status quo becomes unacceptable. There are two main forces that tip an organization to SAFe: a burning platform where the organization is failing to compete or proactive leadership where leaders take a stand for a better future state.

---

7. http://www.scaledagile.com/customer-stories

After reaching the tipping point, forming a guiding coalition is the next critical move. An effective coalition must include the right people from across the organization, especially leaders who can set the vision, remove impediments, and make blocking the change difficult. The people in this coalition need sufficient organizational credibility to be taken seriously and have the expertise and confidence to make fast, smart decisions. The coalition also requires practitioners, managers, and change agents who can implement local and specific process changes. The next step is to design the implementation itself.

13

Designing the Implementation

"Break down barriers between departments."
—W. Edwards Deming

In the previous chapter, we described how the first four steps of the implementation roadmap help form the 'guiding coalition'—a powerful team of knowledgeable and enthusiastic people who can lead a Scaled Agile Framework (SAFe) implementation. In this chapter, we will describe how to design the implementation with the next two steps:

- Step 5: Identify value streams and Agile Release Trains (ARTs).

- Step 6: Create the implementation plan.

Step 5: Identify Value Streams and Agile Release Trains

With a sense of urgency and a powerful coalition in place, it's time to start the implementation. As value streams and ARTs make up the organizational backbone of SAFe, the next step is to pick a value stream and organize the first ART. Although there is no one right way to begin this virtual reorganization, some starting points are more effective than others. An effective way to begin this process is to identify the operational value streams first and then determine what development value streams are needed to support it.

Figure 13-1 highlights the six main steps to identify value streams and ARTs.

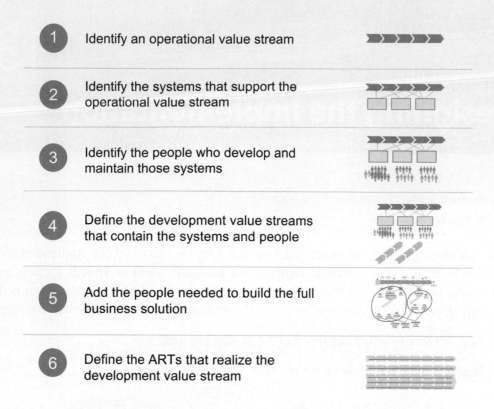

1 Identify an operational value stream	
2 Identify the systems that support the operational value stream	
3 Identify the people who develop and maintain those systems	
4 Define the development value streams that contain the systems and people	
5 Add the people needed to build the full business solution	
6 Define the ARTs that realize the development value stream	

Figure 13-1. A process for identifying development value streams

1. Identify an Operational Value Stream

For some organizations, identifying operational value streams is easy. Many are the set of activities that support the products, services, or solutions that the company sells. In the larger enterprise, however, the task is more complicated. Value flows through various applications, systems, and services—across many parts of the distributed organization to both *internal* and *external* customers. In these cases, identifying operational value streams is a substantial analytical activity. Figure 13-2 provides a set of questions that help stakeholders address the process of identification.

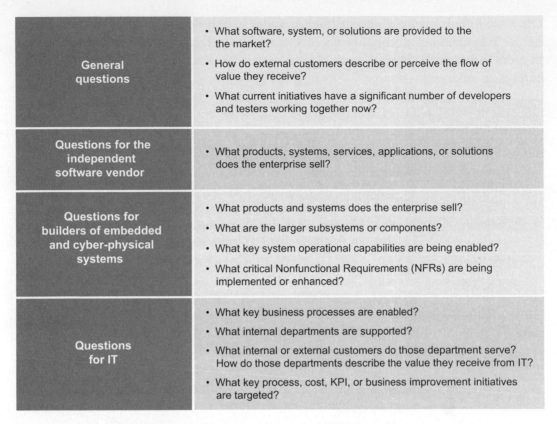

General questions	• What software, system, or solutions are provided to the the market?
	• How do external customers describe or perceive the flow of value they receive?
	• What current initiatives have a significant number of developers and testers working together now?
Questions for the independent software vendor	• What products, systems, services, applications, or solutions does the enterprise sell?
Questions for builders of embedded and cyber-physical systems	• What products and systems does the enterprise sell?
	• What are the larger subsystems or components?
	• What key system operational capabilities are being enabled?
	• What critical Nonfunctional Requirements (NFRs) are being implemented or enhanced?
Questions for IT	• What key business processes are enabled?
	• What internal departments are supported?
	• What internal or external customers do those department serve? How do those departments describe the value they receive from IT?
	• What key process, cost, KPI, or business improvement initiatives are targeted?

Figure 13-2. Questions to help identify operational value streams

In addition, identifying operational value streams in the large enterprise requires an awareness of the organization's broader mission and an explicit understanding of how specific elements of value flow to the customer.

Figure 13-3 illustrates a consumer loan operational value stream, including the trigger (loan need), steps (green chevrons), and people, and value that it generates (repayment plus interest). This operational value stream will be used as an example throughout the remainder of this chapter.

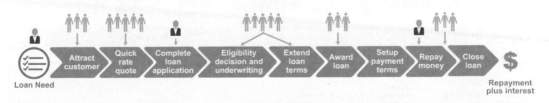

Figure 13-3. An example consumer loan operational value stream

Once identified, Figure 13-4 illustrates a value stream definition template, which can be used to capture information about the operational value stream. It describes the triggers that start the flow of work, the customers involved, and the value they and the enterprise receive.

Name	Consumer Loans
Description	Provides customers with unsecured / secured loans
Customer(s)	Existing retail customer
Triggers	The customer wants to borrow money and approaches the bank through any of the existing channels
Value received to enterprise	Repayment plus interest
Value received to customer	Loan

Figure 13-4. Example value stream definition template for a consumer loan operational value stream

2. Identify the Systems that Support the Operational Value Stream

The next step is to identify the systems that support the operational value stream (see the yellow boxes in Figure 13-5). Lines are drawn to connect each system to the value stream step(s) that it supports. This creates a deeper understanding of what the actual systems are and how the systems support the operational value stream, as our consumer loan example illustrates

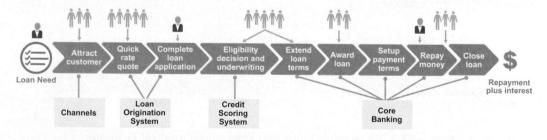

Figure 13-5. Identify the systems that support the operational value stream

3. Identify the People Who Develop and Maintain the Systems

Once the systems that support the operational value stream have been identified, the next activity is to estimate the number and locations of the people that build and maintain those systems (Figure 13-6).

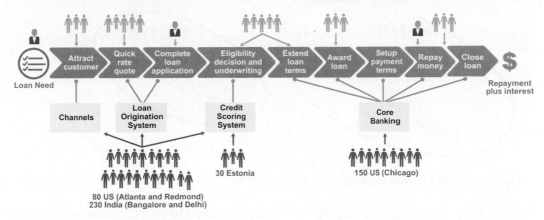

Figure 13-6. Identify the people who develop and maintain the systems

4. Define the Development Value Streams

The next step is to identify and define the development value streams (the blue chevrons in Figure 13-7) and include all the people needed to develop and deliver value. The triggers for the development value streams are the ideas that drive the new features. The value is the new or enhanced features and functionality of the systems. The triggers help identify how many development value streams are needed. If most requirements necessitate touching every system to enable the new functionality, we probably have just one development value stream.

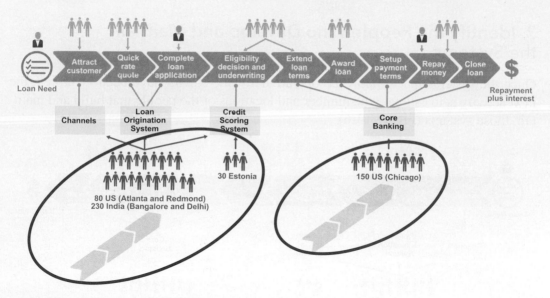

Figure 13-7. Define the development value streams that support the systems and people

However, if the systems are largely decoupled, we might have a few development value streams. Figure 13-7 illustrates that most requirements touch the first three systems or the last one, but rarely all. So, in this case, we would identify two development value streams, each capable of developing, integrating, deploying, and releasing independently, with *minimal* cross-value-stream dependencies.

5. Add the People Needed to Build the Full Business Solution

As described in Chapter 1, business agility requires that everyone involved in business solution definition and delivery—information technology, operations, legal, marketing, finance, support, compliance, security, and others—is considered part of the development value stream. With this in mind, the next step is to identify these additional individuals and teams that are part of the development value streams identified in the previous step. Figure 13-8 illustrates that some people from legal, marketing, and support have joined a development value stream.

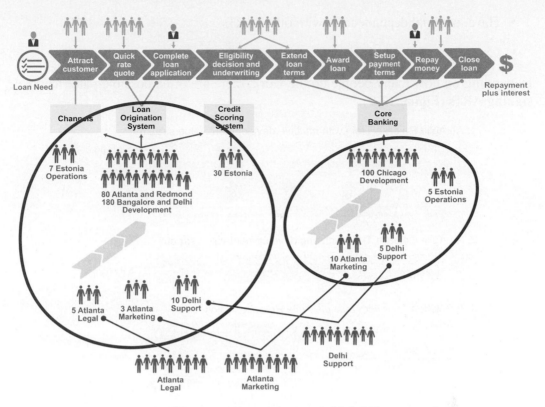

Figure 13-8. Add the people needed to build the full business solution

How business teams are integrated into a value stream or ART depends on the scope and the nature of the work they do. For example, teams such as product marketing may be embedded directly into the ART as whole teams or inside other teams.

6. Defining the ARTs That Realize the Development Value Stream

The final activity is to define the ARTs that deliver the value. Our experience shows that the most effective ARTs have the following attributes:

- Contain 50–125 people

- Focus on a holistic system or related set of products, services, or solutions

- Require long-lived, stable teams to consistently deliver value

- Have minimal dependencies with other ARTs

- Can release value independent of other ARTs

Depending on how many people do the work, there are three possible patterns for designing ARTs (Figure 13-9).

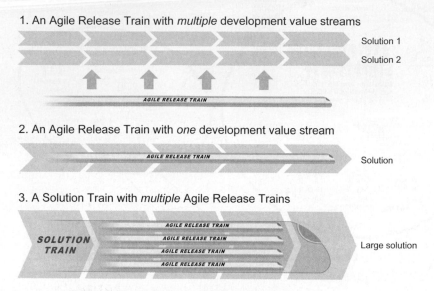

Figure 13-9. Three possible patterns for ART design

- ***An Agile Release Train with multiple development value streams***. When several related products or solutions can be produced with a relatively small number of people, a single ART can often deliver multiple value streams. In this case, everyone in these value streams is part of the same ART.

- ***An Agile Release Train with one development value stream***. Often, a single ART can realize a small value stream (50–125 people). This is common, as many development groups are already organized naturally into units of about that size.

- ***A Solution Train with multiple Agile Release Trains***. When many people are involved, the development value stream must be split into multiple ARTs to form a Solution Train, as described in the next section.

Forming a Solution Train with Multiple ARTs

As we described in Chapter 8, Enterprise Solution Delivery, it often takes multiple ARTs to build a large solution, so forming ARTs within a large solution requires additional analysis.

This leads us to the next decision about organizing ARTs around 'feature areas' or 'subsystems' (Figure 13-10). Solution trains work best when the teams developing features and components that have a high degree of interdependence work together on an ART.

- **Feature-area ARTs** are optimized for flow and speed. But pay attention to subsystem governance; otherwise, the system architecture will eventually decay. As a countermeasure, a system architect (one or more individuals, or even a small team) is dedicated to maintaining platform integrity and subsystem governance.

- **Platform ARTs** (e.g., components, subsystems) are optimized for architectural robustness and reuse of components. However, organizing ARTs this way creates dependencies between them, which can slow the flow of value.

There's no one right way to split value streams into ARTs, and large development value streams typically require both types of ARTs. An example is when multiple ARTs provide services or solutions based on a common platform. In this case, a platform ART may be supporting one or more feature ARTs (Figure 13-10).

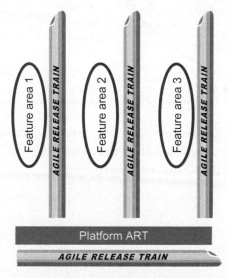

Figure 13-10. Feature area ARTs with a platform ART

There's another familiar pattern, where ARTs realize just a feature area or segment (some value stream steps) of a larger value stream (Figure 13-11). That may not seem like a fully end-to-end practice, but in reality, the beginning and the end of a value stream are relative notions. The different types of systems and operational value streams being served may offer a logical dividing line. And, of course, combinations of all these models often appear in the larger value streams. Figure 13-11 is a good example of this where the loan origination and credit scoring segments of the first development value stream are allocated to separate ARTs, and the second development value stream has a single subsystem ART supporting the core banking platform.

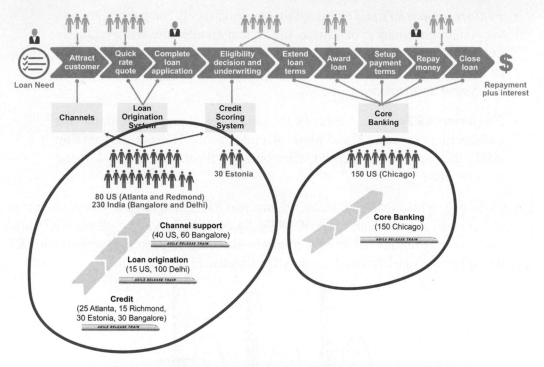

Figure 13-11. Forming ARTs in the consumer loan example

Finally, there are other ART designs and considerations, driven by geography, spoken language, and cost centers—all of which may influence the ART design. Since these designs typically impede flow caution is warranted

As has been shown, identifying value streams and ARTs is a critical step and can sometimes be complicated, especially in large enterprises. To assist with this process SPCs can apply the following toolkit designed for just this purpose.

Step 6. Create the Implementation Plan

The next step involves creating the plan for implementing SAFe. In a smaller portfolio, there may be only one value stream of interest, making the transformation target obvious. Larger enterprises, however, require additional analysis, and leadership often needs to pick the first value stream to be addressed.

Select the First Agile Release Train

It's typical for an organization to initially focus on one value stream (and correspondingly, the first ART). This can create an initial success and knowledge to apply to other value streams. An effective strategy to identify a candidate for the first ART is to consider the intersection of the four factors illustrated in Figure 13-12.

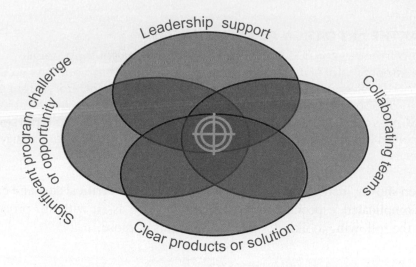

Figure 13-12. Finding an opportunistic ART to start the transformation

Figure 13-12 illustrates that the 'target' for the first ART usually best satisfies the following combination of criteria:

- *Leadership support*. Lean-Agile leaders drive and sustain organizational change by empowering individuals and teams. Selecting an ART that has leadership support is critical for implementing new ways of working and delivering systemic improvements.

- *Clear products or solutions*. ARTs work best when they are aligned around specific products or solutions.

- *Collaborating teams*. Agile teams power the ART. Selecting a first ART where teams already exist and are collaborating will ensure a solid foundation for scaling.

- *Significant challenge or opportunity*. As we noted earlier, creating a sense of urgency is the first step in successful change. A significant program challenge or opportunity provides this urgency and ensures the first ART has the potential to demonstrate significant improvements to business outcomes.

Create a Preliminary Plan for Additional ARTs and Value Streams

Before we move on to launching that first ART, however, it's likely that a broader implementation plan may already be forming. Although it's still early in the process, strategies for rolling out additional ARTs and for launching additional value streams may already be taking shape. In short, change is beginning to happen, and the signs are everywhere.

- The new vision is being communicated and amplified around the company

- Principal stakeholders are aligning

- Something big is in the air, and people are catching on

The Lean-Agile Center of Excellence (LACE) and various SPCs and leaders typically guide the transformation, using Agile and SAFe as their LACE operating model. In keeping with SAFe practices, the LACE holds internal Program Increment (PI) planning and invites other stakeholders, such as Business Owners, to help further define the implementation strategy. One natural output would be a PI roadmap for the implementation, which provides a plan and a PI cadence for implementation (Figure 13-13).

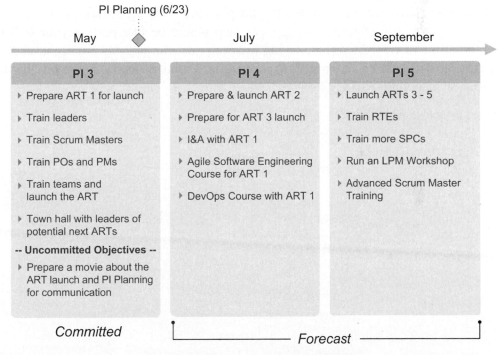

Figure 13-13. An example PI roadmap

Summary

Value streams and ARTs are the organizational backbone of a SAFe implementation and are critically important to the success of this journey. They support the Lean goal of delivering value in the shortest possible time and cut across the functional silos that often inhibit flow.

An effective way to begin the process of moving to this new organizational model is to identify operational value streams first and then determine what development value streams are needed to support them. For some organizations, identifying operational value streams is an easy task. Many are simply the products, services, or solutions the company develops and sells. For others, the process is more complicated, and some additional analysis is required to figure out what value will be delivered and how it flows through the organization.

Creating the implementation plan begins by selecting the first ART in the chosen development value stream—one that fully meets the criteria of leadership support, clear products or solutions, collaborating teams, and a significant challenge or opportunity. Once the first, and perhaps subsequent ARTs, has been identified a broad implementation plan can be drawn up.

Providing the space and time to design and plan the implementation is critical. Attempting to shortcut or breeze through this step would be like putting your foot on the brake at the same time you are trying to accelerate. But get this one right, and the organization will be well on its way to a successful transformation and ready for the next step of launching ARTs.

Implementing Agile Release Trains

14

"Train everyone and launch trains."
— SAFe advice

Introduction

In the previous two chapters of this part of the book, we described steps 1–6 of the implementation roadmap. In this chapter, we'll cover the next three steps, which together is arguably the most important part of the transformation, the part where the enterprise implements Agile Release Trains (ARTs). The steps described in this chapter include the following:

- Step 7: Prepare for the ART launch.

- Step 8: Train teams and launch the ART.

- Step 9: Coach ART execution.

In addition, we'll describe an accelerated, one-week 'quick-start' approach to the ART launch, which—after some preparation—is the fastest way for an ART to begin delivering value.

Step 7: Prepare for ART Launch

By now, the enterprise will have identified their value streams and established an implementation plan. It will also have loosely defined the first ART. This is a *pivotal moment*, as plans are now moving toward implementation. From a change-management perspective, the first ART launch is critical. This will be the first major change to the way of working and will generate the initial short-term wins that help build momentum.

SAFe Program Consultants (SPCs) often lead the implementation of the initial ARTs, supported by SAFe-trained ART stakeholders and members of the Lean-Agile Center of Excellence (LACE). Whoever leads the preparation of the ART launch facilitates the activities described in the following sections.

Defining the ART

In Chapter 13, Designing the Implementation, we described the process for defining the first value stream and the ART. At that stage of planning, the ART is expressed with just enough detail to determine that it's a potential ART. However, its details and boundaries are left to those who better understand the local context. An ART canvas[1] (Figure 14-1) offers a template for this definition.

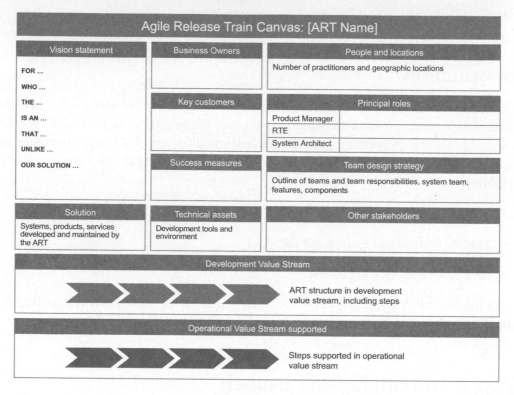

Figure 14-1. Agile Release Train canvas

A key goal of the ART canvas is to help teams identify the principal ART roles, the vision for the train, what solutions it provides, who the customers are, and more. We know from systems thinking that the people, management, and processes of the

---

1. Thanks to SPCT Mark Richards for the ART canvas inspiration.

organization that builds the solution are also a system. By that definition, the ART itself is also a *system*. For this *system* to function properly, the responsibilities of system definition, building, validation, and deployment have to be realized. Filling in the essential roles on the ART canvas fosters these discussions and highlights the new responsibilities.

WHO ARE THE BUSINESS OWNERS?

One critical role on the ART is that of a Business Owner. They are a small group of stakeholders (typically three to five) who have the primary business and technical responsibility for governance, compliance, and return on investment for the ART's solutions. The following questions can help identify the Business Owners:

- Who is ultimately responsible for business outcomes?

- Who can evaluate the technical efficacy of the solution now and in the future?

- Who should participate in PI planning, help eliminate impediments, and speak on behalf of development, the business, and the customer?

- Who can approve, support, and (if necessary) defend a set of committed Program Increment (PI) plans, knowing that they will never satisfy everyone?

- Who can help coordinate the efforts of the ART with other organizations in the enterprise?

The answers to these questions will help identify the Business Owners, who will play a vital role in delivering the ART's value.

Setting the Launch Date and Program Cadence

With the ART definition in hand, the next step is to set a date for the first PI planning event. This creates a forcing function, a 'date-certain' deadline for the launch, which will create a starting point and define the planning timeline.

A development cadence must also be established, including the PI and iteration lengths. Although the SAFe Big Picture shows a ten-week PI, consisting of four regular iterations and one Innovation and Planning (IP) iteration, there is no fixed rule for the PI cadence, nor for how much time should be reserved for the IP iteration.

The recommended duration of a PI is between eight to twelve weeks. Once the cadence is chosen, it should remain stable from one PI to another. This allows the ART to have a predictable rhythm and velocity. The fixed cadence also allows the train's team members and stakeholders to schedule a full year of ART events on their calendars. The PI calendar usually includes the following activities:

- PI planning event

- System demos

- Scrum of Scrums, PO sync, and ART sync meetings

- Inspect and Adapt (I&A) event

The advanced notice provided by the PI calendar reduces travel and facility costs and helps assure that most of the stakeholders will be available to participate. Once the PI calendar is set, team events can also be scheduled, with each team defining the time and place for their DSU, iteration planning, review, and retrospective events. All teams on the train should use the same iteration start and end dates, which facilitates synchronization across the ART.

Training the ART Leaders and Stakeholders

Depending on the scope and timing of the rollout, there may be several ART leaders—Release Train Engineer (RTE), Product Managers, System Architects/Engineers, Business Owners, and other stakeholders—who have not attended *Leading SAFe* training.

It's likely they will be unfamiliar with SAFe, will be unclear on expectations, and may not understand the need and benefits of their participation. It's vital that they understand and support the new model, as well as the responsibilities of their new roles. SPCs will often arrange a Leading SAFe class to educate these stakeholders and motivate their participation. This is usually followed by a one-day implementation workshop, where newly trained stakeholders and SPCs can create the specifics of the launch plan. After all, it's their ART; only they can plan for the best outcomes. Essentially, this is the handoff of primary responsibility from the change agents to the stakeholders of the newly formed ART.

Establishing the Agile Teams

During the implementation planning, questions will arise regarding how to organize the Agile teams around the solution's purpose and architecture. Similar to organizing the ARTs themselves, there are two primary patterns for organizing Agile teams.

- *Feature teams*. Focusing on user functionality, feature teams are optimized for fast value delivery. This is the preferred approach, as each is capable of delivering end-to-end user value. They also facilitate the growth of 'T-shaped' (multiple) skills of the team members.

- *Component teams*. Component teams are optimized to achieve architectural integrity, system robustness, and reuse of assets (e.g., code, components, services). This type of team should be limited to significant reuse opportunities, areas of high technical specialization, and critical Nonfunctional Requirements (NFRs).

Most ARTs have a mix of feature and component teams. However, ARTs should avoid organizing teams around a technical system infrastructure (e.g., architectural layer, programming language, middleware, user interface) as this creates unnecessary dependencies, which reduces the flow of new features and leads to fragile designs.

The next step is to form the Agile teams that will be on the train. One innovative solution is to enable the people on the ART to self-organize with a set of minimum constraints.

SELF-ORGANIZING INTO AGILE TEAMS

In her book *Tribal Unity, Getting from Teams to Tribes by Creating a One Team Culture*, Em Campbell-Pretty, SAFe Fellow at Pretty Agile Pty., Ltd., describes how to facilitate self-organizing an ART into Agile teams. Campbell-Pretty notes, "Whether you already have teams, or you are looking at creating teams, you need to be clear about their mission, and then ensure teams have the right set of skills to deliver on those missions, ideally autonomously. I would add that we want real teams, not just groups of people who work together."

In other cases, management may lead initial team selections based on their objectives, knowledge of individual talents and aspirations, timing, and other factors. This typically requires significant collaboration between the teams and management.

Prior to PI planning, all practitioners who will be joining the ART need to be part of a cross-functional Agile team. The initial roles of Scrum Master and Product Owner also need to be established. The team roster template shown in Figure 14-2 is a simple tool that can help clarify and visualize the organization of each team.

Team #	Team name	Role	Team member name	Geographic location
1	Team A	Scrum Master	LastName, FirstName	City, Country
2	Team A	Product Owner	LastName, FirstName	City, Country
3	Team A	Developer		
4	Team A	Developer		
5	Team A	Developer		
6	Team A	Tester		
7	Team A	Tester		
8	Team A	<role>		
9	Team A	<role>		

Figure 14-2. An Agile team roster template

The simple act of filling out the roster can be quite informative, as it starts to make the more abstract concepts of Agile development concrete. After all, the ideal structure of an Agile team is fairly well defined; the question of who is on the team, and the nature of the specialty roles, can lead to revealing discussions. Even the seemingly simple act of dedicating an individual to a single Agile team can be an eye-opening experience. But there's no going back. The proven success patterns of Agile, including 'one person–one team,' are clear.

The geographic location column is also interesting, as it defines the level of collocation and distribution for each team. Collocation is better, of course. But there may be cases where one or more individuals cannot be physically located with the others. That may evolve over time, but at least everyone understands where the current team members reside, so they can start thinking about Daily Stand-Up (DSU) times and other team events.

Training Product Owners and Product Managers

Product Owners and Product Managers provide the direction for the train and are critical to the success of the ART. So, the people fulfilling these roles have to be trained to learn the new way of working, ensure collaboration, and understand how to best accomplish their responsibilities. In addition, these roles will be responsible for building the initial program backlog, which is a key PI planning artifact.

The *SAFe Product Owner/Product Manager* course teaches Product Owners and Product Managers how to drive the delivery of value together in the SAFe enterprise.

Training Scrum Masters

Effective ARTs rely on the servant leadership of Scrum Masters and their ability to coach Agile team members to improve team performance. Scrum Masters play a vital part in PI planning and help coordinate value delivery through Scrum of Scrums meetings. It's incredibly helpful if Scrum Masters receive appropriate training before starting the first PI.

The *SAFe Scrum Master* course teaches the fundamentals and explores the role of Scrum in the context of SAFe. This course is beneficial for both new and experienced Scrum Masters.

Training System Architects and Engineers

System Architects/Engineers support solution development by providing, communicating, and advancing the broader technology and architectural view of the solution.

The *SAFe for Architects* course teaches senior technical contributors the role of architecture in a Lean-Agile enterprise. Attendees will explore the principles underlying Lean-Agile architecture, DevOps, and continuous delivery. They will also learn how to lead and support Solution Trains and ARTs, extend the principles driving continuous flow to large systems of systems and enable an improved flow of value across an entire portfolio.

Assessing and Evolving Launch Readiness

Training people in their new roles and responsibilities is key to ART readiness, but it's only one element of a successful ART launch. PI planning is a significant event, and preparation is required. The *ART Readiness Workbook* in the SAFe PI planning toolkit provides a checklist for that purpose. It's available to SPCs at https://community.scaledagile.com/.

However, since SAFe is based on the empirical Plan–Do–Check–Adjust (PDCA) model, there is no such thing as perfect readiness for a launch. Trying to be too perfect up front will delay learning, postponing the transformation and benefits realization.

Preparing the Program Backlog

Using the launch date as a forcing function increases the urgency to determine the scope and vision of the PI. This is defined by the vision and program backlog—the set of upcoming features, NFRs, and architectural work that outline the future behavior of the system. Consequently, SPCs and LACE stakeholders often bring the ART stakeholders together to prepare a common backlog. This is often done through a series of backlog workshops and related activities (Figure 14-3).

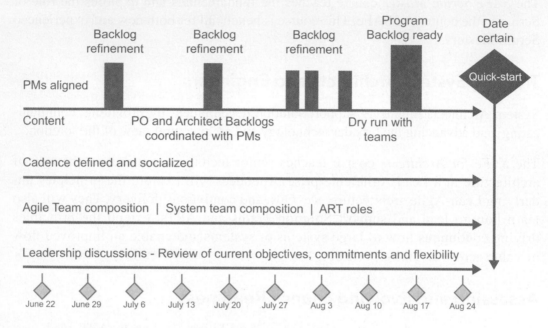

Figure 14-3. Preparing the program backlog and related activities

It's easy to over-invest in backlog readiness, so don't let that slow the process down, as the act of planning with the teams will sort out many issues. Experience shows that a list of well-written features with initial acceptance criteria is sufficient. There can be a tendency to over-plan and create user stories ahead of time, but that often creates waste and disappointment when the vision changes.

Step 8: Train Teams and Launch the ART

Now is the time to focus on the new and tentatively identified Agile teams who will make up the majority of the ART. Since these are the people who create the systems needed by the business, it's critical that they understand their role in the ART and gain the Lean-Agile skills needed to be more effective. These team members may come from different parts of the organization—business, development, operations, support, and other domains—to define, build, test, and deploy their solutions. So, the next significant task is to train all the teams in the SAFe way of working.

Training Teams

It's common that some people will feel that they do not need Agile team training. However, this course is critically important for digital transformation success, as the learning describes how Agile teams work together as a team of Agile teams.

The *SAFe for Teams* course offers an opportunity for team building and provides an introduction to Agile development. It covers the Agile Manifesto, Scrum, Kanban, and built-in quality practices, along with an overview of the Scrum Master and Product Owner roles. It also includes preparation for PI planning and building a Kanban board for tracking stories. In addition, teams prepare their backlog, which helps identify some of the work needed for the upcoming PI planning event.

Understanding the Benefits of Big-Room Training

In some rollouts, teams may be trained separately over an extended time period. However, we recommend a more accelerated approach, where all teams on the ART are trained simultaneously. This practice has created some controversy in the industry. Many compare this approach to the intimate setting of a small group with a single instructor and can't imagine that it delivers equivalent benefits. In reality, it delivers far more. But this is something you have to experience to grasp its full effect, as the following story describes.

BIG-ROOM TRAINING

Mark Richards, SAFe Fellow at CoActivation in Australia, shares his experiences with big-room training: "How on Earth do you get a high-impact training experience with 100 people in the room? I was initially unconvinced, so I worked with my clients to schedule four or five SAFe Agile team courses over the period leading up to the first PI planning. I'd requested that they send entire teams to the same course so they could sit and learn together, and they would promise to do their best. Then the pain would start. First, the teams would often be in flux until the last moment. Then they would be too busy on current commitments to all come together, so they would dribble through two or three people at a time. And distributed team members would go to different courses. Finally, I came to understand the motivation and some of the benefits of the big-room training—and eventually got convinced enough to try it. After the first big-room training, I was 'blown away' [by its effectiveness], and I spent some time sorting through how on Earth it could be so powerful."

The 'big-room' training approach offers the following benefits:

- *Accelerated learning.* This training happens in two days, rather than a few months, which helps the train come together as a team of Agile teams, accelerating the ART launch.

- *A common model for scaling Agile.* All team members receive the same training, at the same time, from the same instructor. This eliminates the variability of different training sessions over time, by different instructors, using different courseware materials.

- *Cost-effectiveness.* One of the challenges with Agile implementation at scale has been the availability and expense of training. Talented, proven instructors are hard to find and not consistently available, and their costs are correspondingly high. The big-room approach is typically three to five times more cost-effective than training one team at a time.

- *Collective learning.* There is no substitute for the face-to-face interaction and learning experience of big-room training. It starts building the social network that the ART relies upon and creates a far better experience than what can be accomplished when working separately from each other. There can be a transformative aspect to it, something you have to experience to believe.

As different as it is, the 'all-in, big-room training' approach is one of SAFe's most cost-effective and valuable implementation strategies.

Launching the ART

There are many ways to start an ART successfully, and there's no specific timeline for the preparation activities we described earlier. However, our experience has shown that the easiest and fastest way to launch an ART is through the ART quick-start approach (Figure 14-4).

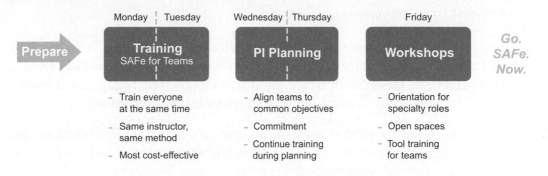

Figure 14-4. The one-week, all-in ART quick-start approach

After the preparation for the ART launch is complete, the quick-start approach trains people on Agile teams and holds the first PI planning event in a single week. Although that may seem daunting, numerous SAFe adoptions demonstrate this is the easiest and most practical way to transition 100-plus people to the new way of working.

Planning The First PI

During the ART quickstart, PI planning helps build team backlogs based on current priorities. It also reinforces the learning from the training. A successful PI planning event is essential to the success of the first PI. It demonstrates a commitment to the new way of working and offers the following benefits:

- Builds confidence and enthusiasm for the SAFe adoption

- Starts to establish the ART as a team of Agile teams and the social network that it relies on

- Teaches the teams how they can take responsibility for planning and delivery

- Creates full visibility into the mission and current context of the ART

- Demonstrates the commitment of Lean-Agile leaders to the SAFe transformation

It's recommended that an experienced SPC co-facilitate PI planning with the RTE to ensure success.

Step 9: Coach ART Execution

"Whenever you let up before the job is done, critical momentum can be lost, and regression may follow."
—John Kotter, *Leading Change*

At this stage of the implementation, the first significant events are now in the rearview mirror. Teams have been trained, the first ART is launched, and the first PI planning event has been held. The result of all this effort is an empowered, engaged, and aligned team of Agile teams ready to begin building solutions that deliver value.

Before moving on to the critical work of the train, it's important to understand that training and planning alone do not make the newly formed teams and ARTs Agile. They simply provide the opportunity to begin the journey. To support this effort, leadership—and SAFe Program Consultants (SPCs), in particular—need to be mindful that classroom *knowledge* does not equal *understanding*. It typically takes several PIs for effective Agile practices and behaviors to become the norm, which is why significant effort is required for coaching ART execution.

Coaching Teams

While SPCs often focus on enabling the ART roles and events, program execution ultimately relies on a competency in team and technical agility. So, SPCs are also needed to provide coaching to Agile teams in the following areas:

- Initial *iteration planning* to learn how to refine and adjust plans developed during PI planning

- *Backlog refinement* to adjust the scope and definition of user stories defined during PI planning

- *Daily meetings* to help the team stay aligned on progress toward iteration goals, raise impediments, and get help

- *Iteration reviews and system demos* to get feedback from stakeholders and assess progress toward PI objectives

- *Iteration retrospectives* to review team practices and identify ways to improve

However, this is only the beginning. To establish a smooth and consistent flow of value, Agile software teams will need to become proficient in the built-in quality practices described in Chapter 6, Team and Technical Agility.

Most of the software practices were established in the Extreme Programming (XP) movement and remain a solid foundation for software craftsmanship. DevOps has made substantial contributions to these practices as well.

Training Software Engineers

The introduction of Lean-Agile and DevOps principles and practices has evolved the discipline of software engineering over the past decade. New skills and approaches will help organizations deliver software-centric solutions faster, more predictably, and with higher quality.

The *SAFe Agile Software Engineering (ASE)* course offers the foundational principles and practices that enable the continuous flow of value and built-in quality, including XP practices, such as BDD, TDD, and test automation.

Attendees also learn how to define, build, and test stories in a SAFe CDP. They will explore abstraction, encapsulation, intentional programming, and the SOLID design principles of object-oriented software development. They will understand how ASE fits into the solution context and learn to collaborate on intentional architecture and DevOps.

Coaching ARTs

Like the approach for Agile teams, coaching the SPCs typically coaches the ART through the following essential events:

- *PI planning.* Creates alignment and shared commitment to a common set of objectives.

- *System demos.* Closes the rapid feedback loop by integrating and validating working solutions

- *Inspect & Adapt (I&A) workshops.* Enables relentless improvement and systems thinking.

- *Scrum of Scrums, PO sync, and ART sync.* Maintains alignment, resolves issues, and facilitates achievement of PI objectives.

But these just scratch the surface of the ART's purpose and potential. To help ARTs optimize the flow of value, SPCs coach ART leaders to look beyond the current PI and capabilities. As the team roles and events are mastered, the focus shifts to Agile product delivery and the CDP. This involves both managing and continuously improving the speed and quality of the ART's capability to do the following:

- *Continuously explore*. Sense and respond to market and business needs and apply design thinking to build and maintain the program vision, roadmap, backlog, and architectural runway.

- *Continuously integrate*. Build, validate, and learn from working system increments.

- *Continuously deploy*. Deliver validated features into production, where they are readied for release.

- *Releasing on demand*. Release value to customers, with frequency and timing based on market and business needs.

While the program Kanban is the primary tool for visualizing and managing the CDP, SAFe DevOps, value stream mapping, and the I&A problem-solving workshop are the coach's primary tools for enhancing these capabilities.

Training SAFe DevOps

To accelerate development of the CDP, DevOps training can be held during the first IP iteration or according to need and opportunity in subsequent PIs.

This course provides a comprehensive overview of the DevOps skills needed to accelerate time to market by improving the flow of value through the CDP. From concept to value, attendees will map the current value stream through their delivery pipeline and identify practices that will eliminate bottlenecks to flow.

The course will build an understanding of the complete flow of value, from continuous exploration to continuous integration and from continuous deployment to release on demand. Attendees will leave with the tools they need to execute an implementation plan for improving their CDP and the knowledge they need to support it.

Training Agile Product Management

Learning the right mindset, skills, and tools to create successful products—from inception to retirement—using Agile techniques to tap into new markets is critical in today's fast-paced digital economy.

The *SAFe Agile Product Management (APM)* course offers advanced product management techniques for applying customer-centricity, design thinking, and continuous exploration to fuel innovation in the Lean enterprise.

Learners will understand how to accelerate the product life cycle to get faster feedback and quickly deliver exceptional products and solutions that delight customers—in alignment with your organization's strategy, portfolio, evolving architecture, and solution intent. They will learn how to manage value stream economics, including licensing and pricing; how to use empathy to drive design; apply product strategy and vision; develop and evolve roadmaps; execute and deliver value using SAFe; and explore innovation in the value stream.

Conducting the Inspect and Adapt

There is no coaching opportunity for continuous improvement more critical than the first I&A event as described in the next section.

 SPCs and coaches can assist the RTE in leading the first I&A event, where the current state of the solution is demonstrated and evaluated by the ART. Teams will then reflect and identify improvement backlog items during a structured, problem-solving workshop.

During the I&A everyone will learn the following:

- How well the organization is adopting SAFe

- How well the PI was executed and the quality of the system increment

- How well the Agile teams and the ART performed against their PI objectives

In addition, SPCs and coaches can help lead the first problem-solving workshop, where corrective actions for the next PI are identified. This workshop gives teams the tools they need to relentlessly improve their performance independently. It also allows teams to work together—along with their management stakeholders—to collaboratively address the larger impediments that they face.

Summary

There is no such thing as 'perfect readiness' for an ART launch. Indeed, trying to be perfect upfront can potentially delay the transformation and the realization of its benefits. To avoid this, setting the launch date ahead of time provides an effective forcing function.

Launching an ART involves three main activities: preparation, training the Agile teams, and conducting the first PI planning. The preparation includes identifying and training ART leaders and specific roles such as Scrum Masters, Product Owners, Product Managers, and System Architects, as well as setting the program cadence and preparing the program backlog.

Following this preparation period, the one-week ART quick-start approach is a proven way to rapidly implement the new way of working. In this approach, the Agile teams are trained, and the first PI planning event is held, all in a single week. Once launched, opportunities are sought to coach the ART, focusing on supporting successful program execution alongside identifying improvements to the continuous delivery pipeline.

Launching and coaching the first ART creates an initial win, which ensures the energy and positive momentum needed to maintain the transformation and move onto the next step, which is to launch more ARTs and extend to the portfolio.

Launching More ARTs and Value Streams; Extending to the Portfolio

15

"Consolidate gains and produce more change."
—John Kotter

Introduction

So far, in Part III of this book, we've covered the first nine steps of the implementation roadmap. In this chapter, we'll describe the next two steps in the transformation.

- Step 10: Launch more ARTs and value streams.

- Step 11: Extend to the portfolio.

Step 10: Launch More ARTs and Value Streams

Launching the initial Agile Release Train (ART) creates the patterns and 'muscle memory' needed to implement additional ARTs in the value stream. And now, the larger business opportunity has arrived, enabling the enterprise to *consolidate gains and produce more change* by launching more ARTs and value streams.

Launch More ARTs

By now, SAFe Program Consultants (SPCs), the Lean-Agile Center of Excellence (LACE), and other stakeholders have the experience needed to launch more ARTs in the next selected value stream. After all, the greater the number of ARTs, the greater the return. The pattern remains the same. Repeat the critical moves that worked the first time.

- Prepare for ART launch.

- Train teams and launch the ART.

- Coach ART execution.

However, a note of caution: *the next few ARTs need to receive the same attention and effort as was paid to the first*. Otherwise, there may be a tendency to assume that 'everyone knows how to do this now.' That's unlikely this early in the transformation; the change leaders will need to give as much love and care to each subsequent ART as they did to their first.

Launch More Value Streams

Launching the first full value stream is a milestone in the company's transformation. Outcomes are improving. People are happier. The new way of working is becoming a habit. The culture is evolving, too. However, in a large enterprise, the job is far from done. The other value streams may be in entirely different businesses, operating units, or subsidiaries. They may be located in different countries, offer different solutions and services, and have different lines of authority that converge only at the highest corporate level.

As a result, even the spread of optimism to other value streams may not evoke an automatic embrace of SAFe across the enterprise. Many may think, 'What worked there may not work here.' So, realistically, each new value stream represents the same challenge and opportunity to incorporate all the change management steps described so far. And each will necessitate the same series of steps (Figure 15-1).

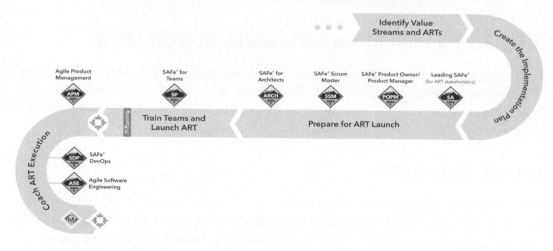

Figure 15-1. Each value stream executes a portion of the implementation roadmap

Also, given the scope of the effort ahead, this is a good time to reflect on earlier principles and apply Principle #6, Visualize and limit work in process, reduce batch sizes, and manage queue lengths. We'll see these principles at work in the SAFe implementation railway, described next.

The SAFe Implementation Railway

Sarah Scott, SPC and Lean-Agile organization coach at Northwestern Mutual Life Insurance & Financial Planning, presented her company's case study at the 2016 SAFe Summit. We were so impressed by their Lean-Agile mindset, how they applied SAFe principles and practices, and the structured way they executed the implementation that we asked if we could share their experience. In turn, we've taken those insights and generalized them into guidance for what we now call the 'SAFe implementation railway' (Figure 15-2). The implementation railway metaphor is a fun and visual Kanban used to manage a large-scale transformation, as is further described in the 'Launch more ARTs and value streams' article[1] on the SAFe website.

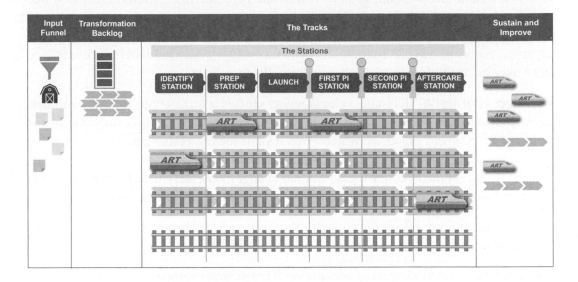

Figure 15-2. SAFe implementation railway

With value streams and trains now running consistently, it's time to proceed to the next critical move in the SAFe implementation roadmap, extend to the portfolio, described next.

---

1. http://www.scaledagileframework.com/launch-more-arts-and-value-streams/

Step 11: Extend to the Portfolio

"Anchor new approaches in the culture."
—John Kotter

It's quite an accomplishment for an organization to have implemented SAFe across a set of value streams. The new way of working is well on its way to becoming second nature to everyone who had a role in the implementation. As a result, the effectiveness of the whole company starts to improve, and the broader goal is coming into sharper focus: a truly Lean-Agile enterprise with a much higher degree of business agility.

This is a critical phase in the rollout. It tests the organization's commitment to transforming the business at all levels. Now is the time to expand the implementation across the entire portfolio to anchor the new approach in the culture. In addition, in large enterprises, a portfolio represents a portion of the business, not the whole business, and there may be multiple portfolios that undergo the transformation.

The success of these ARTs and value streams creates a buzz about the new and better way of working. But this also tends to stimulate greater scrutiny on some of the higher-level business practices, which often reveals legacy, phase-gated processes, and procedures that impede performance. Inevitably, that starts to put pressure on the portfolio and triggers the need for the additional changes necessary to further improve the strategic flow across the portfolio. These issues typically include the following:

- Too much demand versus capacity that jeopardizes throughout and undermines strategy

- Project-based funding, cost-accounting friction, and overhead

- No understanding of how to capitalize expenses in an Agile business

- Overly detailed business cases based on speculative, lagging ROI projections

- Iron triangle strangulation (fixed scope, cost, and time projects)

- Traditional supplier management and coordination—focus on the lowest price, rather than the highest life-cycle value

- Phase-gate approval processes that don't mitigate risk and actually discourage incremental delivery

Nowhere is Lean-Agile leadership more critical than in addressing these remaining legacy challenges. Without modernizing these approaches, the enterprise will not escape the inertia of traditional legacy methods, causing the organization to revert to the old way of doing things. This inevitably leads to attempting Agile development without an Agile mindset, i.e., 'Agile in name only.' The results can be severely compromised. But help is at hand. Figure 15-3 illustrates how these mindsets evolve with training and engagement while implementing SAFe.

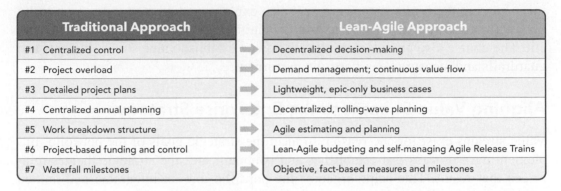

Traditional Approach		Lean-Agile Approach
#1 Centralized control	⇒	Decentralized decision-making
#2 Project overload	⇒	Demand management; continuous value flow
#3 Detailed project plans	⇒	Lightweight, epic-only business cases
#4 Centralized annual planning	⇒	Decentralized, rolling-wave planning
#5 Work breakdown structure	⇒	Agile estimating and planning
#6 Project-based funding and control	⇒	Lean-Agile budgeting and self-managing Agile Release Trains
#7 Waterfall milestones	⇒	Objective, fact-based measures and milestones

Figure 15-3. Evolving traditional mindsets to Lean-Agile thinking

Leading the Transformation

Many of these conventional mindsets exist throughout the organization and, if left unchanged, can sabotage an effective implementation. To help the staff embrace the new way of working, we've described how SPCs and Lean-Agile leaders actively participate in leading the transformation.

Leaders provide the knowledge and purpose needed to inspire people to embrace the new mindset. In addition, Lean Portfolio Management (LPM) and the Agile Program Management Office (APMO) often advance the need for change and provide the knowledge for the new way of working. They sponsor and participate in the LACE and support or encourage the development of the specialty Communities of Practice (CoPs) that focus on and advance the new roles, responsibilities, and behaviors. In so doing, they establish the exemplary Lean-Agile principles, behaviors, and practices described in the following sections.

However, before the LPM team and other stakeholders can transform from traditional mindsets to a Lean-Agile approach for the portfolio, they need to have a deeper understanding of LPM and gain hands-on experience with the tools, techniques, and knowledge needed.

Train Lean Portfolio Management

In this course, attendees gain the practical tools and techniques necessary to implement the *Lean portfolio management competency*. This includes the functions of strategy and investment funding, Agile portfolio operations, and Lean governance.

Participants in the course will have the opportunity to capture the current and the future state with the portfolio canvas tool and identify important business initiatives for achieving the future state. They will also explore methods to establish portfolio flow with the portfolio Kanban and prioritize initiatives for maximum economic benefit. The course also provides insights on how to establish value stream budgets and guardrails and measure Lean portfolio performance.

Aligning Value Streams to the Enterprise Strategy

Value streams exist for one reason: to meet the strategic goals of the portfolio. Implementing a process that establishes and communicates the strategic themes reinforces that result. This helps organize the portfolio into an integrated and unified solution offering. Strategic themes also inform value stream budgeting decisions, as described later.

Establishing Enterprise Value Flow

Managing the flow of work from portfolio epics is an important step in the maturity cycle. This requires implementing the portfolio backlog and Kanban system. This facilitates the role of Epic Owners by adopting the epic backlog, Lean business case, and build-measure-learn Lean Startup cycle. Also, Enterprise Architects establish enabler epics needed to extend the architectural runway to support future business functionality across the full portfolio.

Implementing Lean Financial Management

Traditional governance carefully controlled the definition and cost of development via the 'project' construct. But the project model provided only temporary work for temporary people; the usual cost and schedule overruns caused undesirable disruption in personnel and financial management. As the enterprise improves its methods, however, and discovers the long-lived nature of most work, the move to a more persistent flow-based model will be natural. The new approach minimizes overhead, gives people a stronger sense of purpose, and facilitates the growth of institutional knowledge.

This is the larger purpose of the portfolio's development value streams, funded by following SAFe strategy and investment funding practices.

Aligning Portfolio Demand to Capacity and Agile Forecasting

Lean thinking teaches us that any system operating in a state of overload will deliver far less than its potential capacity. This is certainly true for any development process in which excess Work In Process (WIP) produces multitasking (lowering productivity), unpredictability (lowering trust and engagement), and burnout (lowering everything).

By consistently applying the concept of velocity to the team, ART, and Solution Train, the emerging SAFe enterprise uses this valuable knowledge to limit portfolio WIP until demand matches capacity. That increases throughput and the value delivered to the customer. And in place of detailed, long-range commitments, the SAFe enterprise applies Agile forecasting to create a portfolio roadmap, a baseline of expectations communicated to internal and external stakeholders.

Evolving Leaner and More Objective Governance Practices

As we noted in Figure 15-3, customary governance practices were often based on conventional waterfall life-cycle development. This usually included passing various phase-gate milestones, along with proxy, document-driven measures of completion. The Lean-Agile model, however, works differently. As explained in SAFe Principle #5, Base milestones on objective evidence of working systems, the focus of governance evolves, establishing and measuring the appropriate objective measures at the conclusion of each PI.

Fostering a Leaner Approach to Supplier and Customer Relationships

The Lean-Agile mindset informs another group of business practices: how the enterprise treats its suppliers and customers. The Lean enterprise takes the long view. It enters into long-term partnerships with suppliers, which produces the lowest overall cost of ownership versus a series of near-term maneuvers that lower only the price of a current deliverable. Indeed, the enterprise will help its suppliers adopt Lean-Agile thinking and may even participate in developing a supplier's capabilities in that area.

The SAFe enterprise also recognizes the critical importance of customers to the value stream. That realization means they are included in such crucial events as PI planning, system and solution demos, and I&A. They take on the responsibilities incumbent on a customer in a Lean-Agile ecosystem.

Traditional contracting changes as well, evolving to a leaner approach with Agile contracts, which fosters healthier—and more profitable—long-term relationships.

Summary

Launching the first ART creates a short-term win. However, in the large enterprise, the job is just beginning. To continue the journey, the critical moves that worked the first time need to be repeated.

The same level of attention and effort should be devoted to the launch of each subsequent train as for the first, focusing initially on ARTs within the same value stream before moving onto the next value stream.

Once the Lean enterprise has realized a fully implemented set of SAFe value streams, these new ways of working must then be extended to the portfolio to create alignment between strategy and execution. Establishing Lean portfolio management provides a comprehensive governance approach to ensure that each portfolio fulfils its role in supporting the enterprise to achieve its broader business objectives.

The journey does not end here however, as with this structure in place the enterprise can now focus on how to measure, grow, and accelerate the journey toward the goal of business agility.

16

Measure, Grow, and Accelerate

"Excellent firms don't believe in excellence—only in constant improvement and constant change."
—Tom Peters

In the previous chapters of this part of the book, we covered steps 1–11 of the implementation roadmap. In this chapter, we'll cover the last and most persistent step—step 12: accelerate. However, this final step is not the end. Instead, it's the start of a new beginning! Now the goal is to accelerate the enterprise's growth toward business agility.

To reinforce and accelerate the SAFe transformation, leaders must now 'measure and grow' the implementation. To do that, they'll need to maintain the energy and enthusiasm they're devoting to the short cycles of iterations and Program Increments (PIs) while setting their sights on the larger goals of true business agility.

Organizations that have followed the first 11 steps of the implementation roadmap deserve congratulations! There's no doubt that substantial progress has occurred; for example:

- A sufficiently powerful coalition of change agents is in place.

- The majority of stakeholders are trained in Lean-Agile practices.

- Leaders are 'thinking lean' and 'embracing agility.'

- The portfolio has been reorganized around value streams.

- Agile Release Trains (ARTs) have been launched and are continuously delivering value.

- The new way of working is becoming the norm for individual teams and those responsible for managing portfolio concerns.

Most importantly, substantial business benefits are accumulating every day. Improvements in quality, productivity, time to market, and employee engagement are meeting or exceeding expectations. The first results of business agility are becoming apparent. It can be tempting to think that the work of transformation is done, since most of the steps in the implementation roadmap have been followed.

However, building on these benefits allows the enterprise to accelerate its business agility journey. This requires a commitment to basic and advanced practices, self-reflection, and retrospection. Here are some activities the enterprise can use to ensure its relentless improvement:

- Measure and grow

- Reinforce the basics with Essential SAFe

- Anchor new behaviors in the culture

- Apply learnings across the enterprise

Each of these is described in the following sections.

Measure and Grow

'Measure and grow' is the term we use to describe how a portfolio evaluates its progress toward business agility and determines improvement steps. It describes how to measure the current state and grow to improve overall business outcomes. There are two separate assessment mechanisms, which are designed for different audiences and different purposes.

1. The SAFe business agility assessment is designed for Lean Portfolio Management (LPM), Lean-Agile Center of Excellence (LACE), and other portfolio stakeholders to assess their overall progress toward the ultimate goal of true business agility.

2. The SAFe core competency assessments are used to help teams and trains improve on the technical and business practices they need to help the portfolio achieve its goals.

Each assessment follows a standard process pattern of running the assessment, analyzing the results, taking action, and celebrating the victories.

SAFe Business Agility Assessment

The SAFe business agility assessment is a high-level assessment that summarizes how Agile the business is at any point in time. The assessment report provides a visualization that shows progress measurements along the 21 dimensions. An example report is shown below in Figure 16-1.

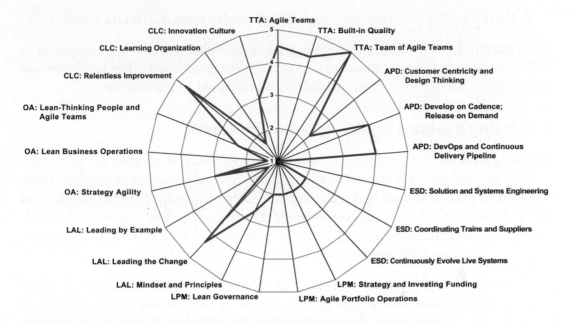

Figure 16-1. Example business agility assessment showing low LPM proficiency

Running the Business Agility Assessment

The business agility assessment contains a series of questions that help identify the current state of the portfolio. Typically, portfolio, business, and technology stakeholders take it, together with the LACE. After choosing the target audience and deciding which competencies the group should assess, it's essential to set the context before starting the assessment, ensuring that all participants understand the 21 dimensions, as well as the SAFe terminology used.

Assessing business agility progress is not a trivial feat. Opinions abound, the data is lumpy, and the ways of working are evolving at the same time as the assessment is taking place. Therefore, simply sending the assessment out to various participants and asking them to fill in the data will probably not provide the right experience or accurate results. Instead, we recommend a facilitated session with someone trained in the nuances of SAFe and the assessment process. An experienced SAFe Program Consultant is probably a good choice.

Two assessment patterns can be used:

- Fill out the assessment individually and then come together to discuss and analyze the results

- Work together to discuss each question and reach a consensus on the score

Both patterns have their benefits and disadvantages. Either way, having a facilitator to set the context and answer questions during the assessment is vital. The facilitator also helps ensure that the assessment workshops are engaging and actionable.

Analyzing Business Agility Assessment Results

With the data from the assessment in hand, the next step is to analyze the results. During the analysis, it is important to identify significant variances in opinion. These might stem from a different understanding of the statement itself, or from disagreement about the current state in relation to a specific dimension. The goal is to explore the differences to get better alignment of where improvement is needed. This is a significant part of the collaborative learning experience.

Dimensions that the group has assessed as problematic can then be explored to understand the reasons that drove people to score themselves low. In addition to pointing out areas needing improvement, the assessment allows portfolios to see visible improvements in performance or 'wins.' The wins or small milestones, when multiplied, encourage teams to consolidate those gains and produce more change, as Kotter's model suggests.

The facilitator should also be aware of the Dunning-Kruger effect,[1] in which people tend to assess their ability as greater than reality. In turn, dimensions that seem unnaturally high should be reviewed to ensure the group understands the meaning of the statements in question and are being realistic in their assessment.

---

1. https://en.wikipedia.org/wiki/Dunning%E2%80%93Kruger_effect

Taking Action on the Business Agility Assessment

Although high level, taking the business agility assessment is, in itself, a learning experience. Many questions directly set expectations of behaviors, activities, or outcomes that can be reasoned about and discussed. For example, a question about continuous learning such as "the organization provides dedicated time and space for people to explore and experiment" is fairly clear, and the implied corrective action is fairly obvious. Further in Figure 16-1, the enterprise scored low in LPM. That could be because they are ineffective at it, but it's more probable that that enterprise hasn't started that part of the journey yet. In most cases, a quick look at the implementation roadmap will identify some fairly obvious next steps, with the goal being to steadily improve proficiency across all seven core competencies.

The portfolio or the LACE should routinely re-evaluate their progress toward business agility, perhaps every other PI, and plan the next steps. The measurement frequency depends on the opportunities pursued and how fast the portfolio can reasonably achieve progress. Creating a baseline early on in the transformation, followed by periodic assessments, will illustrate improvement trends and allow everyone to communicate successes.

SAFe Core Competency Assessments

In most cases, assessing progress toward business agility spurs the enterprise to greater, and deeper, improvement efforts. That leads the business to explore and start to measure and take more specific action on some or all of the seven core competencies. Structured similarly to the business agility assessment, each core competency assessment has a set of statements, organized by dimension, that are rated on the same scale as the above. The questions go one step deeper to specific aspects and areas of opportunity and concern along each of the three dimensions of that specific competency. An example report is illustrated in Figure 16-2.

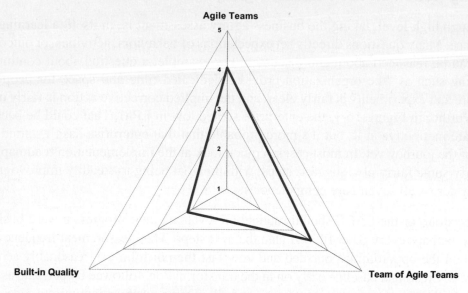

Team and Technical Agility Self-Assessment

Figure 16-2. A report from a team and technical agility competency assessment

Running a Core Competency Assessment

As with the business agility assessment, the scope, audience, and process for an individual competency assessment must be purpose built. Perhaps low results in the Agile product delivery competency might suggest that each Agile Release Train assess its progress in that dimension. Or perhaps it's an LPM assessment that needs to bring in the right stakeholders. In any case, all the guidance and caveats provided earlier still apply and attention to culture and careful facilitation is necessary to get the right experience and results.

Each of these more detailed assessments can be downloaded from the bottom of each competency article on the SAFe website.

Analyzing Results of a Core Competency Assessment

The results of a competency assessment are summarized along the three dimensions. But again, there is far more detail in the assessment and far more learnings than the figure alone implies. For example, here's a sample of questions from the built-in quality dimension, which by themselves inform stakeholders and imply improvement activities:

- Teams share responsibility for design

- Teams reduce technical debt in each iteration

- Teams foster cross-training and T-shaped skills

- Continuous integration and automated tests run at team and system levels

To reiterate, taking the business agility or core competency assessment is not a routine, mechanical effort. It's a facilitated collaborative session filled with learnings, and it sets expectations and communicates intent. Therefore, even the apparently simple act of taking the assessment will be a significant step in moving toward improvement.

Taking Action from a Core Competency Assessment

Based on the analysis of the core competency assessment, the team identifies the areas needing the most improvement. For example, in Figure 16-2, the built-in quality dimension of the team and technical agility competency has a low score, while the other areas appear solid.

Each competency article contains a 'grows' link, which opens a page that has recommendations for each dimension (Figure 16-3). The grows represent an activity (e.g., watch a video, run a workshop) that helps the team improve in that dimension.

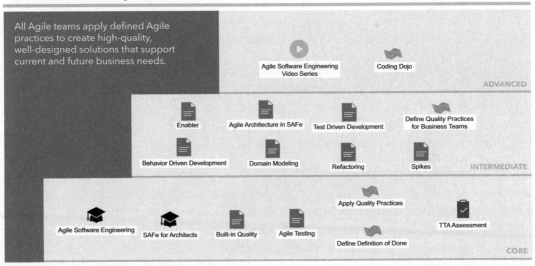

Figure 16-3. Built-in quality grows from the team and technical agility competency

The grows in Figure 16-3 are organized into three groups (core, intermediate, and advanced) to provide a logical order for selecting improvement actions. It's also helpful to prioritize the opportunities using Weighted Shortest Job First (WSJF) and choose one or two activities to limit work in process and gain the most value in the shortest time. The top, highest priority items go into the appropriate backlog (e.g., LACE, program) based on the size and scope of the improvement.

Celebrate Successes

Lastly, change is hard. Continuous change is harder still. A smart enterprise uses small wins to celebrate progress and inspire people to achieve the next milestone. There are many opportunities to celebrate: such as when a portfolio, ART, or team move from one level to the next in each dimension; or perhaps even manage to change a single assessment statement from 'mostly false' to 'mostly true.' Celebrating successes creates the fuel needed for more improvement and advancement on the journey toward business agility.

These milestones can also provide an opportunity for organizations to gamify the process. This, in turn, can motivate individuals and teams to intensify their focus on the activities that will help them and their portfolio to achieve goals.

In addition, tying the improvement to changes in the value stream KPIs and other busness metrics connects the effort to the portfolio's measures of success. This way, the entire portfolio can focus on results and celebrate growth and positive outcomes.

Reinforce the Basics with Essential SAFe

The business agility and individual competency assessments provide a comprehensive framework to help the enterprise 'measure and grow.' But there's often an intermediate path as well. In virtually every sport, when teams start to struggle, coaches will refocus their players on the fundamentals of their positions. This first step on the path back to winning is also often the same for organizations adopting SAFe.

At the beginning of the transformation, everyone was trained, and the initial emphasis was on learning the fundamentals of SAFe. However, as more trains are launched and the organization's attention moves to new challenges, steps in the implementation roadmap may be skipped. Practices that were closely followed in the beginning may have been altered or discontinued. Whether it's lack of understanding, a desire to shortcut the path to agility, or the natural ebb and flow of a company's attention to performance, often one or more of the ten critical success factors in Essential SAFe (Figure 16-4) is not being followed.

Experience from thousands of SAFe implementations has shown that skipping any factor will lead to the portfolio achieving less than exemplary results. To overcome these challenges, the following ten critical success factors (Figure 16-4) are a subset of Essential SAFe that describe the basics necessary to achieve positive business outcomes.

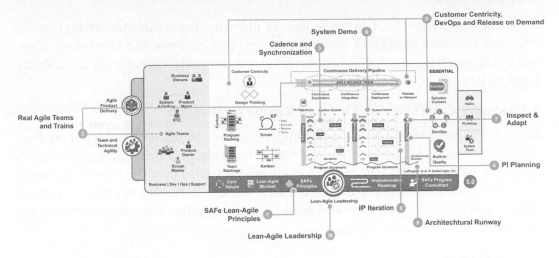

Figure 16-4. The ten critical success factors of Essential SAFe

Each of these elements is described next.

1. Lean-Agile Principles

SAFe practices are grounded in fundamental Lean-Agile principles. As organizations adopt SAFe, their continuous improvement activities find even better ways of working. These principles guide those efforts and ensure that adjustments are moving on a steady path to the 'shortest sustainable lead time, with the best quality and value to people and society.'

2. Real Agile Teams and Trains

Real Agile teams and ARTs are fully cross-functional. They have everything, and everyone, necessary to produce working, tested increments of the solution. Self-organizing and self-managing, they flow value more quickly, with a minimum of overhead. Agile teams that cannot define, build, test, and deliver their work are not fully functional Agile teams. ARTs that cannot deliver solutions or parts of them are not fully capable ARTs.

3. Cadence and Synchronization

As described in Principle #7, cadence provides a rhythmic pattern—a steady heartbeat for the development process. It makes routine those things that can be routine.

Synchronization allows multiple perspectives to be understood and resolved at the same time. For example, synchronization is used to pull the various assets of a system together to assess solution-level viability.

4. PI Planning

No event is more powerful in SAFe than PI planning. It provides the rhythm for the ART and connects strategy to execution by ensuring business and technology alignment. Aligning the entire ART to a common vision and goal creates energy and a shared sense of purpose.

5. Customer Centricity, DevOps, and Release on Demand

SAFe enterprises create a positive customer experience across their full set of products and services. They adopt a DevOps mindset, culture, and applicable technical practices to enable more frequent and higher-quality releases whenever the market demands. Customer centric, they apply design thinking to their work. These practices provide faster validation of hypotheses and produce greater profits, increased employee engagement, and more satisfied customers.

6. System Demo

The primary measure of the ART's progress is the objective evidence from a working solution in the system demo. Every two weeks, the full system—the integrated work of all teams on the train for that iteration—is demoed to the train's stakeholders. Stakeholders then provide the feedback the train needs to take corrective action and stay on course. This replaces other forms of governance that create additional work and impede flow.

7. Inspect and Adapt

Inspect and Adapt (I&A) is a significant event held every PI and is a predetermined time to reflect, collect data, and solve problems. The I&A event assembles teams and stakeholders to assess the solution and define the improvements and actions needed to increase the velocity, quality, and reliability of the next PI.

8. Innovation and Planning (IP) Iteration

The IP iteration serves multiple purposes. It acts as an estimating buffer for meeting PI objectives and provides dedicated time for innovation, continuing education, PI planning, and I&A. IP iteration activities support many Lean-Agile principles that enable business agility.

9. Architectural Runway

The architectural runway consists of the existing code, components, and technical infrastructure necessary to implement high-priority, near-term features, without excessive delay and redesign. Insufficient investment in the architectural runway slows the train and makes the ART's delivery less predictable.

10. Lean-Agile Leadership

For SAFe to be effective, the enterprise's leaders and managers take responsibility for Lean-Agile adoption and success. Executives and managers become Lean-Agile leaders trained in—and then become trainers of—these Leaner ways of thinking and operating. Without leadership taking responsibility for the implementation, the transformation will be unlikely to achieve the full benefits.

Anchor New Behaviors in the Culture

Implementing SAFe and achieving mastery of the seven competencies will inevitably shift the culture of the organization. Anchoring this shift to make it permanent is critical to ensuring that the organization keeps progressing and doesn't regress to old patterns of behavior. As portfolios advance toward higher degrees of mastery, there will be a natural tendency to assume that the new way of working has become habit and to shift the focus of the organization to the 'next big thing.'

But beware. Until all of the new principles and practices spread throughout the entire portfolio become the default way of working, there will be an ongoing risk that some or all of the organization's gains will be lost. The portfolio could easily revert to legacy mindsets and practices. Changes in leadership, threats that create an emergency response environment, or the organization not having enough time and experience for the new habits to take root are all possible causes.

So, how can this pitfall be avoided?

Once again, the wisdom of W. Edwards Deming points the way. "Transformation is not automatic. It must be learned; it must be led." Leaders must do more than 'change the system.' Leaders have to understand the principles and practices of change leadership and organizational change management. They must become curators, caretakers, and defenders of the new way of working. When the heat is on and the pressure to revert to old habits escalates, everyone will look to leaders from the top of the organization down to see how they respond. Has leadership transformed how it thinks, acts, and makes decisions—even in moments of crisis? When leaders demonstrate that real change has occurred and going backward is not an option, no matter the circumstances, the changes become part of the organization's DNA. Then, the new way of working is likely to withstand similar challenges in the future.

Many of these new behaviors are modeled and exemplified by two specialty roles: the Scrum Master and the RTE. It takes a combination of coaching, experience, and training to develop them.

Advance Scrum Master Servant Leadership

Scrum Masters are servant leaders and coaches for an Agile team. They help educate the team in Scrum, XP, Kanban, and SAFe built-in quality practices. They also help remove impediments and foster an environment for high-performing team dynamics, continuous flow, and relentless improvement. Consequently, Scrum Masters play a critical role in the adoption of SAFe.

After a Scrum Master has been in the role for a while, at least three to five PIs, it's time for them to apply advanced learning to their experience to solve the next level of problems.

The *SAFe Advanced Scrum Master* course prepares current Scrum Masters for their leadership role in facilitating Agile team, program, and enterprise success in SAFe implementation.

The course covers facilitation of cross-team interactions in support of ART execution and relentless improvement. It enhances the Scrum paradigm with an introduction to scalable engineering and DevOps practices, the application of Kanban to facilitate the flow of value, and supporting interactions with System Architects, Product Management, and other critical stakeholders in the larger enterprise context. The course also offers actionable tools for building high-performing teams and explores practical ways of addressing Agile and Scrum anti-patterns in the enterprise.

Advance Agile Release Train Servant Leadership

The RTE is a servant leader and coach for the entire ART. Their major responsibilities are to facilitate the ART events and processes and assist the teams in delivering value. RTEs communicate and interact with everyone on the ART, including executives, Business Owners, and many other stakeholders to escalate impediments, help manage risk, and drive relentless improvement to deliver value. It's an incredibly difficult and important role. RTEs are vital to the success of the entire ART and therefore are critical to the adoption of SAFe. It's typical for an RTE to be informally trained and coached by an experienced SPC. After an RTE has conducted at least three to five PIs, it's important that they can spend time to advance their skills and knowledge by learning with other similar or more experienced people.

The *SAFe Release Train Engineer* course helps RTEs learn how to build a high-performing ART by becoming a true servant leader and coach through experiential learning and examining the RTE role in a Lean-Agile transformation with other peers. Moreover, RTEs will learn advanced tech-niques for facilitating ART processes and execution; coach leaders, teams, and Scrum Masters in new processes and mindsets; and be the primary enabler of alignment throughout all levels of a SAFe enterprise. Although the course can be valuable for people new to the role, this course relies on train-ing from the back-of-the room techniques where the majority of the learning comes from the experiences of the other course participants.

Apply Learnings Across the Enterprise

It's common for the world's largest organizations to have many portfolios. However, success in one portfolio does not ensure success in the others. As the initial portfolio adopting SAFe progresses toward business agility, the next step of accelerate is to leverage the insights and successes of the pioneering organization to transform the remaining portfolios. The recommended pattern is to provide change agents from the initial portfolio with the opportunity to help transform future portfolios, bringing with them all of the experience and understanding of implementing SAFe. For this pattern to succeed, organizations need to invest in cultivating the next generation of leaders in every role so they are prepared to step in when their counterparts move on to launch the transformation in other portfolios. Planned well, these transitions can be smooth and can create great opportunity and upward mobility for these leaders. They can also assure that the existing portfolio continues making progress toward the never-ending journey of mastering business agility.

Summary

Although it might appear so in the implementation roadmap, the accelerate step of SAFe is not the last in the transformation journey. Rather, it's the beginning of a new and larger journey of relentless improvement.

The emerging Lean enterprise has started to build a new operating model. Persistent progress is becoming the norm, but it can't be taken for granted. Accelerating the transformation requires continuous retrospection and identification of opportunities for improvement. The business agility and core competency assessments provide a means to measure this progress and identify areas for growth. In addition to the ten critical

ART success factors, specific 'grows' provide activities to increase proficiency in each core competency. Over time, the new behaviors that emerge will become anchored in a new organizational culture, thereby creating the opportunity to spread learnings wider across the enterprise.

Taken together, the 'accelerate step' and the 'measure and grow' guidance provide a comprehensive strategy that will help the enterprise achieve the full business benefits of a SAFe implementation.

Glossary

The Scaled Agile Framework (SAFe) glossary defines all of the terms on the Big Picture.

Agile Product Delivery
Agile product delivery is a customer-centric approach to defining, building, and releasing a continuous flow of valuable products and services to customers and users.

Agile Release Train (ART)
The Agile Release Train (ART) is a long-lived team of Agile teams, which, along with other stakeholders, incrementally develops, delivers, and where applicable operates one or more solutions in a value stream.

Agile Teams
In SAFe, an Agile team is a cross-functional group of 5 to 11 individuals who define, build, test, and deliver an increment of value in a short timebox.

Architectural Runway
The architectural runway consists of the existing code, components, and technical infrastructure needed to implement near-term features without excessive redesign and delay.

Built-in Quality
Built-in quality practices ensure that each solution element, at every increment, meets appropriate quality standards throughout development.

Business Agility
Business agility is the ability to compete and thrive in the digital age by quickly responding to market changes and emerging opportunities with innovative business solutions.

Business Owners
Business Owners are a small group of stakeholders who have the primary business and technical responsibility for governance, compliance, and Return On Investment (ROI) for a solution developed by an Agile Release Train (ART). They are key stakeholders on the ART who must evaluate fitness for use and actively participate in certain ART events.

Capabilities

A capability is a higher-level solution behavior that typically spans multiple Agile Release Trains (ARTs). Capabilities are sized and split into multiple features to facilitate their implementation in a single Program Increment (PI).

Communities of Practice (CoPs)

Communities of Practice (CoPs) are organized groups of people who have a common interest in a specific technical or business domain. They collaborate regularly to share information, improve their skills, and actively work on advancing the general knowledge of the domain.

Compliance

Compliance refers to a strategy and a set of activities and artifacts that allow teams to apply Lean-Agile development methods to build systems that have the highest possible quality, while simultaneously ensuring they meet any regulatory, industry, or other relevant standards.

Continuous Delivery Pipeline

The Continuous Delivery Pipeline (CDP) represents the workflows, activities, and automation needed to shepherd a new piece of functionality from ideation to an on-demand release of value to the end user.

Continuous Deployment (CD)

Continuous Deployment (CD) is the process that takes validated features in a staging environment and deploys them into the production environment, where they are readied for release.

Continuous Exploration (CE)

Continuous Exploration (CE) is the process that drives innovation and fosters alignment on what should be built by continually exploring market and customer needs, and defining a vision, roadmap, and set of features for a solution that addresses those needs.

Continuous Integration (CI)

Continuous Integration (CI) is the process of taking features from the program backlog and developing, testing, integrating, and validating them in a staging environment where they are ready for deployment and release.

Continuous Learning Culture

The continuous learning culture competency describes a set of values and practices that encourage individuals—and the enterprise as a whole—to continually increase knowledge, competence, performance, and innovation.

Core Values

The four core values of alignment, built-in quality, transparency, and program execution represent the fundamental beliefs that are key to the effectiveness of SAFe. These guiding principles help dictate behavior and action for everyone who participates in a SAFe portfolio.

Customer

Customers are the ultimate beneficiaries of the value of the business solutions created and maintained by the portfolio value streams.

Customer Centricity

Customer centricity is a mindset and a way of doing business that focuses on creating positive experiences for the customer through the full set of products and services that the enterprise offers.

Design Thinking

Design thinking is a customer-centric development process that creates desirable products that are profitable and sustainable over their life cycle.

DevOps

DevOps is a mindset, a culture, and a set of technical practices. It provides communication, integration, automation, and close cooperation among all the people needed to plan, develop, test, deploy, release, and maintain a solution.

Enablers

An enabler supports the activities needed to extend the architectural runway to provide future business functionality. These include exploration, architecture, infrastructure, and compliance. Enablers are captured in the various backlogs and occur throughout the framework.

Enterprise

The enterprise represents the business entity to which each SAFe portfolio belongs.

Enterprise Architect

The Enterprise Architect establishes a technology strategy and roadmap that enables a portfolio to support current and future business capabilities.

Enterprise Solution Delivery

The enterprise solution delivery competency describes how to apply Lean-Agile principles and practices to the specification, development, deployment, operation, and evolution of the world's largest and most sophisticated software applications, networks, and cyber-physical systems.

Epic Owners

Epic Owners are responsible for coordinating portfolio epics through the portfolio Kanban system. They collaboratively define the epic, its Minimum Viable Product (MVP), and Lean business case, and when those items are approved, they facilitate implementation.

Epics

An epic is a container for a significant solution development initiative that captures the more substantial investments that occur within a portfolio. Because of their considerable scope and impact, epics require the definition of a Minimum Viable Product (MVP) and approval by Lean Portfolio Management (LPM) before implementation.

Essential SAFe

Essential SAFe contains the minimal set of roles, events, and artifacts required to continuously deliver business solutions via an Agile Release Train (ART) as a team of Agile teams.

Features

A feature is a service that fulfills a stakeholder need. Each feature includes a benefit hypothesis and acceptance criteria and is sized or split as necessary to be delivered by a single Agile Release Train (ART) in a Program Increment (PI).

Foundation

The foundation contains the supporting principles, values, mindset, implementation guidance, and leadership roles needed to deliver value successfully at scale.

Full SAFe

Full SAFe is the most comprehensive configuration, including all seven core competencies needed for business agility.

Innovation and Planning Iteration

The Innovation and Planning (IP) iteration occurs every Program Increment (PI) and serves multiple purposes. It acts as an estimating buffer for meeting PI objectives and provides dedicated time for innovation, continuing education, PI planning, and Inspect and Adapt (I&A) events.

Inspect & Adapt (I&A)

The Inspect and Adapt (I&A) is a significant event, held at the end of each Program Increment (PI), where the current state of the solution is demonstrated and evaluated by the train. Teams then reflect and identify improvement backlog items via a structured, problem-solving workshop.

Iteration

Iterations are the basic building block of Agile development. Each iteration is a standard, fixed-length timebox, where Agile teams deliver incremental value in the form of working, tested software and systems. The recommended duration of the timebox is two weeks. However, one to four weeks is acceptable, depending on the business context.

Iteration Execution

Iteration execution is how Agile teams manage their work throughout the iteration time-box, resulting in a high-quality, working, tested system increment.

Iteration Goals

Iteration goals are a high-level summary of the business and technical goals that the Agile team agrees to accomplish in an iteration. They are vital to coordinating an Agile Release Train (ART) as a self-organizing, self-managing team of teams.

Iteration Planning

Iteration planning is an event where all team members determine how much of the team backlog they can commit to delivering during an upcoming iteration. The team summarizes the work as a set of committed iteration goals.

Iteration Retrospective

The iteration retrospective is a regular meeting where Agile team members discuss the results of the iteration, review their practices, and identify ways to improve.

Iteration Review

The iteration review is a cadence-based event, where each team inspects the increment at the end of every iteration to assess progress, and then adjusts its backlog for the next iteration.

Large Solution SAFe

Large Solution SAFe describes additional roles, practices, and guidance to build and evolve the world's largest applications, networks, and cyber-physical systems.

Lean Budget Guardrails

Lean budget guardrails describe the policies and practices for budgeting, spending, and governance for a specific portfolio.

Lean Budgets

Lean budgets provide effective financial governance over investments, with far less overhead and friction, and support a much higher throughput of development work.

Lean Enterprise

The Lean enterprise is a thriving digital age organization that exhibits business agility—responding quickly to market changes and emerging opportunities by delivering innovative systems and solutions to its customers in the shortest sustainable lead time.

Lean Portfolio Management

The Lean portfolio management competency aligns strategy and execution by applying Lean and systems thinking approaches to strategy and investment funding, Agile portfolio operations, and governance.

Lean User Experience (Lean UX)

Lean User Experience (Lean UX) design is a mindset, culture, and a process that embraces Lean-Agile methods. It implements functionality in minimum viable increments and determines success by measuring results against a benefit hypothesis.

Lean-Agile Leadership

The Lean-Agile leadership competency describes how Lean-Agile leaders drive and sustain organizational change and operational excellence by empowering individuals and teams to reach their highest potential.

Lean-Agile Mindset

The Lean-Agile mindset is the combination of beliefs, assumptions, attitudes, and actions of SAFe leaders and practitioners who embrace the concepts of the Agile Manifesto and Lean thinking. It's the personal, intellectual, and leadership foundation for adopting and applying SAFe principles and practices.

Lean-Agile Principles

SAFe is based on 10 immutable, underlying Lean-Agile principles. These tenets and economic concepts inspire and inform the roles and practices of SAFe.

Measure and Grow

Measure and grow is the way portfolios evaluate their progress toward business agility and determine their next improvement steps.

Metrics

Metrics are agreed-upon measures used to evaluate how well the organization is progressing toward the portfolio, large solution, program, and team's business and technical objectives.

Milestones

Milestones are used to track progress toward a specific goal or event. There are three types of SAFe milestones: Program Increment (PI), fixed-date, and learning milestones.

Model-Based Systems Engineering (MBSE)

Model-Based Systems Engineering (MBSE) is the practice of developing a set of related system models that help define, design, and document a system under development. These models provide an efficient way to explore, update, and communicate system aspects to stakeholders, while significantly reducing or eliminating dependence on traditional documents.

Non-Functional Requirements (NFRs)

Non-Functional Requirements (NFRs) define system attributes such as security, reliability, performance, maintainability, scalability, and usability. They serve as constraints or restrictions on the design of the system across the different backlogs.

Organizational Agility

The organizational agility competency describes how Lean-thinking people and Agile teams optimize their business processes, evolve strategy with clear and decisive new commitments, and quickly adapt the organization as needed to capitalize on new opportunities.

PI Objectives

Program Increment (PI) objectives are a summary of the business and technical goals that an Agile team or train intends to achieve in the upcoming Program Increment (PI).

Portfolio Backlog

The portfolio backlog is the highest-level backlog in SAFe. It provides a holding area for upcoming business and enabler epics intended to create and evolve a comprehensive set of solutions.

Portfolio Kanban

The portfolio Kanban system is a method to visualize and manage the flow of portfolio epics, from ideation through analysis, implementation, and completion.

Portfolio SAFe

Portfolio SAFe aligns strategy with execution and organizes solution development around the flow of value through one or more value streams.

Portfolio Vision

The portfolio vision is a description of the future state of a portfolio's value streams and solutions and describes how they will cooperate to achieve the portfolio's objectives and the broader aim of the enterprise.

Pre-and Post-PI Planning

Pre- and post–Program Increment (PI) planning events are used to prepare for, and follow up after, PI planning for Agile Release Trains (ARTs) and suppliers in a Solution Train.

Product Management

Product management is responsible for defining and supporting the building of desirable, feasible, viable, and sustainable products that meet customer needs over the product-market life cycle.

Product Owner (PO)

The Product Owner (PO) is a member of the Agile team responsible for defining stories and prioritizing the team backlog to streamline the execution of program priorities while maintaining the conceptual and technical integrity of the features or components for the team.

Program Backlog

The program backlog is the holding area for upcoming features, which are intended to address user needs and deliver business benefits for a single Agile Release Train (ART). It also contains the enabler features necessary to build the architectural runway.

Program Increment (PI)

A Program Increment (PI) is a planning interval during which an Agile Release Train (ART) delivers incremental value in the form of working, tested software and systems. PIs are typically 8–12 weeks long. The most common pattern for a PI is four development Iterations, followed by one Innovation and Planning (IP) iteration.

Program Increment (PI) Planning

Program Increment (PI) planning is a cadence-based, face-to-face event that serves as the heartbeat of the Agile Release Train (ART), aligning all the teams on the ART to a shared mission and vision.

Program Kanban

The program and solution Kanban systems are a method to visualize and manage the flow of features and capabilities from ideation to analysis, implementation, and release through the continuous delivery pipeline.

Release on Demand

Release on demand is the process that deploys new functionality into production and releases it immediately or incrementally to customers based on demand.

Release Train Engineer (RTE)

The Release Train Engineer (RTE) is a servant leader and coach for the Agile Release Train (ART). The RTE's major responsibilities are to facilitate the ART events and processes and assist the teams in delivering value. RTEs communicate with stakeholders, escalate impediments, help manage risk, and drive relentless improvement.

Roadmap

The roadmap is a schedule of events and milestones that communicate planned solution deliverables over a planning horizon.

SAFe for Government

SAFe for Government is a set of success patterns that help public sector organizations implement Lean-Agile practices in a government context.

SAFe for Lean Enterprises

SAFe for Lean Enterprises is a knowledge base of proven, integrated principles, practices, and competencies for achieving business agility by implementing Lean, Agile, and DevOps at scale.

SAFe Implementation Roadmap

The SAFe implementation roadmap consists of an overview graphic and a 12-article series that describes a strategy and an ordered set of activities that have proven to be effective in successfully implementing SAFe.

SAFe Program Consultants (SPCs)

Certified SAFe Program Consultants (SPCs) are change agents who combine their technical knowledge of SAFe with an intrinsic motivation to improve the company's software and systems development processes. They play a critical role in successfully implementing SAFe. SPCs come from numerous internal or external roles, including business and technology leaders, portfolio/program/project managers, process leads, architects, analysts, and consultants.

Scrum Master

Scrum Masters are servant leaders and coaches for an Agile team. They help educate the team in Scrum, Extreme Programming (XP), Kanban, and SAFe, ensuring that the agreed Agile process is being followed. They also help remove impediments and foster an environment for high-performing team dynamics, continuous flow, and relentless improvement.

ScrumXP

ScrumXP is a lightweight process to deliver value for cross-functional, self-organized teams within SAFe. It combines the power of Scrum project management practices with Extreme Programming (XP) practices.

Set-Based Design

Set-based design (SBD) is a practice that keeps requirements and design options flexible for as long as possible during the development process. Instead of choosing a single point solution up front, SBD identifies and simultaneously explores multiple options, eliminating poorer choices over time. It enhances flexibility in the design process by committing to technical solutions only after validating assumptions, which produces better economic results.

Shared Services

Shared services represent the specialty roles, people, and services required for the success of an Agile Release Train (ART) or Solution Train but that cannot be dedicated full-time.

Solution

Each value stream produces one or more solutions, which are products, services, or systems delivered to the customer, whether internal or external to the enterprise.

Solution Architect/Engineer

The Solution Architect/Engineer is responsible for defining and communicating a shared technical and architectural vision across a solution train to help ensure the system or solution under development is fit for its intended purpose.

Solution Backlog

The solution backlog is the holding area for upcoming capabilities and enablers, each of which can span multiple ARTs and is intended to advance the solution and build its architectural runway.

Solution Context

Solution context identifies critical aspects of the operational environment for a solution. It provides an essential understanding of requirements, usage, installation, operation, and support of the solution itself. Solution context heavily influences opportunities and constraints for releasing on demand.

Solution Demo

The solution demo is where the results of development efforts from the Solution Train are integrated, evaluated, and made visible to customers and other stakeholders.

Solution Intent

Solution intent is the repository for storing, managing, and communicating the knowledge of current and intended solution behavior. Where required, this includes both fixed and variable specifications and designs; reference to applicable standards, system models, and functional and nonfunctional tests; and traceability.

Solution Management

Solution management is responsible for defining and supporting the building of desirable, feasible, viable, and sustainable large-scale business solutions that meet customer needs over time.

Solution Train

The Solution Train is the organizational construct used to build large and complex solutions that require the coordination of multiple Agile Release Trains (ARTs), as well as the contributions of suppliers. It aligns ARTs with a shared business and technology mission using the solution vision, backlog, and roadmap, and an aligned Program Increment (PI).

Solution Train Engineer (STE)

The Solution Train Engineer (STE) is a servant leader and coach for the Solution Train, facilitating and guiding the work of all ARTs and suppliers in the value stream.

Spanning Palette

The spanning palette contains various roles and artifacts that may apply to a specific team, program, large solution, or portfolio context.

Stories

Stories are short descriptions of a small piece of desired functionality, written in the user's language. Agile teams implement small, vertical slices of system functionality and are sized so they can be completed in a single iteration.

Strategic Themes

Strategic themes are differentiating business objectives that connect a portfolio to the strategy of the enterprise. They influence portfolio strategy and provide business context for portfolio decision-making.

Supplier

A supplier is an internal or external organization that develops and delivers components, subsystems, or services that help Solution Trains and Agile Release Trains provide solutions to their customers.

System Architect/Engineer

The System Architect/Engineer is responsible for defining and communicating a shared technical and architectural vision for an Agile Release Train (ART) to help ensure the system or solution under development is fit for its intended purpose.

System Demo

The system demo is a significant event that provides an integrated view of new features for the most recent iteration delivered by all the teams in the Agile Release Train (ART). Each demo gives ART stakeholders an objective measure of progress during a Program Increment (PI).

System Team

The system team is a specialized Agile team that assists in building and supporting the Agile development environment, typically including development and maintenance of the toolchain that supports the continuous delivery pipeline. The system team may also support the integration of assets from Agile teams, perform end-to-end solution testing where necessary, and assist with deployment and release on demand.

Team and Technical Agility

The team and technical agility competency describes the critical skills and Lean-Agile principles and practices that high-performing Agile teams and teams of Agile teams use to create high-quality solutions for their customers.

Team Backlog

The team backlog contains user and enabler stories that originate from the program backlog, as well as stories that arise locally from the team's local context. It may include other work items as well, representing all the things a team needs to do to advance their portion of the system.

Team Kanban

Team Kanban is a method that helps teams facilitate the flow of value by visualizing workflow, establishing Work In Process (WIP) limits, measuring throughput, and continuously improving their process.

Value Stream Coordination

Value stream coordination defines how to manage dependencies and exploit the opportunities that exist only in the interconnections between value streams.

Value Stream KPIs

Value stream Key Performance Indicators (KPIs) are the quantifiable measures used to evaluate how a value stream is performing against its forecasted business outcomes.

Value Streams

Value streams represent the series of steps that an organization uses to implement solutions that provide a continuous flow of value to a customer.

Vision

The vision is a description of the future state of the solution under development. It reflects customer and stakeholder needs, as well as the features and capabilities proposed to meet those needs.

Weighted Shortest Job First (WSJF)

Weighted Shortest Job First (WSJF) is a prioritization model used to sequence jobs (e.g., features, capabilities, and epics) to produce maximum economic benefit. In SAFe, WSJF is estimated as the Cost of Delay (CoD) divided by job size.

Index

tooling and automation, 178
working environments, 175–176

Collective learning, benefits of 'big room' training, 238

Collective ownership, built-in quality, 85

Communities of Practice. See CoPs (Communities of Practice)

Compensation
    in motivation of knowledge workers, 55
    people operations, 173

Compliance
    continually addressing, 130–131
    coordinating, 165
    defined, 268

Component teams, 233

Components, building and integrating, 131

Confidence vote
    making commitment based on, 135
    in PI planning, 107

Configuration options, SAFe
    Essential SAFe configuration, 17
    Full SAFe configuration, 19–20
    Large Solution SAFe configuration, 18
    overview of, 16–17
    Portfolio SAFe configuration, 18–19

Continuous Delivery Pipeline. See CDP (Continuous Delivery Pipeline)

Continuous Deployment. See CD (Continuous Deployment)

Continuous engagement, people operations, 172

Continuous Exploration. See CE (Continuous Exploration)

Continuous Integration. See CI (Continuous Integration)

Continuous Learning Culture
    as core competency, 16
    defined, 268
    experimentation and feedback, 193
    fact-based improvement, 199
    Go See (gemba), 192–193
    innovation culture, 191–192
    innovation riptides, 194–195
    learning organizations, 189–191
    optimizing the whole, 196
    pivoting, 193–194
    problem-solving, 196–198
    reasons for, 187–189
    reflection at key milestones, 198–199
    relentless improvement, 195
    summary, 199

Contracts
    Agile contracts, 184–185
    collaboration over contract negotiation, 33
    people operations, 172

CoPs (Communities of Practice)
    defined, 268
    leading transformation, 249

making time and space for innovation, 192
spanning palette elements, 21

Core competencies. See also by individual types
    analyzing assessment, 258–259
    assessing, 23, 254, 257
    illustration of, 63
    running assessment, 258
    summary of, 15–16
    taking action, 259–260

Core values
    defined, 269
    foundation elements, 22
    SAFe, 68–69

Cost centers, measuring portfolio performance, 164

Cost-effectiveness, benefits of 'big room' training, 238

Cost of Delay (CoD), 100–101

Costs, ignoring sunk, 184

Courses
    Agile Product Management, 243
    training executives, managers, and leaders, 207–208
    training product owners and product managers, 234
    training Scrum Masters, 235
    training teams, 237

Cross-domain planning. See also PI (program incremental) planning, 52–54

Cross-functional teams
    collaboration spaces, 175
    LACE and, 211
    realizing value streams, 60

Culture
    anchoring new behaviors in, 263
    continuous learning. See Continuous Learning Culture
    embracing DevOps, 111
    hiring for fit with, 172
    innovation. See Innovation culture
    problem-solving, 196–198
    respect for, 28
    types of (Westrum), 70–71

Culture, Automation, Lean flow, Measurement, and Recovery (CALMR), 111–112

Customer centricity
    in Agile product delivery, 90
    as casualty of hierarchical structure, 7
    reinforcing the basics, 262
    team actions resulting from, 91

Customer journey maps, 96–97

Customers
    Agile team roles, 83
    collaboration over contract negotiation, 33
    coordinating, 138–139
    defined, 269
    identifying operational value streams, 216
    identifying personas, 95
    leaner approach to customer relations, 251–252

making time and space for innovation, 192
pre-PI planning, 134
refining personas and establishing empathy, 95–96
Solution Train roles, 132
visualizing, 177

D

Daily meetings, coaching teams, 240

Daily Stand Up (DSU), Agile teams, 81

DBA (Database Administrators), 84

Decentralization
decision-making, 57–58, 71
LACE organizational models, 212

Decision-making
decentralizing, 57–58
qualities of generative cultures, 71

Definition of Done (DoD), 86

Delivery, early and often. *See also* Agile Product Delivery;
CDP (Continuous Delivery Pipeline), 40–41

Demand, aligning to capacity and forecasts, 251

Deming, W. Edwards, 11, 39, 42, 45, 61, 65, 207, 215, 263

Deployment. *See also* CD (Continuous Deployment)
Deploy phase of CD, 114
to production, 117

Deployment period, technology disruption and, 4

Design feedback, prototyping for, 98

Design thinking
defined, 269
in learning organizations, 190
in product delivery, 92–93

Designing the implementation
ARTs that deliver value, 221–222
creating implementation plan, 225
development value streams, 219–220
identifying value streams, 215–216
operational value streams, 216–218
overview of, 215
people for building full business solution, 220–221
people for developing and maintaining systems, 219
planning ARTs and value streams, 227
selecting first ART, 225–226
Solution Train with multiple ARTs, 223–225
summary, 228
systems for operational value streams, 218

Development
aligning development cadence, 53
on cadence and releasing on demand, 98–99
Continuous Development, 114
delivery early and often, 40–41
Develop phase of CI, 113
improving system development, 12
incremental, 46–47

integrated development environments, 178
practices in PI planning, 105
Test-Driven and Behavior-Driven, 51, 87

Development value streams
ART design patterns, 222
identifying, 216, 219–220
overview of, 179
people for building full business solution, 220–221

DevOps
continuous delivery pipeline and, 90
defined, 269
embracing, 110–112
enterprise solutions, 122
goal of SAFe, 11
managing batch size, 51
reinforcing the basics, 262
SAFe drawing from, 12
training, 242

The DevOps Handbook, 110

DevSecOps, 112

Discovery, finding better ways (Agile Manifesto), 32

Documentation
minimal but sufficient, 126–127
working software vs., 32–33

Done
DoD (Definition of Done), 86
establishing portfolio flow, 160

Draft plan, reviewing in PI planning, 105–106

Drucker, Peter, 55, 57

DSU (Daily Stand Up), Agile teams, 81

Dual operating system (Kotter), 7

Dweck, Dr. Carol S., 25–26

E

Earned authority, of generative leaders, 71

Economic framework (or view)
comprehensive nature of, 41–42
delivery early and often, 40–41
primary elements, 42

Eight-step model for leading change (Kotter), 23

Emotional intelligence, qualities of generative cultures, 71

Empathy, 95–96

Empathy maps, 95–96

Enablers
defined, 269
defining epics, 154
stories in team backlog, 78

End-to-end testing, 114

Value stream coordination, 278

Value stream KPIs
  celebrating success, 260
  defined, 278
  informing LPM of progress, 160
  measuring portfolio performance, 164

Values
  Agile Manifesto, 31–33
  Lean-Agile mindset, 27
  SAFe core, 68–69

Variability, assuming, 45

Verification/validation
  CD (Continuous Development), 114
  in program Kanban, 117

Video conferencing, 175

Vision
  for change, 72, 209
  defined, 278
  disciplines of learning organizations, 189–190
  maintaining portfolio vision and roadmap, 150
  product vision, 105
  spanning palette elements, 21

Visualizing work, 49–50, 176–177

VMO (Value Management Office), 161

W

Ward, Allen C., 45, 180

Weighted Shortest Job First. *See* WSJF (Weighted Shortest Job First)

Westrum, Ron, 70–71

White boards, in collaboration spaces, 175

WIP (Work In Process)
  aligning demand to capacity and forecasts, 251
  blending Agile methods, 79
  establishing flow, 85, 159
  estimating, 80
  implementing flow, 181
  Lean flow, 111
  managing queue lengths, 51–52
  portfolio Kanban, 159
  program Kanban, 116
  reducing batch size, 50–51
  visualizing, 49–50, 177

Working environments
  cross-team collaboration spaces, 175
  overview of, 173–174
  PI planning and ART collaboration space, 175–176
  remote workers, 174–175

Workplace engagement, in motivation of knowledge
  workers, 56

WSJF (Weighted Shortest Job First)
  defined, 278
  in portfolio Kanban, 159–160
  program backlog, 100–101
  solution backlog, 133

X

XP (Extreme Program)
  blending Agile methods, 79
  Scrum XP, 275
  servant leaders, 264–265

Credits

Page 3: "Those who master large-scale software delivery will define the economic landscape of the 21st century." Mik Kersten, Project to Product (IT Revolution Press, 2018).

Page 7: "The solution is not to trash what we know and start over but instead to reintroduce a second system." John P. Kotter, Leading Change (Harvard Business Review Press, 1996).

Page 57: "Knowledge workers themselves are best placed to make decisions about how to perform their work." Peter F. Drucker, The Essential Drucker (Harper-Collins, 2001).

Page 58: "The world is now changing at a rate at which the basic ... no matter how clever, are not up to the job." John P. Kotter, Leading Change (Harvard Business Review Press, 1996).

Page 72: "Nothing undermines change more than behavior by important individuals that is inconsistent with the verbal communication." John P. Kotter, Leading Change (Harvard Business Review Press, 1996).

Page 205: "A strong guiding coalition is always needed. One with the right composition, level of trust, and shared objective." John P. Kotter, Leading Change (Harvard Business Review Press, 1996).

Page 207: "People are already doing their ... responsibility cannot be delegated." Edwards Deming, W. Out of the Crisis (MIT Center for Advanced Educational Services, 1982).

Page 213: "If you can't communicate the vision to someone in five minutes or less and get a reaction that signifies both understanding and interest, you are not done." John P. Kotter, Leading Change (Harvard Business Review Press, 1996).

Page 240: "Whenever you let up before the job is done, critical momentum can be lost, and regression may follow." John P. Kotter, Leading Change (Harvard Business Review Press, 1996).

Page 245: "Consolidate gains and produce more change." John P. Kotter, Leading Change (Harvard Business Review Press, 1996).

Page 248, "Anchor new approaches in the culture." John P. Kotter, Leading Change (Harvard Business Review Press, 1996).

SCALED AGILE®
Provider of SAFe®

scaledagileframework.com

The world's leading framework for enterprise agility

- Freely available knowledge base of proven, integrated principles and practices for Lean, Agile, and DevOps

- Configurable and scalable for Teams, Programs, and Portfolios

- Role-based curriculum, worldwide Partner Network, and global community

---

SCALED AGILE®
LEARNING AND CERTIFICATION

scaledagile.com/learning

A comprehensive role-based curriculum for successfully implementing SAFe

- Actionable learning for every SAFe role

- Globally consistent courseware and certification

- Skills validation through professional certification

SCALED AGILE®
PARTNER NETWORK

scaledagile.com/partners

Worldwide SAFe expertise and support through 180+ Partners

- Training and coaching for all SAFe roles

- Implementation and consulting services across industries and disciplines

- Platforms for SAFe automation, visibility, and flow

COMMUNITY

scaledagile.com/community

Continuous learning, tools, and connections for SAFe professionals

- Network and learn with 200,000 SAFe professionals

- Advance your career with in-demand skills and certification

- Access tools, guidance, and role-based Communities of Practice

SAFe role-based curriculum

Scaled Agile offers a portfolio of professional credentials designed to meet the needs of Lean-Agile professionals. Each certification is supported by world-class courseware and value-added resources that prepare the individual to succeed as a key player in a SAFe enterprise.

SAFe courses and certifications include:

- **Implementing SAFe®**
  with SAFe® 4 Program Consultant certification

- **Leading SAFe®**
  with SAFe® 4 Agilist certification

- **SAFe® for Teams**
  with SAFe® 4 Practitioner certification

- **SAFe® Scrum Master**
  with SAFe® 4 Scrum Master certification

- **SAFe® Advanced Scrum Master**
  with SAFe® 4 Advanced Scrum Master certification

- **SAFe® Release Train Engineer**
  with SAFe® 4 Release Train Engineer certification

- **SAFe® Product Owner/Product Manager**
  with SAFe® 4 Product Owner/Product Manager certification

- **SAFe® DevOps**
  with SAFe® 4 DevOps Practitioner certification

- **More courses in development!**

FOR COURSE INFORMATION AND REGISTRATION, VISIT

 scaledagile.com/**learning**

Photo by Marvent/Shutterstock

VIDEO TRAINING FOR THE **IT PROFESSIONAL**

LEARN QUICKLY
Learn a new technology in just hours. Video training can teach more in less time, and material is generally easier to absorb and remember.

WATCH AND LEARN
Instructors demonstrate concepts so you see technology in action.

TEST YOURSELF
Our Complete Video Courses offer self-assessment quizzes throughout.

CONVENIENT
Most videos are streaming with an option to download lessons for offline viewing.

Learn more, browse our store, and watch free, sample lessons at
informit.com/video

Save 50%* off the list price of video courses with discount code **VIDBOB**

Photo by izusek/gettyimages

Register Your Product at informit.com/register

Access additional benefits and save 35% on your next purchase

- Automatically receive a coupon for 35% off your next purchase, valid for 30 days. Look for your code in your InformIT cart or the Manage Codes section of your account page.

- Download available product updates.

- Access bonus material if available.*

- Check the box to hear from us and receive exclusive offers on new editions and related products.

Registration benefits vary by product. Benefits will be listed on your account page under Registered Products.

InformIT.com—The Trusted Technology Learning Source

InformIT is the online home of information technology brands at Pearson, the world's foremost education company. At InformIT.com, you can:

- Shop our books, eBooks, software, and video training
- Take advantage of our special offers and promotions (informit.com/promotions)
- Sign up for special offers and content newsletter (informit.com/newsletters)
- Access thousands of free chapters and video lessons

Connect with InformIT—Visit informit.com/community

the trusted technology learning source

Addison-Wesley • Adobe Press • Cisco Press • Microsoft Press • Pearson IT Certification • Que • Sams • Peachpit Press

 Pearson